Faiths and Faithfulness

Pluralism, Dialogue and Mission in the Work of Kenneth Cragg and Lesslie Newbigin

D1354287

PATERNOSTER THEOLOGICAL MONOGRAPHS

A full listing of all titles in this series
appears at the close of this book

PATERNOSTER THEOLOGICAL MONOGRAPHS

Faiths and Faithfulness

Pluralism, Dialogue and Mission in the Work of Kenneth Cragg and Lesslie Newbigin

Nicholas J. Wood

Foreword by Timothy J. Gorringe

Paternoster:
thinking faith

MILTON KEYNES · COLORADO SPRINGS · HYDERABAD

Copyright © Nicholas J. Wood 2009

First published 2009 by Paternoster

Paternoster is an imprint of Authentic Media
9 Holdom Avenue, Bletchley, Milton Keynes, MK1 1QR, UK
1820 Jet Stream Drive, Colorado Springs, CO 80921, USA
OM Authentic Media, Medchal Road, Jeedimetla Village,
Secunderabad 500 055, A.P., India

www.authenticmedia.co.uk
Authentic Media is a Division of IBS-STL UK, a company limited by guarantee
(registered charity no. 270162)

15 14 13 12 11 10 09   7 6 5 4 3 2 1

The right of Nicholas J. Wood to be identified as the Author of this Work
has been asserted by him in accordance with the Copyright, Designs
and Patents Act 1988

British Library Cataloguing in Publication Data
A catalogue record for this book is available from the British Library

ISBN 978–1–84227–371–5

Typeset by A.R. Cross
Printed and bound in Great Britain
for Paternoster
by AlphaGraphics Nottingham

PATERNOSTER THEOLOGICAL MONOGRAPHS

Series Preface

In the West the churches may be declining, but theology—serious, academic (mostly doctoral level) and mainstream orthodox in evaluative commitment—shows no sign of withering on the vine. This series of *Paternoster Theological Monographs* extends the expertise of the Press especially to first-time authors whose work stands broadly within the parameters created by fidelity to Scripture and has satisfied the critical scrutiny of respected assessors in the academy. Such theology may come in several distinct intellectual disciplines—historical, dogmatic, pastoral, apologetic, missional, aesthetic and no doubt others also. The series will be particularly hospitable to promising constructive theology within an evangelical frame, for it is of this that the church's need seems to be greatest. Quality writing will be published across the confessions—Anabaptist, Episcopalian, Reformed, Arminian and Orthodox—across the ages—patristic, medieval, reformation, modern and counter-modern—and across the continents. The aim of the series is theology written in the twofold conviction that the church needs theology and theology needs the church—which in reality means theology done for the glory of God.

Series Editors

To my parents
who taught me the meaning of faith

Contents

Foreword

It is not yet a century since the Edinburgh International Missionary Conference spoke confidently of 'the evangelization of the world in this generation'. Most of what today is called 'the Third World' or 'the global South' was under one or another form of European colonialism – mostly British. There were voices which denounced imperialism, including that of the Catholic Social Union, for which it was the principal of all sins, but they certainly did not represent the consensus. Christian mission, even when critical of imperialism, followed the flag. Today, though we have what David Harvey has called a 'new imperialism', that whole view of the world lies in ruins. Within the constraints of the total market difference is what we celebrate. The very idea of Christian mission is somehow not respectable. Sharp challenges to Christianity's claim to speak of salvation come not only from other religions and ideologies, and from secular humanism, but from psychotherapy. Christian confidence, when it is expressed, often has a hollow note. In this context it is good to pause and consider two of the great missionary bishops of the past century – Kenneth Cragg and Lesslie Newbigin. Both were men of great intellectual ability, superb linguists who spoke the language of the people amongst whom they worked with perfect fluency. Both could have had quite different careers, the one as a literary scholar, the other as a 'captain of industry'. Both chose instead to work in what used to be called 'the mission field'. Both wrote profound studies which remain classic expositions of the grounds of Christian engagement. Both men had the greatest respect for the religions amongst which they shared the gospel. The morning I left for South India Newbigin came to see me and told me two things: 'Eat anything within reason, but always boil your water; and always respect Hinduism'. This courtesy and respect was a hallmark of everything these two men did.

Nick Wood rightly calls our attention to what these two great figures have to teach us, inviting us to learn from them in our very different and much less confident times. Complacent pluralism is a dead end, a fig leaf for the hegemony of the total market. What we can learn in this study are ways to struggle for the truth without stridency, to pay attention to the other whilst holding fast to one's own vision of the truth, to recover some of that gracious sense of mission which we find in the first centuries of the Church. This recovery is vital not only to the Church's integrity but to its survival. Let us hope the study has the hearing it deserves.

Timothy J. Gorringe,
Exeter,
May 2009.

Preface and Acknowledgements

How are people of faith to be faithful to their various traditions in today's diverse society? How may we live together as neighbours and yet remain true to our differing religious convictions? How is it possible for the contemporary Christian to confess the Lordship of Jesus Christ in a world of many faiths? These are some of the fundamental questions which this volume seeks to explore.

In a way that can no longer be ignored we live in a world of many faiths and ideologies. In a globalised society we are aware of many paths towards truth, enlightenment, spiritual fulfilment and salvation. How are Christians to respond to this pressing global reality, acknowledging the power, and perhaps even the truth and beauty of much of the world's religious heritage, whilst at the same time retaining the Church's historic allegiance to the Lordship of Christ? The serious nature of the questions is reflected in the growing volume of literature within the Christian tradition, both in the academic theology which will be the main focus of this volume, but also in more popular works aiming to assist Christians reflect on these issues.[1]

While many religions affirm the unity of God, and while many Christians acknowledge that all monotheists (at least) worship the one God, Christianity has always interpreted the nature of God by the measure of Jesus Christ. This is not to restrict God to Christ, for the doctrine of the Trinity has always underlined that the reality of God is greater than all human formulations of the divine mystery. But, at heart, Christianity affirms that the Triune God is Christ-like: the Father is revealed by the Son in the power of the Spirit.[2] This knowledge of God has not been understood as one vision among many; an idea that reflects only a particular cultural or historical stream. Rather it has been understood as a universally valid revelation, true for the whole world, for all peoples and for all time. Indeed Christians have believed that the salvation offered by God through the life, death, resurrection and exaltation of Jesus has cosmic significance. Through the Christ-event the universe is reconciled to God and the divine purposes in creation and redemption are fulfilled. This is the essence of the Good News with which the Church has been entrusted. This Gospel is not a treasure to be locked away and preserved, but an announcement to be proclaimed throughout the world in which all nations are called to turn to the living God and receive salvation in Christ.

The mission of the Creating and Redeeming God thus defines the mission of the Church. In this book I will argue that for a Christian theology of religions, such a missiological perspective is vital, retaining the centrality of Christ within a Trinitarian framework. In the following chapters I will therefore discuss the issue of religious pluralism from a Christian missiological point of view; what I am offering is an avowedly confessional study. As a Christian within the Baptist tradition this

---

[1] E.g. M. Green, *But don't all religions lead to God?* (IVP, Nottingham, 2002); R. Zacharius, *Jesus Among the Other Gods*, (Nelson, Nashville, Th 2000).

[2] Cf. J.V. Taylor, *The Christ-Like God* (SPCK, London, 1992).

reflects something of the approach that has been a major factor in shaping my own reflection. I will also argue that for all people of faith, engagement with people of other traditions always takes place within such a confessional framework. But I am equally clear that this approach does not mean that God is not to be known in other ways. Indeed I will argue that if Jesus Christ is the definitive revelation of God as self-giving love, then we should positively expect to find such a God at work among all peoples, in all places and at all times.

In the last forty years or more there has been an explosion of important theological reflection on this issue, much of it abandoning the missiological framework in which, historically, the discussion was often conducted, and adopting what has become a new orthodoxy of liberal pluralism in which personal commitments are apparently to be set aside. But I shall argue that questions of inter-faith relationships are actually best rooted in encounter between people with firm faith commitments. Indeed it has often been the missionaries of the Church who have first made tentative suggestions of appropriate responses to the realities they have experienced in a world of many faiths.

No one today would wish to endorse all the methods or theological assumptions of the missionaries of a generation or two ago; we can see all too clearly the arrogance, imperialism and even the racism of some. It is this, along with a close and sometimes compromising association with the Western colonial enterprise, which has led to the discrediting of any missiological approach in some circles. True mission, however, must ultimately be measured not by political or economic power but by the powerlessness of the crucified Christ and it is this perspective I shall try to bring to bear.

Part One of the discussion will examine this historical background in some detail and I will identify two broad strands of Christian missiological thinking about other religious traditions in the modern period, through the work of J. N. Farquhar (the 'continuity' strand) and Hendrik Kraemer (the 'discontinuity' strand). I shall then examine an approach which has discarded such a framework, the pluralistic theology of scholars such as John Hick. This part will conclude with a review of the current debate.

The central sections of the book will offer a critical account of two key twentieth century missionary-theologians who, in different ways, attempted to address the issue of pluralism within a confessional framework: the (Anglican) Bishop Kenneth Cragg, and the (Reformed) Bishop Lesslie Newbigin. Part Two will consider the contribution of Cragg, which, I will argue, represents a development of the first strand, the continuity tradition, of Christian mission, which looks for points of contact with the world's religious traditions in order to communicate the Gospel of Christ. Part Three will be an examination of the position of Newbigin, standing, I will suggest, in a tradition of radical discontinuity which emphasises the distinctiveness of Christ as a means of presenting the Gospel; that is the second strand of the missiological approach.

In Part Four I will discuss the vital issue of Christology around which much of the debate is framed, and I will argue for a reconsideration of the biblical themes of fullness and fulfilment, which may offer a way of holding together the traditions of continuity, which Cragg shows can never be total, and of discontinuity, which Newbigin argues can never be absolute. In this way I will try to address some of the implications for the development of an appropriate missiological approach to inter-faith issues in the twenty first century which requires us to take people of faith seriously but allows us to be faithful to the Christian gospel.

This book is a revision and updating of material I first developed in my doctoral thesis for the University of Oxford *Confessing Christ in a Plural World* (1996) and outlined in my Whitley Lecture (2002) under the same title. The research and reflection has been undertaken during pastoral ministry at South Oxford and Eynsham Baptist Churches, and more recently alongside my responsibilities as Fellow in Religion and Culture at Regent's Park College, Oxford. I am grateful to the Principal, Governing Body and all my colleagues at Regent's for a period of study leave in which to complete the final text for this book and I am thankful for all these communities of faith and learning which have sustained and challenged me in equal measure.

It has also been written in the context of wide-ranging church and interfaith experience and responsibilities and this too has never been far from my mind, especially my friends and colleagues in Southern Counties Baptist Association, the Joppa Group - the Baptist Interfaith Network, and the Christian Muslim Forum of England. I am grateful for many conversations, lively discussion and dialogue, and deep friendships. I do not think that all my friends in churches, mosques, synagogues and temples are likely to agree with everything I have written. But I hope I have not said anything here which I would not also say in their company.

I am grateful to the original supervisor of my research, Prof. Tim Gorringe, now of Exeter University, both for his initial encouragement and ultimate patience and now for his willingness to contribute the Foreword to this book. Thanks also to my doctoral examiners, Prof. Keith Ward and Prof. Gavin D'Costa, for their continued interest and kind words. Particular thanks to my friend and colleague Dr Anthony R. Cross for typesetting the book and constant support.

During the original research it was my privilege to have several conversations with both Kenneth Cragg and with the late Lesslie Newbigin. I am glad that this book appears in 2009, the centenary of Newbigin's birth. Happily the conversations have continued with Kenneth Cragg, a friend and sometime neighbour in Oxford, to the present day. Both of these distinguished servants of church and academy received me with unfailing courtesy and kindness for which I remain profoundly grateful. Family and friends have also been patient and gently supportive and encouraging for a long time. To all these people these reflections on *Faiths and Faithfulness* are offered in appreciation.

Nicholas J. Wood,
Regent's Park College,
University of Oxford,
Easter 2009.

Part 1

Christian Mission in a Plural World

CHAPTER 1

Mission and Dialogue in the Colonial Era

It had been the dream of William Carey, pioneer Baptist missionary, eminent linguist, educationalist, botanist, and so-called "father of modern missions", that a world missionary conference should be held at the Cape of Good Hope in 1810.[1] It was too ambitious a notion even for someone of Carey's energy and vision,[2] but a century later it was an idea come of age. Of course it had already been anticipated in some of the lesser conferences regularly held in the latter half of the nineteenth century, either regionally, such as the Bengal Conference of 1855, or internationally such as those of Liverpool 1860 and Mildmay, London, in 1878. Yet the World Missionary Conference of 1910, held finally in Edinburgh rather than South Africa, is widely recognised as a significant event in modern church history. This is not just because of the breadth of representation from both sending and receiving countries, including for the first time at such a gathering High Church Anglicans together with the Archbishop of Canterbury. In many ways Edinburgh 1910 can be seen as a watershed occasion, looking in one direction back to the enormous achievements, for all its many flaws, of the nineteenth century missionary movement, "the Great Century" as K. S. Latourette characterised it; and in the other looking forward to some of the major concerns of the church in the century ahead.

The 1910 Conference is well-known as the origin of both the International Missionary Council and the 'Faith and Order' Movement which met in conference at Lausanne in 1927 and which led to the founding of the World Council of Churches in Amsterdam some twenty-one years later. These two bodies recognised their common origin and concerns by their subsequent merger at the WCC Assembly in New Delhi in 1961 (in which Lesslie Newbigin played a considerable part). The Edinburgh Conference not only gave the Ecumenical Movement the impetus it required to attain institutional expression, it captured an atmosphere of energy and expectancy characteristic of the days of empire. Yet at the same time, through its breadth of representation and by its willingness to hear the views of the younger churches, it also anticipated the end of western dominance and the close of the colonial era.

---

1 In a letter to Andrew Fuller of 15 May 1806 he called for a "general association of all denominations of Christians from the four quarters of the world" to be held every ten years beginning in 1810. See the Preface by E.A. Payne to Carey's *Enquiry* (BMS, Didcot, 1961 reprinted 1991) p26.

2 See Max Warren, *The Missionary Movement from Britain in Modern History* (SCM, London, 1965) p146.

The Conference met to consider eight reports, four of which dealt with aspects of mission abroad, and four of which concerned the 'Home Base' and the interests of the various missionary societies and boards. Temple Gairdner in his famous account of the Conference suggests that the most remarkable of this series of reports was that presented by the Scottish theologian, Professor David S. Cairns on "The Missionary Message in Relation to the Non-Christian Religions."[3] The report concludes with an anticipation of the conquest of the five great religions[4] by Christianity, in militaristic imagery typical of an earlier generation of mission thinking and subsequently characterised by E.C. Dewick as 'war-attitudes'.[5]

In the body of the report, however, another attitude is revealed, typified by the words 'fulfil' and 'fulfilment', which often recurred in the two hundred responses from the field in reply to the questions of the Commission. Eric Sharpe's analysis of these replies shows that some missionaries were wary as to how far a more sympathetic approach to other faiths ought to go, but most were agreed that greater understanding was required even if for some it was no more than simple expediency.[6] For others the notion of 'fulfilment' provided an interpretative key by which the Christian relation to other faiths was to be understood and this is reflected in Temple Gairdner's comment: "Christianity, the religion of the Light of the World, can ignore no lights however 'broken' – it must take them all into account, absorb them all into its central glow".[7]

The name most commonly associated with this fulfilment theology of religions is that of another Scot, John Nicol Farquhar, the subject of Eric Sharpe's magisterial study *Not to Destroy but to Fulfil*.[8] Elsewhere Sharpe has commented that more than any other individual it was Farquhar who was responsible for creating decisive changes in Christian thinking about other faiths.[9] A member of the Evangelical Union, a small Scottish independent church, Farquhar was accepted for service in India by the London Missionary Society following education at Aberdeen University and Christ Church, Oxford. After some years as a teacher in Calcutta he was offered a Y.M.C.A. post by J. R. Mott, which involved him more directly in evangelistic work and in literature. In 1903 he became the editor of the journal *"The Inquirer"* and published a series of articles under the heading "Is Christianity the Only True Religion?" Already he was prepared to admit the 'partial truth' of other religions,

3 W.H.T. Gairdner, *'Edinburgh 1910' An Account and Interpretation of the World Missionary Conference* (Oliphant, Anderson & Ferrier, Edinburgh, 1910) p134.

4 That is, Animism, Chinese Religion, Japanese Religion, Islam and Hinduism; the subject of successive chapters in the Report.

5 E.C. Dewick, *The Christian Attitude to Other Religions* (CUP, Cambridge, 1953).

6 E.J. Sharpe, *Not to Destroy But to Fulfil* (Gleerup, Lund, 1965) pp279-80.

7 Gairdner, *Edinburgh 1910*, p137.

8 The title is of course a reference to the words of Jesus in Matthew 5:17 which read: "Think not that I have come to destroy the law or the prophets: I am come not to destroy but to fulfil." KJV. Farquhar went on to apply this verse not only to Judaism but also to other faiths.

9 E.J. Sharpe, *Faith meets Faith* (SCM, London, 1977) p20.

although such recognition served mainly to demonstrate the universality of Christianity. In the fourth article of the series, Farquhar concluded that, "the belief that Jesus Christ, the Son of God, died for our sins on Calvary, produces a religion which satisfies the modern mind, and which also proves to be the fulfilment and goal of all the religions of the world, the crudest as well as the loftiest".[10] This particular use of the word 'fulfilment' goes back to the evangelical *Orientalist* scholar Sir Monier Monier-Williams who used it both in a general sense to express the relationship of Christianity to the human religious instinct, and more specifically to establish the relationship of the Christian faith to Hinduism.[11] Farquhar develops this second, more specific, sense of the term in considerable detail in his book *The Crown of Hinduism*.[12]

Although not published until 1913, Farquhar had anticipated this title in an article for *The Contemporary Review* in 1910 where he explicitly describes Christianity as "the evolutionary crown of Hinduism".[13] Other contributors to this stream of nineteenth century thought include Max Mueller, another Oxford scholar and the editor of the influential series *Sacred Books of the East*; William Miller, the pioneering Principal of the Madras Christian College who argued that Christ was the friend of all that was good and true wherever it was found, and that it was Christ rather than Christianity who was the fulfiller of Hinduism; and the evangelist T. E. Slater who died just two years after the Edinburgh Conference, and whose aim was to present Christianity, "as that in which Hindus would find realised and satisfied the noblest and earliest ideas of their sages, and the truest sentiments and yearnings of their hearts".[14]

Again the double sense of 'fulfilment' (general and particular) is clear, together with the notion that somehow the earliest expressions of the human religious instinct were purer than the later corruptions. Such thinking can be seen as early as William Carey who used such arguments, together with textual evidence from the Hindu scriptures, to persuade the Hindu reformer Ram Mohan Roy to join the campaign against *sati*, the self-immolation of widows on the funeral pyre of their husbands.

Max Warren suggested that this awareness of ancient, and possibly less crude and corrupt, tradition was also a contributory factor in the more positive evaluation of the non-Christian religions during the nineteenth century, although it fitted ill with current views about evolution and progress.[15] He even goes so far as to suggest that this is where the roots of dialogue are to be found. This is perhaps to overstate the case, but it does serve to underline an important point, that positive appreciation begins with personal encounter. It is relatively easy to dismiss an ideology, but

---

10 'The Inquirer' V:1 p6.

11 See Sharpe, *Not to Destroy*, p52; Sharpe also notes that Monier-Williams later withdrew from this position under pressure from the Evangelical lobby, p57.

12 J.N. Farquhar, *The Crown of Hinduism* (OUP, London, 1913).

13 Contemporary Review, XCVIII:1 (1910), p57.

14 T.E. Slater, *God Revealed* (London, 1876) piii.

15 Max Warren, *Social History and Christian Mission* (SCM, London, 1967) pp81-2.

people require a more adequate human response. Arguments are often abstract and while they may compel assent they do not demand a response in the same way as do human beings in all their complexity. This is particularly true for the many sincere men and women caught up in the fervour of the missionary movement out of deep pastoral and evangelistic concern. It is noticeable that changes of attitude towards people of other faiths are most apparent among those missionaries and others who had experienced at first hand a genuine and deep association with people of other faiths.

The question of the relationship of Christian faith to other religions is regularly raised during the missionary conferences of the second half of the nineteenth century and it was in an attempt to address the issue that it formed one of the eight Reports for Edinburgh. It is the name of Farquhar that has dominated the discussion since, although not all have been as careful in their scholarship or their evaluation as was Farquhar himself. He begins by suggesting that the new-found unity of humanity must be paralleled by a Christian recognition of "a certain underlying unity in all religions" which links the lowest to the highest, for in every society religion is the highest thing known to the human race.[16] Indeed, he argues, through the great religions, truth has been revealed, saints have been trained, "and multitudes of men and women have found God. We rejoice in the true and fruitful religious experience of these good men".[17]

Farquhar is not one to gloss over genuine differences and contradictions and because of these it is not possible to refer to the religions as *true* in any absolute sense. He is confident that just as any 'thinking man' is able to see the superiority of the higher religions over the lowest faiths, so too the Christian sees the superiority of his faith over the other great religions. It is interesting to note that this clear view is afforded by the practical experience of mission-field contact.[18] The wide-spread interaction made possible by modern technology would lead, so Farquhar argued, to a new era in which the religious needs of the human race could be met only by the highest thing known to humanity, the Christian faith. The aim of the book is to demonstrate that claim in respect of the Hindu religion with which he has become familiar, but not in any destructive sense. Loss of faith in one system does not mean the automatic transfer of trust elsewhere.[19] The image that he favours is that of death and resurrection, not of individuals but of whole systems: "Hinduism must die in order to live, it must die into Christianity".[20]

In much the same way as Christians retain and read the Jewish Scriptures in the light of Christ, so too the 'gleams of light' in Hindu faith and practice find in him 'their explanation and consummation'. It is in this context that Farquhar uses his key text: "I am come not to destroy but to fulfil" (Matthew 5:17).[21] Farquhar is

---

16 Farquhar, *Crown*, p26.
17 Farquhar, *Crown*, p28.
18 Farquhar, *Crown*, p31.
19 Farquhar, *Crown*, p34.
20 Farquhar, *Crown,* p51.
21 Farquhar, *Crown*, p54, see further chapter 10.

conscious that this affirmation requires some qualification if it is not to seem both arrogant and patently untrue. He refers, therefore, to Christianity "as it springs living and creative from Christ himself", rather than to what he terms the elaborations of the historic denominations. This emphasis on Christ rather than Christianity reflects a similar approach to that of Miller, and there is also a parallel in Farquhar's talk of some 'pristine' Christianity to Slater's comments about early versions of other faiths. More positively (and presciently) he suggests that the embryonic churches of Asia may help to recover aspects of Christian faith lost by the West.[22]

In the main body of the book he draws on the widespread nineteenth century notions of evolution, progress and development to apply his fulfilment theology to various aspects of Hindu religion. Christ is able to transfigure the Hindu Scriptures, its pattern of family life, and even the much maligned caste system, where the ideals of highest and lowest, *Brahmin* and *Sudra*, are universalised in Christ the priestly-servant. Such thinking is bold enough, but he goes on to make an even more daring comparison in his comments on idolatry, the focus of considerable venom and scorn in much missionary literature. Farquhar argues that something which has won the respect and affection of some of India's greatest philosophers, including Sankara and Ramanuja, cannot be readily dismissed as the outworkings of primitive minds. Rather it reflects the universal human instinct for religious worship and devotion and this too may be fulfilled in Christ, the image of the Father: "Jesus actually takes in the Christian's life the place which is held by idols in idolatrous systems".[23]

Such views were bound to be controversial in the generation for which Farquhar wrote, but it serves to illustrate the rigour and integrity with which he was prepared to pursue the argument. In almost every aspect of Hinduism he was able to see Christian parallels, but always on a 'higher' degree of development and with a 'deeper' level of satisfaction. He concludes:

> Every true motive which in Hinduism has found expression in unclean, debasing or unworthy practices, finds in Him fullest exercise in work for the downtrodden, the ignorant, the sick, and the sinful. In Him is focused every ray of light that shines in Hinduism. He is the Crown of the faith of India.[24]

As we have already noted many of the missionaries who responded to the Cairns' Commission for the World Missionary Conference were adopting this sort of language, but most were wary of pushing the argument to the sort of conclusions that Farquhar was advocating. A.G. Hogg, a close associate of Cairns, anticipated much of the later criticism of fulfilment theology by drawing a distinction between beliefs *about* God, and faith *in* God. Much missionary endeavour had failed because it concentrated upon presenting a body of belief about God, rather than attempting to share a living faith in God. In any case he suggests that, in his attempts to relate Hindu tradition to Christian doctrine, Farquhar has misunderstood the predominantly

---

22 Farquhar, *Crown*, pp58-64.
23 Farquhar, *Crown*, p350.
24 Farquhar, *Crown*, p458.

social religion that Hinduism is. In his paper for the Edinburgh Conference Hogg argues forcefully that Christian doctrines do not fulfil Hindu doctrines, and Christian rites do not fulfil Hindu rites. He is prepared to concede to Farquhar that revelation cannot be restricted to Christianity, but he goes on from this to draw the contrast between the two faiths rather than to make comparisons.

In two reviews of *The Crown of Hinduism*,[25] Hogg stated that Farquhar's position must be taken seriously, but he reiterated his fundamental disagreement that Christianity did in fact fulfil Hinduism. Christ omits a good deal of what constitutes Hindu faith and practice, and includes a good deal of what was never in Hinduism. Christ certainly satisfies human need, but that is universal and not specific to any one faith.

There was considerable debate on these issues reflected in the missionary literature of the day. Some reacted fiercely against the line which Farquhar developed, especially over the question of idolatry, but others wanted to take the argument a stage further. The suggestion was made that in the Indian context for example, the Old Testament might be replaced by a suitable selection from the Hindu Scriptures. The Methodist J. W. Burton asked, "Should we be wrong in allowing the more evolved races to place their Old Testament where we place the Jewish?"[26] However, Farquhar himself did not agree with such proposals. Fulfilment was a one-way process and Christianity was not in need of supplementing from other sources, nor did he believe that all religions were virtually the same.

In a follow-up article in the *International Review of Mission*, Farquhar clarified the point that not every element of the old religion reappears in the new. Indeed fulfilment can mean replacement. What Farquhar was after was a new approach, rather than a change in the content of the message.[27] But he also wanted not just a sympathetic attitude to other faiths but a theory of the relationship between Christianity and other religions, and this is what he had set out with such detail and clarity in *The Crown of Hinduism*. The crucial question, identified by Hogg, was that of continuity and discontinuity, and this was to prove central to the next stage of the debate. If movement towards a continuous understanding of the relationship between Christian faith and other faiths was characteristic of the latter part of the Colonial period, then discontinuity was the counter-theme as the foundations of European Christian civilization were rocked and shaken.

---

25 For *Madras Christian College Magazine* XIII:8; and *International Review of Mission* III, both 1914.

26 See Sharpe, *Not to Destroy*, p326.

27 *International Review of Mission* III, 1914, p354.

CHAPTER 2

Mission and Dialogue in the Aftermath of the 1914-18 War

The context for this next phase of Christian response to other faiths was very different to that of the early years of the century. The bitter fighting and colossal loss of life in the trenches of the Great War had given the lie to the old Liberal Protestant dream of a newly united humanity that recognised "the Fatherhood of God and the brotherhood of Man". It had exposed some naïve thinking which underlay the atmosphere of progress and development, fostered by the evolutionary thought of Darwin and others, and it triggered the neo-orthodox school of theology associated particularly with Karl Barth.

The collapse of European domination and the undermining of the whole notion of "Christian civilization" raised in a sharp form the question of colonial government for so much of the world's population, colonies largely governed by the same European powers which had squandered so much potential and so many resources, financial, material and human, often drawn from their various colonies, in a wasteful war. The Western Christian Missions, so closely associated with the colonial expansion of Europe, were hard put in this context to justify the Christian religion as the 'crown' of anything.

The application of neo-orthodox theology to the theology of mission and the question of religious pluralism is most closely linked with the name of the great Dutch missiologist Hendrik Kraemer (1888-1965). In recent discussion he is all too readily dismissed as an uncritical follower of Barth, and is often viewed as a narrow 'exclusivist'. Kraemer's position is actually more subtle and complex than is sometimes allowed, so first let us reconsider Kraemer's contribution to the debate. I will aim to show how his discussion of the crucial question of continuity and discontinuity remains vital for a proper consideration of the relation of Christianity and other religions.

Kraemer trained at Leiden as an Orientalist for the Dutch Bible Society with whom he went to Java, Indonesia, in 1922. He was an expert linguist and a considerable scholar in many forms of oriental religion and culture. He spent the bulk of his time from 1922 to 1937 in various parts of Indonesia writing reports for the Dutch Bible Society.[1] Through contact with many of the leading ecumenical and missionary figures of his day, he was asked to prepare a study document for the World Missionary Conference due to be held at Tambaram, Madras in 1938. The task

---

1 See *From Missionfield to Independent Church* (SCM, London, 1958).

was to outline the "fundamental position of the Christian Church as a witness-bearing body in the modern world".[2] The result was *The Christian Message in a Non-Christian World* in the dialectic method of Barth and Brunner. It gave powerful expression to Kraemer's basic position that in Jesus Christ, God has revealed *the Truth* for the whole of humankind, and that in the event of the incarnation God had acted in a unique and unrepeatable way.

In 1937 Kraemer returned to Leiden as Professor of the History and Phenomenology of Religion, a post he retained through the difficult war years during which he was interned by the Nazis for his part in the resistance movement. His esteem in the worldwide Church led to his appointment as the first director of the World Council of Churches Ecumenical Institute at Bossey (1948-55) during which time he produced a more sophisticated statement of his views, which he saw as clarifying, rather than materially altering, his earlier position. This was published as *Religion and the Christian Faith*.[3] From 1955-57 he was Visiting Professor at Union Theological Seminary, New York, and he then retired to Holland during which period his last short account of the subject was published as *Why Christianity of All Religions?*[4]

Kraemer was a more than able exponent of the science of religion, but he was adamant that neither philosophy nor phenomenology could decide between the truth claims of the various faiths. Nor was he content with an agnostic relativism. He believed that Christian theology had both the competence and the responsibility to discriminate between the truth claims of the various religions which are essentially theological in character. For the Christian theologian the ground of all truth was revealed by God in the Person of Jesus Christ who was the judge of all religions *including Christianity*.

In neo-orthodox thought Jesus Christ is not the supreme realisation of human potential, but the wholly new, hitherto unknown, Eternal Word made flesh. Any other source of revelation, whether so-called natural theology or the witness of the various religions, pales into insignificance by comparison with the self-disclosure of God in Christ. Like Farquhar, Kraemer recognized the newfound unity of the world, 'planetary' unity as he termed it. But writing for 1938, with the experience of the Great War in the recent past and the Nazis already in power in Germany, the outlook was very different than it had appeared to people of Farquhar's generation. He referred to "the frightful tensions which are harassing the world of today",[5] and recognized the 'crisis' situation in which the third World Missionary Conference would meet. Neo-orthodoxy has often been rightly characterised as 'theology of crisis', emerging as it did out of crisis, but also recognizing that the Church always lives under the divine judgement (*krisis*) within the Kingdom of God. Kraemer wrote, "According to its essential nature [the Church] is not one of the many religious and moral

---

2 Kraemer, *The Christian Message in a Non-Christian World* (Edinburgh House Press, London, 1938, 2nd Ed. 1947) pv.

3 Lutterworth Press, London, 1956.

4 Lutterworth Press, London, 1962.

5 Kraemer, *The Christian Message*, p5.

institutions that exist in the world. It is a divine-human society, which always, and not only in periods of worldly crisis, is living 'between the times'".[6]

Kraemer's affinities with the thinking of Barth have frequently been noted, and his agreement with Barth on many points has often led to an assumption of dependency. For example, Paul Knitter in his influential study *No Other Name?*[7] mentions Kraemer only in connection with Barth. But such assumptions are wide of the mark. Kraemer wrote *The Christian Message* quite independently in 1937 and whilst acknowledging the importance of much of what Barth was saying, in many places he sides with Brunner against Barth. Moreover, Barth was writing principally about religion as he knew and experienced it, that is European Christianity, and not particularly about 'the Religions' which Kraemer had studied at first hand. Therefore what certainly became *the* Protestant attitude owes at least as much to Kraemer's independent advocacy as to Barth's 'heavy artillery'.

Kraemer is clear that the Christian theologian must study religion *theologically*, that is:

> ... in being a faithful interpreter of God's self-disclosure in Christ and thereby exercising that interpretation of religion which is implied in his primordial, undemonstrable starting-point...We are, in saying this, not invoking the right to prejudice. On the contrary, by full recognition and avowal of one's bias one is comparatively speaking the better armed against the temptations of prejudice and partiality, to which every scholar without exception is constantly exposed.[8]

In other words the Christian assumption and 'given' is as tenable as the 'scientific' starting point of relativism. He defends himself against those who at Tambaram called for just such a 'neutral' basis, "as if a Christian has the possibility and the right to have a 'starting-point' whence he may judge Jesus Christ" for "Christians cannot behave as if there is an ultimate religious *a priori*, under which Jesus Christ is subsumed. For them Christ is the religious *a priori*.[9] Again and again Kraemer stresses that the criterion of Christ reveals the distinction between Christian faith and other religious belief and practice. To maintain the unity of all religions is to do justice neither to Christianity nor to the other religions.

This is his main complaint about the report of the *Laymen's Enquiry* chaired by W. E. Hocking.[10] Kraemer characterises this report as a total distortion of the Christian message, the suicide of mission, and the annulment of the Christian faith – he was not one to mince his words! The *Laymen's Report* had achieved considerable influence in the 1930s and it was the principal background against

---

6 Kraemer, *The Christian Message*, p25.

7 Paul F. Knitter, *No Other Name? A Critical Survey of Christian Attitudes Towards the World Religions* (SCM, London, 1985).

8 Kraemer, *Religion and the Christian Faith* p52.

9 Kraemer, *Religion and the Christian Faith* p143.

10 *Re-thinking Missions: A Laymen's Enquiry after One Hundred Years* (Harper & Brothers, New York, 1932).

which Kraemer was writing *The Christian Message in a Non-Christian World*. He argued that the Christian faith does not relate to the spiritual world reflected in the religions merely, or even mainly, through fulfilment or continuity: "we must, out of respect for the proper character of the Christian Faith and the other religions, begin by pronouncing emphatically the word 'discontinuity'."[11] Hocking's enquiry had been inadequate because it had not involved sufficient cultural encounter at any real ·depth. The report: "is the product of urbane, liberal-minded gentlemen, devoid of any real estimate of the divine and the diabolic in man as conceived in the gospel, and therefore living under the illusion that a world-religion is born out of benevolent consultation and unanimous agreement".[12]

However, Kraemer recognised that some, at least, of his critics had misunderstood what he meant by 'discontinuity'. Certainly he did not mean to imply contempt or indifference to other religious traditions, for "undeniably God works and has worked in man outside the sphere of Biblical revelation".[13] For Kraemer, however, what is at stake is the issue of truth, and vital questions of universal destiny and of historical particularity. The Christian Gospel makes clear that God's concern is for the whole world; the Church, which is the bearer of that Gospel, is only provisional, although it is too self-centred to realise it. Kraemer believes that the Church is the current, and indeed the final (but not always the best), example of that pattern of God's activity in history which began with the Hebrew patriarchs. Kraemer is alive to the possibility that for many people in the world the actual 'discontinuity' of the Christianity which is presented to them, is nothing to do with the radical message of the Gospel, but rooted in the European thought and practice in which it is dressed. Missionaries are themselves frequently blind to this, but Kraemer insists that:

> ...the Gospel can neither be heard nor felt by taking the focal points of the Gospel as they are clearly formulated to European ears and minds, and expressing them in a tolerable fashion in an indigenous language. They [the missionaries] did not see that the true appeal of the Gospel may be *heard and responded to only* by starting out from a formulation of spiritual problems as *living* in the indigenous soul, and thus touching *existing* chords.[14]

Such thinking not only underlines the possibility of the wrong sort of 'discontinuity', but also implies a fundamental continuity of relationship of the Christian Gospel to the basic spiritual condition and needs of humanity. This is illuminated by his discussion of the whole question of 'points of contact', a notion famously rejected by Barth because of the radical nature of the Christian revelation, yet seen as essential by Kraemer, the experienced missionary. In this discussion he sides with Brunner against Barth in the well-known and highly personal confrontation between the two great theologians.

---

11 Kraemer, *Religion and the Christian Faith*, p224.
12 Kraemer, *Religion and the Christian Faith*, p224.
13 Kraemer, *Religion and the Christian Faith*, p232.
14 Kraemer, *From Missionfield to Independent Church*, p106.

In his essay *Nature and Grace* Brunner argued that the divine image in humanity is destroyed by sin on the *material* level, but on the *formal* level humankind remains in the *imago dei*, and therefore can receive revelation. Despite sin human beings remain a subject, a state of being derived from God, the source of all subjectivity.[15] God remains in relationship to his fallen creation by means of 'preserving grace' and addresses to humanity his 'saving grace' through his Word. What makes humanity capable of being addressed by this Word is the 'point of contact' of the *formal imago dei*. Brunner is firm that:

> No one who agrees that only human subjects but not sticks and stones can receive the Word of God and the Holy Spirit can deny that there is such a thing as a point of contact for the divine grace of redemption. This point of contact is the formal *imago dei*, which not even the sinner has lost.[16]

Barth not only denies this, but does so with his emphatic *Nein!*[17] (although he modifies his position somewhat in *Church Dogmatics III: 1 and 2*). For Barth the divine image is not so much a quality belonging to humanity as our divine purpose and destiny through redemption. There is no 'point of contact'; humanity is of its own effort unable to gain access to God's revelation: "The fact that we become hearers and doers of the Word of God signifies the realisation of a divine possibility, not of one that is inherent in our human nature".[18] For Barth the 'given' is always God rather than humanity.

Barth writes against the background of the Nazi creation ordinances, and this explains his reluctance to concede any ground to natural theology. Whilst Kraemer understands the reasons for Barth's emphatic response, he suggests that such absolutism renders activities like preaching, religious education and missions "rather absurd".[19] Without some form of contact-point the missionary has nowhere to start. This illustrates the point that Kraemer is not simply engaging in discussion with the concerns of European systematic theology, but bringing to the debate his missionary experience of other cultures and religions. For example even the apparently simple word 'God' must have reference for the non-Christian. Kraemer views 'points of contact' as that human element to which God can attach his Word,[20] and which the missionary can use as his starting-point. By the very nature of a shared humanity there are those questions which are common to both Christian and non-Christian and to which the Gospel supplies its own answers. No doubt these would conflict with other answers, this was not only inevitable but also important, illuminating the

---

15 Brunner in 'Nature and Grace', in *Natural Theology* (Geoffrey Bles: The Centenary Press, London, 1946) pp23f.

16 Brunner, 'Nature and Grace', p31.

17 Barth's essay 'No!' is also printed in *Natural Theology*, pp65-128.

18 Barth, 'No!' p117.

19 Kraemer, *Christian Message*, p132.

20 See Carl F. Hallencreutz, *Kraemer Towards Tambaram - A Study in H. Kraemer's Missionary Approach* (Gleerup, Uppsala, 1966) p300.

distinctive Christian message. But there were certainly what Kraemer termed 'values' in other world-views which could be 'converted' to the Christian cause.

Kraemer insisted that such conversion is not to be equated with 'fulfilment'.[21] Certainly the world's great religions could no longer be regarded as altogether without God, but in Christ, God was acting in a way that was the consummation and fulfilment of *all human history*, not merely human religion. Christ is the centre, background and fulfilment of history, Saviour of the *world*. Such a universal perspective would necessarily entail conflict with other world-views, but this process could serve to bring to the fore new aspects of the Christian message. Kraemer is ever aware of what he terms the 'divine-human drama', the interaction of God with humanity throughout history. It is in this context that the phenomenon of religion must be understood, never forgetting that like all human enterprises religion will be characterised by that reality which the Bible calls sin.[22]

Although he consistently rejects the concept of an 'Essence of Religion' or the *idea* of religion, in his later work Kraemer does accept the notion of a universal religious consciousness, which expresses itself both subjectively and objectively. The former is reflected in a particular piety or inner religious life, and the latter as doctrine, myth, rite and cult within an established religious pattern.[23] Such religious consciousness is underived, a 'given' of human existence.[24] This concession is made in response to the criticisms of H.H. Farmer who from the start argued that Kraemer had overlooked the awareness of God which is found in the religions.[25]

Following various examples from the religions of their part in the 'divine-human drama', Kraemer goes on to say:

> Man wants God, but somehow he wants Him in his own way. Therefore the deepest *Ahnungen* [intuitions], the highest flights, the sincerest contrition, remain in the sphere of a lofty moralism or spirituality. Nowhere do we find a radical repudiation of every possible man-made spiritual world, which is the uncanny power of the gospel. Just where we seem to be nearest to the gospel, it appears often that we are farthest away from it.[26]

He suggests that even after the Fall the whole human race continues under God's purposes of partnership in creation, and the whole of human culture, including religion, lies within the compass of God's concern, for "God is not absent from them". This is the objective existential situation in which mankind and its religions

---

21 Hallencreutz, *Kraemer Towards Tambaram*, p307.

22 Kraemer, *Why Christianity*, p99.

23 See Kraemer, *Religion and the Christian Faith*, pp78ff.

24 Kraemer, *Religion and the Christian Faith*, p81.

25 See the comments by Farmer in *The Authority of the Faith* (Tambaram, Madras Series Reports, Volume 1, OUP, London, 1939) pp163-180, and the response by Kraemer in *Religion and the Christian Faith*, p316.

26 Kraemer, *Religion and the Christian Faith*, p334.

are, "and it makes religion and the religions, conscious or unconscious responses to God, wrong, partly right, sometimes really right".[27]

The scientific study of religion has made possible a true assessment of the value of the religions, and the approach must be fair and honest, but it must also have to do with truth. It will also necessarily entail recognition of the trivial, the petty and the questionable, for all religion, including Christianity", is a mixture of "sublimity and perversion, of evil, falsehood and sheer absurdity".[28] All this belongs to the realm of 'unredeemed man', awaiting judgement and fulfilment in Christ. Despite their nobility and character, which Kraemer freely recognizes, by the measure of Christ all religions are in fundamental error, because they always want to pose and to answer essential questions in their own terms. Such ventures are inevitably doomed to failure for, "these are mysteries which, so far as His purpose with and pose with and attitude towards men and the world are concerned, God *makes* known in Christ".[29]

Kraemer thus sides with Brunner in holding a positive concept of religion.[30] As Hallencreutz points out in his survey of the early Kraemer, "he preferred the situation of religious man to that of secular man".[31] Kraemer is, however, prepared to admit that secular thinking may have the purpose of liberating people from the "petrification of Christian thought".[32] Like Brunner, Kraemer also pays special attention to the other 'prophetic religions', Judaism, Zoroastrianism and Islam, which have not only phenomenological affinities, but, according to Brunner, a "blood relationship" with Christianity.[33] Although Kraemer suggests that special sensitivity is required here, these are not exceptions to the general rule. In the last resort all are religions of self-justification.[34]

It is not possible to draw up an inventory of which aspects of religions are erroneous or otherwise. Religion includes humanity, and base humanity at that, but also has nobler aspects, which aspire to Jesus Christ and point to Him who is 'full of grace and truth'. As Kraemer summarizes his views, religion is:

> A fundamental 'being in error'; a field in which we can trace God's own footsteps; noble aspiration and a tremendous capacity for creative action; and, in the light of Jesus Christ, humiliating aberration: these form the main outline of what I have

---

27 Kraemer, *Religion and the Christian Faith*, p257.

28 Kraemer, *Why Christianity*, p89.

29 Kraemer, *Why Christianity*, p93.

30"Behind all religion, therefore, there lies, on the side of God, truth, communication, the testimony of the Creator-God to himself." E. Brunner, *Revelation and Reason* (SCM, London, 1947) p262.

31 Hallencreutz, *Kraemer Towards Tambaram*, p228.

32 Kraemer, *The Christian Message*, pp235ff.

33 Brunner, *Revelation and Reason*, pp226ff.

34 Kraemer, *Why Christianity*, pp104-9.

been trying to say...they are sufficient index to my views on the whole question...[35]

Or, rather more succinctly, all religion is ambiguous, and requires some measure or standard by which it can be judged, not so much on the intellectual level as on the existential. Such a criterion is not to be found in Christianity as a religion, for there is no true *religion*. Humanity hungers after such absolutes and creates them as idols. Christianity, as an historical phenomenon is a religion in this idolatrous sense, and is therefore not in itself the criterion for such judgement. The only 'absolute' for Kraemer is not Christianity but "the Revelation of God in Jesus Christ He has no need of our proofs. He simply reigns from the cross, even were no-one to recognize the fact".[36]

In all this Kraemer is attempting to maintain a doctrine of grace, though he does not appear to use this term much. He is trying to emphasize the inability of humanity to arrive at a knowledge of God by its own efforts. So, for example, he comments that "knowledge of the truth in a religious context is not an achievement on the part of man ... It rests – and this is the whole basis of Christianity – upon God's self-communication, upon His self-disclosure in Jesus Christ, in whom and through whom 'grace and truth' are come".[37]

Kraemer insists that "the truth is revealed *in* Him and not just *by* Him",[38] and therefore "when the question is raised of the *truth* and *value* of the different religions, it is there, i.e. in the Person of Jesus Christ *and in whatever is comprehended in that*[39] that he [the Christian] finds his standard of reference".[40] This is a crux for Kraemer's position and a serious problem for his interpreters in that he never really spells out in sufficient detail just what 'the Person of Jesus Christ' really does comprehend. Once again we see Kraemer sides with Brunner against Barth. The latter had viewed Biblical revelation as the annulment of religion. For Barth Religion, because it is a human striving for the ultimate, is, in the last analysis, unbelief. As we have seen above, Kraemer felt that Barth overemphasised divine sovereignty and grace (hence, perhaps, his own restrained use of that term). The priority of grace may well be theologically correct, but when pushed with full Barthian weight and rigour Kraemer found it to be over-schematic and almost inhuman. He suggests that Barth lacked Calvin's appreciation of the divine sense within humanity, and quotes Scripture in defence of his own position.[41] Kraemer prefers Brunner's description of

35 Kraemer, *Why Christianity*, p104.

36 Kraemer, *Why Christianity*, p116.

37 Kraemer, *Why Christianity*, p76.

38 Kraemer, *Why Christianity*, p73.

39 My emphasis.

40 Kraemer, *Why Christianity*, p74.

41 See Kraemer's critique of Barth in *Religion and the Christian Faith*, pp185ff, and his reference to Mal 1:11: "unworthy priests are reminded of the fact that God has everywhere in the world, from east to west, true worshippers and sacrificers who worship with their hearts." p194.

the Christian revelation as the *crisis* of all religion, but also as fulfilling those prophetic faiths in which humankind is in contact not merely with its own imagination, but also with God.[42]

Kraemer is fully aware that any verdict reached by such a method will be subjective, but in dealing with existential truth claims such as this it is inevitable that people will use existential criteria. Christianity itself must stand or fall by the same criterion, and Kraemer willingly concedes that it does not always provide the 'best' expression of aspects of the truth. He suggests, for example, that in Islam we find better expression of the Sovereignty of God. However, Christianity is a special case because it is the locus for the activity of God, under the Lordship of Christ, endowed with the Holy Spirit, and with the light of God's Word in Scripture. For these reasons it is open to sterner judgement as well as "greater possibilities for good".[43] And because of this also "the Evil One is more interested and more active in tempting the Church in order to destroy it".[44] Christianity is 'best' in the sense that it is there that the Gospel is to be heard.

In connection with this at Tambaram the veteran A.G. Hogg (whom we saw earlier criticize Farquhar for over-emphasis on continuity) now questioned whether Kraemer is too emphatic about discontinuity. He asked whether a distinction needed to be made between non-Christian *religion* and non-Christian *faith*.[45] Hogg believed that God was indeed revealed beyond the Christian tradition, but to *faith* rather than *religion*. Kraemer agreed that such a distinction should be made, but argued that *Biblical* faith is not a psychological faculty, but a response to the divine activity in salvation. The questions raised by Hogg, suggested Kraemer, are too individualistic and do not decide questions of Truth, nor does he truly face "the mystery of iniquity, precisely in the 'highest' expression of the human mind".[46]

The relationship between Christianity and the other faiths is not a static relationship, because the Church lives in communion with Christ by whom it is constantly being formed, judged and renewed. Therefore it is always open to see with clearer insight and to judge "more profoundly, truly and honestly than before".[47] Equally the reverse is also possible depending on the quality of the Church's relationship to Christ and its living of his life. The process is a continual round of reappraisal, searching out the 'revelatory' and the 'demonic' in all religion, including Christianity itself.

In sum for Kramer sin and 'the Fall' have disrupted true communication between God and humanity, and between human cultures. The communication of the Christian message is in obedience to a divine imperative, and, like the Christian revelation and the Christian Church, it is *sui generis*, to adopt Kraemer's characteristic phrase. If the missionary Church can find the true means to

---

42 On Brunner see Kraemer, *Religion and the Christian Faith*, pp182ff.
43 Kraemer, *Why Christianity*, p116.
44. Kraemer, *Religion and the Christian Faith*, pp336-7.
45 See *The Authority of the Faith*, pp102-25.
46 Kraemer, *Religion and the Christian Faith*, p227.
47 Kraemer, *Why Christianity*, p90.

communicate the revelation of God in Christ, then the path to true relationship and unimpaired communication is open once more. The Church is *sui generis* because of its relationship to Jesus Christ, and the Christian message is *sui generis* because of the presence within it, at least theologically and theoretically, of the Holy Spirit. But this does not guarantee the success of either, because of the possibility of 'cardiosclerosis', that is the hardening of the heart to the Gospel, both by those within the Church and those outside it.

As we have already noted, Kraemer was well aware of the barriers to communication posed by culture, and his experience in Indonesia and elsewhere gave him insight into the need to allow the Gospel to 'take root' and find expression in non-European soils. He argued for a process of 'Christianisation' by which he meant, "digging channels for the expression of normal religious needs".[48] In a report on the controversial mission to Bali, he argued that missions could neither preserve nor annihilate Balinese culture rather, "the aim of mission is to preach the Gospel and to be engaged in building religious and moral foundations. In this work it will have to direct its honest efforts towards finding a Balinese form in which Christianity can be expressed."[49] He was in the vanguard of the movement to encourage the maturity and development of indigenous churches as the prime agencies of mission. In an era in which growing nationalism was an issue both for the Indonesians and the Dutch colonists, Kraemer did not shrink from the political implications of his thinking. The missionary must be open to nationalist claims, for the prime loyalty must be to 'the people of God', whose servants the missionaries are. Kraemer also recognised that communication is a two way process. Christianity grown and developed in a new situation will not only be different from say, European Christianity, but will also in time change and influence the new culture in which it is living.

All this requires sensitivity and patience on the part of the missionary, and Kraemer was critical of those who were quick to condemn, especially those who passed hasty judgement on the effect of another faith on the life and morals of a nation. Kraemer suggested that given the record of Christianity and the 'Christian' nations, Christians were hardly in a position to criticize. So, for example, of Islam:

> It is neither our task nor our duty to say ... that Mohammed is not the true prophet. Our witness on this point is merely taken as slanderous and offensive. It does not stimulate reflection but resentment. We cannot say this to a Mohammedan [sic], we must let him discover it for himself.[50]

On the other hand Kraemer was not one to offer a gospel so bland that it contained neither challenge nor offence. It must be recognised that however careful and sensitive the missionary may be, the gospel message carries an inherent challenge which will inevitably cause offence. This neither can nor should be

48 Kraemer, *From Missionfield to Independent Church*, p21.
49 Kraemer, *From Missionfield to Independent Church*, p183.
50 Kraemer, *From Missionfield to Independent Church*, p61.

avoided. But this consideration must never be taken as an excuse for an insensitive and deliberately offensive presentation of the Christian message. Kraemer was well aware of the historical background to this particular controversy, and he suggested that in the encounter with Islam, Christianity failed to be true to itself. He argued that Islam is *by its nature* the ideology of a cultural, social and political system, and met as its opponent a Christendom, which also behaved, *against the nature of the Christian faith*, as the 'ideology of a cultural, social and religious system'.[51] Kraemer was convinced that the proper attitude towards encounter or dialogue, must be that of openness and willingness for frank communication. Mere tolerance, or a neutrality rooted in apathy and indifference, was not enough. This had as much to do with the way the Church was, as with what it said.

A purely analytical method was also inadequate, what was necessary was 'the approach of love'. That is why there was the need to discover the 'values' of the non-Christian religions, in order to enter into the alien spiritual life and communicate the Gospel in all its depth. Such encounter with the religions, and indeed with secularism, served as a sharp reminder to the Church as to her true nature and business:

> ... the whole process of secularisation is one of the ironic ways of God to call the Church back to its true nature and calling, to knowing better its legitimate pretension to proclaim and assert Christ's claim of Kingship over all realms of life, but to do this, just as its Lord, as a servant, ever ready to be a suffering servant, and not as a power dependent on its rights and privilege.[52]

True Christian tolerance is not a recognition of human finitude and the relativity of human apprehension and experience, but is a recognition of the nature of God and the Gospel as one of love and freedom. Exclusivism too belongs to the heart of the Biblical message, and this has nothing to do with intellectual or any other certainty. It is rather the expression of being possessed by the Truth of God in Christ, by faith, "an act of joyful, obedient loyalty to Him".[53]

Kraemer was *the* protestant missiologist of the 1940s and 1950s, and, with his close links with the World Council of Churches, his views were widely held. For example, WCC General Secretary W. A. Visser 't Hooft, a fellow Dutchman, held a Kraemerian position, reflected in a statement shortly before his retirement in 1966 that, "it is the duty of every Christian to proclaim the divine Lordship of Jesus Christ; that this Gospel is to be addressed to every man, whatever his religious or cultural background may be; that it is to be given in its purest form, that is, in accordance with the biblical witness and unmixed with extraneous or cultural

---

51 Kraemer, *The Communication of the Christian Faith* (Lutterworth, London, 1957) p46.
52 Kraemer, *The Communication of the Christian Faith*, p87.
53 Kraemer, *Religion and the Christian Faith*, p373.

elements".[54] Visser 't Hooft's retirement coincided with the beginnings of what Kenneth Cragg has called 'conscious pluralism',[55] that is, a new awareness of the plurality of world-wide religious experience, and a new willingness to take it seriously. Assertion of the uniqueness of the Christian revelation and the supremacy of Christ in this new climate seemed arrogant and intolerant, and views like those of Kraemer and Visser 't Hooft were dismissed as such. However, in recent years it has become fashionable to include Kraemer within surveys of Christian approaches to other faiths, usually as the prime example of the so-called 'Exclusivist' position, and in conclusion to this section we must briefly review his treatment in recent discussion.

We have already mentioned one of the most comprehensive recent surveys of Christian attitudes to the world religions, Paul Knitter's *No Other Name?* Regrettably he pays scant attention to Kraemer, clearly regarding him as a mouthpiece for Barth. As we have already seen, Knitter's exposition fails to understand the differences between Barth and Kraemer and overlooks totally his affinities to Brunner, and the Calvinist background of his position.

A better account of Kraemer's work and influence is to be found in Alan Race's *Christians and Religious Pluralism*,[56] in which he recognises Kraemer's independent position within the overall method of dialectical theology, and his similarity to Brunner in accepting that there is truth in non-Christian religion, but maintaining *the Truth* in Jesus Christ. Both Brunner and Kraemer wish to make the distinction between revelation and religion, but Race is critical of the latter's view of revelation, with its simple appeal to biblical witness as internally coherent and externally cogent. Kraemer wants to use the 'Person of Jesus Christ' as his criterion for judgement, but Race argues that it cannot be done unless some doctrinal content is given to that phrase. This Kraemer never does, because he is trying to avoid importing into the discussion the doctrinal controversies of the early Church, which would complicate his argument through the introduction of the whole question of cultural relativity.[57] For Race the 'exclusivist edifice' is dependent on the doctrine and concept of Incarnation, and if this is challenged then exclusivism falls with it. However, it should be noted that for Kraemer the 'doctrine and concept' of Incarnation was basic to Christianity. If that fell then not just exclusivism but Christianity itself would be finished.

Perhaps the best recent account of Kraemer is found in the work of Gavin D'Costa. In his book *Theology and Religious Pluralism*,[58] he follows Race's categories of 'Exclusivism', 'Inclusivism' and 'Pluralism' and uses Kraemer as his prime example of the exclusivist paradigm. He notes Kraemer's warnings against over-simple comparisons between religious phenomena, and his stress on religions

---

54 In an interview given to *Christianity Today* and quoted by J.D. Douglas, *New International Dictionary of the Christian Church* (IVP, Leicester, 1975) p1021.

55 K. Cragg, *The Christian and Other Religion* (Mowbrays, Oxford, 1977) p7.

56 A. Race, *Christians and Religious Pluralism* (SCM, London, 1983).

57 See Race's discussion in *Christians and Religious Pluralism*, pp21-4 and pp30-2.

58 D'Costa, *Theology and Religious Pluralism* (Blackwell, Oxford, 1986).

as 'totalities'. However, he suggests that Kraemer himself is blind to some genuine similarities because of his assumption about the *sui generis* nature of the Christian revelation. D'Costa comments "There are, I believe, many points of contact and similarities which Kraemer obscures by his reductive hermeneutic".[59] He recognises the importance of Kraemer's plea for more scientific study of religion in order better to understand genuine differences and contradictions, but suggests that Kraemer underestimates the dynamic character of religion, which precludes any final analysis. D'Costa also highlights Kraemer's stress on the event of the Christian revelation, but notes, as we have already done, Kraemer's unwillingness to give the event much specific content. Given that Kraemer accepts revelation outside of Christ, certainly the Old Testament at the very least, then surely, pleads D'Costa, the stress must be on the *content* of revelation rather than the event.

Essential to Kraemer's stance is the recognition of the strange paradox, that in rejecting relativism one is left with subjectivism. He acknowledges throughout his work that it is carried out by a subjective method, and argues strongly that it *can* only be done in this way. Of course, he would claim that for the Christian the criterion of Jesus Christ is given rather than chosen, but nevertheless this criterion is available only to the committed Christian. In fact, Kraemer is even more subjective than this, for his criterion is really *his own interpretation* of the biblical witness, recognised as early as 1938 by that pioneer in this field E. C. Dewick.[60] Herein lies a major problem with Kraemer's method, for a Christocentric approach demands an articulated Christology, precisely that, which, according to his modern critics he fails to provide.

D'Costa believes that the Christian cannot easily dismiss Kraemer's insistence on Christ as the criterion for judging truth, but he argues for a less restrictive interpretation. Christ can be 'normative and definitive', but not 'exclusive'.[61] The difficulty for D'Costa and others is Kraemer's "excessively Pauline" interpretation of the Christian message which means that Kraemer must constantly reject non-Christian insights because they "lack the consciousness of sin and the need for forgiveness".[62] We shall return to this in a moment, but there does certainly seem to be a genuine difficulty in discerning what 'the biblical witness' really is. Kraemer's assertion that the Bible presents not theology but witness is, we agree with Race, over-simple and naïve.[63]

The question thus seems to hinge on what we believe is happening in God's revelation in Christ. In what sense is it *sui generis* and in what sense a completion or fulfilling of what God is everywhere seeking to do? Is it to do with the actual events in themselves or is it to do with the content of these events? Kraemer would find it impossible to make such a distinction. It is in the event of Christ that the

59 D'Costa, *Theology and Religious Pluralism*, p63.
60 See *The Modern Churchman*, 1938, p328.
61 D'Costa, *Theology and Religious Pluralism*, pp71-2.
62 D'Costa, *Theology and Religious Pluralism*, p72.
63 See Kraemer, *The Christian Message*, p65; and Race, *Christians and Religious Pluralism*, pp30-1.

content is made plain. Time and again he denies that he means by revelation 'saving *knowledge*', rather God gives Himself utterly *in* the event as well as *through* the event. It is this that is unique and gives to the Christ event its *sui generis* character.

The questions that ought to be asked are therefore to do with what God is accomplishing in and through Christ, rather than with the individual question of personal salvation implicit in the whole categorisation of 'Exclusivism, Inclusivism and Pluralism'. It is interesting that Lesslie Newbigin, the most frequently cited contemporary 'exclusivist', wanted to pose the same sort of questions. He urged us to see Christ as the one who is given to us as the centre of the human story, "the one who 'through the blood of his cross' can reconcile all people and all things". In this way God gives meaning and unity to history and the whole of creation, an affirmation not made imperialistically by the Church, but "in the name of the one who reigns from the tree", words amazingly redolent of what Kraemer has been trying to say.[64]

Newbigin does not believe that to see Jesus as the divine centre of human history is to exclude everyone else from the human story; in fact the reverse is the case. Like Kraemer, Newbigin views Jesus as the one who fulfils all history and in his life, death and resurrection, calls for a response of faith from the whole human race. Who will be judged to have made such a response is not ours to know, but the implications of the teaching of Jesus himself are that there will be surprises in store for all, and the criterion will be obedience to the will of God. Apparent 'outsiders' will discover that they are now inside for, "the first will be last and the last will be first".[65]

The question of sin and forgiveness is impossible to avoid in all this, for the content of the revelation of God in Christ, must have to do with what God *needed* to do in order to accomplish the divine purpose. This in turn depends upon what we perceive the human situation to be. Kraemer certainly believes that all human enterprises are flawed because humanity is fundamentally flawed, and he would seem to have in his favour not only the weight of biblical and Christian tradition, but also that of empirical evidence. D'Costa wants to argue that "because of the dynamic nature of religion brought about through the interaction of practice and belief, it follows that one cannot say, *a priori*, that all religions, past and future, exhibit human-made structures of self-justification".[66] But how unreasonable is it to assume that what has always been the case will, in all probability, continue to be the case in the future? Most ordinary life proceeds on this assumption and is generally correct to do so. If something proves not to fit with this then assumptions are modified in line with the new situation. Although Kraemer may not succeed in proving the *a priori* nature of his assumption, it may still provide a working hypothesis that continues to explain the known facts.

---

64 Newbigin, 'The Christian Faith and the World Religions' in G. Wainwright (ed), *Keeping the Faith* (SPCK, London, 1989), pp310-340; for Kraemer's comment see p16 above.

65 Newbigin, 'The Christian Faith and the World Religions', p333.

66 D'Costa, *Theology and Religious Pluralism*, p64.

The fundamental question remains as to whether the activity of God in Christ is so unambiguous as to provide the sort of clear-cut criterion that Kraemer claims. By definition Christ must be the starting point for the Christian, but in what sense do we have access to Christ? Can we really separate Christ from the tradition or the religion as Kraemer seems to suggest? Is it not rather through the tradition that we have access to Christ, and is it not by the tradition that we are able to fill out Kraemer's 'whatever is comprehended in that'? (In fact, to do him justice, Kraemer's phrase about God's self-revelation in Christ's 'Person, work, teaching, death and resurrection' is probably as comprehensive as possible, although rather too sketchy.) This difficulty is not unique to the so-called 'exclusivist' position, it also raises problems for those who would uphold Jesus Christ as the measure of what Kenneth Cragg calls 'the Christic' wherever it may be discerned in human life.

CHAPTER 3

Mission and Religious Pluralism in a Post-Colonial World

The years immediately following the Second World War saw the hope of a united world exemplified in the formation of the United Nations in 1945 and the creation of the World Council of Churches in 1948. There was also the recognition that scientific development might provide a common culture which would bridge the divide of continent, language and tradition. Some even considered the possibility that in a united world there might be a common faith and such thinking is reflected by titles like Lesslie Newbigin's *A Faith for this One World?*[1]

However, it was not just the fascist era that was at an end, all imperialisms had been undermined by the events of the previous twenty years. So too had movements like Christianity which seemed in the eyes of many to be too closely aligned with the Western colonial powers. The early 1960s saw a number of books by senior missionary figures such as Max Warren and Stephen Neill and this flurry of activity suggest something of the sharpness of the questions being faced by Christian missions in this period.[2] In his re-examination of the issue the mission historian Brian Stanley has noted that from the late Sixties onwards the debate took place within "an increasingly polarized and highly charged ideological context".[3] It is perhaps not surprising to note therefore, that the parallel debate about the relationship of Christianity to other faiths became detached from the missiological context in this period, and transferred to university faculties and departments increasingly labelled 'Religious Studies', rather than 'Theology' in order to show their independence of any church or religious institution.

Within this setting the dominant theory of inter-faith relationships over the past thirty-five years or more has been that usually described as 'pluralism', and the leading advocate of a pluralist theology of religions since the publication of his *God*

---

1 Newbigin, *A Faith for this One World?* (SCM, London, 1961); the faith in question was of course Christianity!

2 See Warren, *The Missionary Movement from Britain in Modern History* (SCM, London, 1965) and *Social History and Christian Mission* (SCM, London, 1967); Neill, *A History of Christian Missions* (Penguin, Harmondsworth, 1964) and *Colonialism and Christian Missions* (Lutterworth, London, 1966).

3 B. Stanley, *The Bible and the Flag: Protestant Missions and British imperialism in the nineteenth and twentieth centuries* (Apollos/IVP, Leicester, 1990) p19.

and the Universe of Faiths[4] has been Professor John Hick. It was here that he first advocated what he labelled a 'Copernican Revolution' in the Christian understanding of the relationship between Christianity and other faith systems. This meant an initial movement from a Christocentric view of the 'universe of faiths' to a theocentric model, but he subsequently developed this theory further to take account of the non-theistic belief systems of Advaita Vedanta and Theravada Buddhism among others. His theology is built on the twin foundations of a soteriological approach to religion, and an epistemology borrowed and adapted from Kant and Wittgenstein. Hick would also argue that his view is firmly grounded in the phenomenology of religion, but this claim is somewhat suspect.

This section will outline Hick's essential position as it has developed from *God and the Universe of Faiths*, through to the very full statement in his magnum opus *An Interpretation of Religion*, based on his Gifford Lectures 1986-87.[5] It will then consider the various criticisms of his approach, especially the sustained critique of his former pupil Gavin D'Costa and the careful analysis by Chester Gillis.

The soteriological foundation for much of Hick's thinking on this issue is clearly stated in *God and the Universe of Faiths* where he argues that the Christian understanding of God with its teaching on the universality of divine love must, "exclude the idea that salvation occurs only in one strand of human history, which is limited in time to the last nineteen centuries and in space virtually to the western hemisphere. If God's love is universal in scope, he cannot thus have restricted his saving encounter with humanity. If God is the God of the whole world, we must presume that the whole religious life of mankind is part of a continuous and universal human relationship to him".[6] Here we are presented with the old, yet still pressing, problem of 'the scandal of particularity', which actually Hick makes even more particular by reference only to *'the religious life of mankind'*, why not the whole life of the whole planet? His rejection of the cosmological argument for the existence of God[7] seems to have left him without a doctrine of creation in which his soteriology might be grounded.

Hick follows Wilfred Cantwell Smith in treating the religious faiths as human phenomena, historically, geographically and culturally conditioned. What is true of religions in general must be true of each religion in particular, so Christianity, for example, may be characterised as "an ongoing movement of life and thought, defined by its origin in the Christ-event and by its consciousness of that origin". It cannot be defined in terms of adherence to any doctrinal standard, for its doctrines are historically and culturally conditioned and have changed as the church has entered

---

4 J. Hick, *God and the Universe of Faiths* (Fount, London, Rev. Ed., 1977; 2nd Ed. Macmillan, London, 1993).

5 J. Hick, *An Interpretation of Religion* (Macmillan, London, 1989).

6 Hick, *Universe of Faiths*, pp100-1.

7 E.g. Hick's brief review in *Interpretation of Religion*, pp79-81, which concludes: "Thus it seems that the cosmological family of arguments, although richly suggestive, nevertheless does not constitute a compelling theistic proof."

new historical and cultural situations.[8] This approach seems to rule out any definitive self-revelation of God.

At this stage in the development of his argument, Hick believes that it is not necessary to 'water down' the essential Christian understanding of Christ, for to recognize the divine presence in Christ need not preclude "an *equally valid* awareness of God in other religions".[9] He argues that the religious life of the human race is part of a continuum of relationship to the divine Reality. To be truly comprehensive and global in approach, the theologian must include all forms of religious experience and all types of religious ideas within the hypotheses that he suggests. All that matters is that it should be genuine. Hick is well aware that this leaves open the question as to what data is to be acceptable as 'genuine religious experience' and by what criteria it may be judged. He returns to this question over again because his critics repeatedly raise it, but essentially he wants to use soteriological criteria. In other words, religious experience is 'genuine' in so far as it promotes human salvation-liberation, by which he means, "the realisation of that limitlessly better quality of human existence which comes about in the transition from self-centredness to Reality-centredness".[10]

The concern for salvation is actually at the root of all that Hick is trying to achieve in the 'Copernican revolution', and it is a considerable moral argument that he brings to bear in recognising that a large majority of the human race who have lived and died up to the present moment have lived either before Christ or outside the borders of Christendom. Hick wonders how a God of love who seeks to save all mankind apparently ordains that only a small minority can in fact receive this salvation.[11]

In response to this issue, many Christian thinkers have adopted what has been termed an 'inclusivist' approach. Recognising the reality of the divine life in many cultures and religions, Catholic thinkers especially have sought to include such people by means of theories such as 'anonymous Christians' (Rahner) and 'ordinary and extraordinary salvation' (Küng). Hick sees all this in terms of his astronomical analogy. The old (exclusivist) theology is like the Ptolemaic astronomy, struggling to match up to the new awareness of reality. Theories such as those of Rahner and Kung are like the complex epicycles added by ingenious astronomers to retain a geocentric astronomy. In the end the simpler explanation of Copernicus cut through the knots in which the old approach had tied itself.

In this initial stage of his thinking, Hick argues that the theological equivalent of the Copernican Revolution will see a Christocentric model of the universe of faiths replaced by a theocentric model. It will involve "a shift from the dogma that Christianity is at the centre to the realisation that it is *God* who is at the centre, and that all the religions of mankind, including our own, serve and revolve around

---

8 Hick, *Universe of Faiths*, p119

9 Hick, *Universe of Faiths*, pp106-7; my emphasis.

10 See 'On Grading Religions' in J. Hick, *Problems of Religious Pluralism* (Macmillan, London, 1985) p86.

11 Hick, *Universe of Faiths*, pp122-3.

him".[12] Such a revolution needs to happen for all other faiths too, because they are equally 'Ptolemaic': theology and religious faith are dictated by the accidents of birth and geography.

Hick tends to take a broadly 'evolutionary' approach to the history and development of religion, and, following Karl Jaspers, finds the period c800BC to c200BC to be the 'axial period' for the development of religious thought and practice the world over. The 'axial age' he defines as "a concentration of events which, although without exact boundaries, forms a large-scale event in its own right".[13] He characterises the early period as "religion without revelation", and he describes it as mainly concerned with the preservation of the cosmic and social order. Post-axial religion in contrast, is mainly concerned with the quest for salvation or liberation, and thus marks a new stage in the development of the human consciousness. In all traditions during this period there begins the search for transformation of the human condition from self to reality-centredness, and each strain of human religious thought exhibits a "soteriological structure", concerned with moral weakness or the pervasive insecurity and inherent suffering of human life. Each tradition also proclaims a limitlessly better possibility arising from another, transcendent, reality, and the teaching of a way, whether humanistic or gracious, to its realisation.[14]

Such 'post-axial' religion thus embraces what Hick describes as 'cosmic optimism'. That is, the conviction that the human condition can indeed be transformed and liberation experienced. This marks the second stage in the development of Hick's argument, where 'theocentricity' gives way to 'soteriocentricity', the centrality of the search for salvation. This shift of consciousness, Hick argues, is due to revelation or rather, "a remarkable series of revelatory experiences",[15] over a period of some five hundred years. The geographical and cultural isolation of the time made it inevitable that such revelation would have a pluriform character, developing independently within different streams of human history. Hick traces 'the golden age of religious creativity' from the early Jewish prophets Amos, Hosea and first Isaiah, through the Persian prophet Zoroaster, eastwards through the Upanishadic India of Gotama the Buddha to the China of Confucius and Lao-Tzu. Towards the end of this period he notes the writing of the *Bhagavad-Gita* and the activity of the great Greek philosophers. Unfortunately, this scheme fails to include the ministry of Jesus of Nazareth or the activity of the Prophet Muhammad, so these are 'tagged on' at the end, somewhat lamely given that their followers are the most numerous of all the world faiths.

Hick argues that all of these events can be regarded as 'revelatory' of the divine transcendent within different strands of human consciousness, they are thus not rivals but complementary dimensions of humanity's religious experience. Hick is of course aware that they can also be regarded in humanistic terms as the development of crude religious fantasy into sophisticated metaphysical speculation, but from the

---

12 Hick, *Universe of Faiths*, p131.
13 Hick, *Interpretation of Religion*, p31.
14 Hick, *Interpretation of Religion*, p56.
15 Hick, *Universe of Faiths*, p135.

viewpoint of faith the interpretation of this sketch of human religious history as 'a movement of divine self-revelation' is a 'reasonable hypothesis'. Such opposing conclusions are generated by what Hick terms 'the religious ambiguity of the universe', especially in a post-Enlightenment world: "the universe maintains its inscrutable ambiguity. In some aspects it invites whilst in others it repels a religious response. It permits both a religious and a naturalistic faith, but haunted in each case by a contrary possibility that can never be exorcised".[16]

This opens up the significant area of epistemology within Hick's discussions and he carefully analyses how we know what we claim to know, and why we opt for one interpretation of reality rather than another. He makes the important point that in some ways, objectively and philosophically, we recognize that life and the universe are capable of a variety of interpretations. But practical living demands that we actually interpret life and the universe "as meaningful in a particular way which, whilst it operates, excludes other possible ways".[17] Meaning and interpretation are in this sense existential and practical, and they create a particular disposition towards life, which is reflected in human behaviour patterns. It is in this context that he develops Wittgenstein's theory of 'seeing-as'. When we 'see' a picture, we absorb shade, shape and texture and so on; but in 'seeing-as' we use an interpretive element, especially where the picture is unclear, as in Wittgenstein's famous examples of puzzle-pictures such as the well-known 'duck-rabbit'. Hick suggests that this process is true not just of seeing, but equally of all our sense perception. In fact he suggests that in our living we rarely if ever just 'experience', but inevitably 'experience-as', that is we *interpret* our experience as it happens. Equally inevitably cultural conditioning operates in this process, especially in those complex relational situations in which we find ourselves and which may be interpreted in aesthetic, ethical and religious terms.

He notes that many people in the world experience places, people and situations as 'religious', often articulated as "living in the presence of the unseen God".[18] This is to 'experience-as' within situations that are often ambiguous and capable of alternative explanation. We are left with considerable freedom and responsibility in our response to such experience. Even though only one interpretation may be correct, in the sense of appropriate to actuality, its true character does not force itself upon us, and the vindication of our cognitive choices will only be discovered in the future unfolding of reality. It is this process which Hick labels 'eschatological verification'. To relate this specifically to religious experience, Hick argues that, for example, the Christian response to Jesus "was and is an uncompelled interpretation, experiencing an ambiguous figure in a distinctive way as mediating the transfiguring presence of God".[19] As we move from the physical through the ethical to the religious, so human cognitive freedom becomes greater, correlated as it is to the greater claim upon our lives of this aspect of reality.

---

16 Hick, *Interpretation of Religion*, p124.
17 Hick, *Interpretation of Religion*, p129.
18 Hick, *Problems of Religious Pluralism*, p22.
19 Hick, *Interpretation of Religion*, p157.

Hick argues strongly for the right of the religious believer to claim that such religious response to experience, whether one's own or that of the saints, is as valid as a naturalistic or non-transcendent interpretation of reality. And religious language must be viewed as an attempt to articulate in some sense 'how things are'; it is 'realistic'. The views of the non-realist, such as Don Cupitt, or the anti-realist, such as Dewi Phillips, suggest that religious language merely reflects the subjective state of the believer. Hick argues that such an approach does not allow for the ultimate fulfilment of the vast majority of humankind, only for the elite who attain salvation-liberation in this life, that is those who achieve a subjective state of liberation here and now. As the Californian poet Thom Gunn put it, only "birds and saints complete their purposes".[20] While this is not impossible, such a pessimistic creed "cannot credibly claim to represent the message of the great spiritual traditions" in their "cosmic optimism".[21]

Hick's soteriological criterion is never clearer than in such places where he defends the rights of the "ordinary believer" to trust religious experience, whether their own or that of their tradition. Just as daily life requires us to assume the veridical character of our perceptual experience and "experiencing-as", so too with religious experience, especially for those "mahatmas" or saints whom we cannot conceive as interpreting their life in any other way. The ordinary believer too is entitled to trust those moments of intensified meaning in public worship or private devotion, or at one of the "deep points" of human life such as birth or death. Hick goes on to argue:

> Thus if in the existing situation of theoretic ambiguity a person experiences life religiously, or participates in a community whose life is based on this mode of experience, he or she is rationally entitled to trust that experience and to proceed to believe and to live on the basis of it.[22]

This applies equally to theistic and non-theistic belief and experience.

This sort of approach clearly raises the question of the truth claims of these varying experiences and traditions, for at the very least there is conflict between concepts of 'the Real' as personal or impersonal and human life as cyclical or linear. In the end one or other of these various alternatives must be closer to actuality than the other. Hick responds in a number of ways to this point. First he argues that all great religious traditions recognize that because the Real is infinite it transcends the grasp of finite human minds, therefore all claims to truth must be partial and not absolute. Thus the different claims of these traditions may all be encounters with the one genuine divine reality. This is illustrated by the famous Indian parable, of the blind men and the elephant. Each of the blind men encounters a different part of the elephant and his description seems at first to contradict the testimony of the others

---

20 From Gunn's poem, 'On the Move' first published in *The Sense of Movement* (Faber, London, 1957).
21 Hick, *Interpretation of Religion*, pp207-8.
22 Hick, *Interpretation of Religion*, p228.

which also contradict each other. It turns out that of course all are true, but limited, descriptions of the whole reality. Hick does not suggest that the various traditions have encountered only *part* of the Real, but that each encounter has been clothed in different cultural packaging.

Secondly, Hick claims that the probability of this explanation is increased when we realise that in worship and prayer and in the mystical aspects of all the religions there is considerable agreement and overlap between them, suggesting a common encounter with the same divine reality. Thus all are, or can be, "soteriological 'spaces' within which, or 'ways' along which, men and women can find salvation, liberation, fulfilment". For Hick there can be no separation of the truth-claim from the salvation-claim: rather the truth-claim must be seen as the 'packaging' in which the 'goods' of the salvation-claim are wrapped in order for the whole 'parcel' to be transmitted and received. Truth-claims are essential but secondary to the process. What is primary and vital is the receiving of salvation – soteriology again.

Hick suggests that the absolute language in which religious truth-claims are usually packaged testifies to the ultimate nature of the religious experience that they reflect. Psychologically this is perfectly understandable and is akin to national pride, an expression of the natural parochialism and residual tribalism of human community. This has many commendable features within it, prompting us to work and sacrifice for the good of the community. As such "it may be accepted and taken into account as an inevitable feature of human life".[23] However, we should not make the harmful mistake of elevating this sort of thinking to the level of the absolute, which happens when the religious experience of salvation-liberation within one tradition, is doctrinally expressed in terms of exclusive or superior access to the truth. This means for Christianity that it must take a long hard look at those doctrines that suggest exclusivity and superiority, central to which is the whole notion of the unique Incarnation of Christ.

He recognises that many contemporary theologians are attempting to mitigate the old absolutist and exclusivist doctrines by demonstrating that the salvation won by Christ is made available to the whole of the human race, but whilst these are admirable in their intention, they simply do not go to the heart of the matter. In addition to his astronomical analogy already mentioned above, he compares such theologies to the pharmacist who advocates the use of the pure unadulterated medicine, Christ, wherever possible, but recognises the value of other products which may contain Christ, albeit in dilute and compound form, where pure Christ is not available. In the end such approaches must be rejected in favour of religious pluralism, and doctrines such as the Incarnation must be subject to radical revision.

Hick argues that the 'substance' language of the Nicean and Chalcedonian formulas was perfectly rational and understandable in the thought world of the early Church Fathers. This is not so for our generation, indeed there is no corresponding universal philosophical language. He suggests that there is a logical similarity and parallel in the dogma of transubstantiation which for most Christians, both Catholic

---

23 Hick, *Problems of Religious Pluralism*, pp49-50.

and Protestant, is now redundant. Hick goes on to argue for an identity of purpose or action, rather than substance, which he claims is closer to the biblical Hebraic world-view. He prefers H.H. Farmer's term 'inhistorisation' to that of the traditional 'incarnation' because it brings out more forcefully this functional identity between the activity of Jesus and the activity of God. In Christ God is at work within and through human history, rather than upon it or into it. The result is a functional Christology in which Jesus has a single, human, nature, but which is directed by God's agapé; Christ has a single will whose ruling motive was God's agapé for mankind. The continuity between Jesus and God is one of event rather than entity.

In any case, whether we use the language of substance or agape, the talk is mythological rather than metaphysical. It is not the language of explanation but the language of attitude. In a similar way to that in which 'the Fall' has come to be seen as mythology over the last century, so too will the notion of 'Incarnation'. The classical Christological formulas reaffirm the mystery but in fact explain nothing, and all attempts at explanation have been condemned as heresy for one reason or another. Hick argues that the fundamental heresy always rejected by the Church has been to treat the myth as an hypothesis.[24] Hick suggests that the absoluteness of the language reflects the absoluteness of the experience; indeed it is this 'absolute' character that defines the moment of 'divine revelation'. But, "The question that now has to be raised, however, in the context of our new map of the universe of faiths, is whether we properly understand the function of this Christian myth of incarnation if we take it to make an exclusive claim for Christianity as the *only* way of salvation".[25] The answer to this question for Hick is clearly 'no', but this does not alter for him the truth of the myth, for if the attitude that this myth creates is appropriate then the myth is true, and the experienced salvation is indeed a reality.

Thus far Hick has notably ignored the question of the resurrection of Jesus Christ and so he begins with this in his contribution to *The Myth of God Incarnate*. Hick is willing to concede post-death appearances of Jesus to his disciples, which can be described as 'resurrection'. Indeed, in view of the survival and growth of the tiny Jesus movement, this "seems virtually certain".[26] He argues, however, that this did not in fact suggest divinity to his contemporaries, and compares the resurrection of Jesus to the other raisings from death recorded in the New Testament.[27] He affirms that "Jesus' specially intimate awareness of God, his consequent spiritual authority and his efficacy as Lord and as *giver of new life*,[28] required in his disciples an adequate language in which to speak about their master".[29] What we see in the New Testament and the Patristic literature is the search for this language and the arrival at the classical formulas, which Hick has argued, will no longer do. It should now be

---

24 Hick, *Universe of Faiths*, p171.
25 Hick, *Universe of Faiths*, p172.
26 J. Hick (ed), *The Myth of God Incarnate* (SCM, London, 1977) p170.
27 Cf. the dismissal of this argument by S. Neill in (ed) M. Green, *The Truth of God Incarnate* (IVP, Leicester, 1977) p69.
28 My emphasis.
29 Hick, *Myth*, p173.

seen for the metaphor that it is and no longer regarded as 'fact-asserting'. But he is willing to suggest that the 'Logos' language of Christianity may yet have some mileage within it:

> If, selecting from our Christian language, we call God-acting-towards-mankind the Logos, then we must say that *all* salvation, within all religions, is the work of the Logos and that under their various images and symbols men in different cultures and faiths may encounter the Logos and find salvation. But what we cannot say is that all who are saved are saved by Jesus of Nazareth. The life of Jesus was one point at which the Logos has acted; and it is the only point that savingly concerns the Christians; but we are not called upon nor are we entitled to make the negative assertion that the Logos has not acted and is not acting anywhere else in human life.[30]

Rather what is required is the sharing of the various revelations of God for mutual enrichment. One of the dangers of the 'exclusive' approach is that it confines Christ within the Church instead of freeing him into the world.[31] Jesus must not be imprisoned behind an 'iron mask' of western incarnational mythology. Hick believes that the so-called 'degree Christologies' of Baillie and Lampe may offer a way forward for the development of a Christology appropriate to a theocentric map of the universe of faiths.

In his later writings on understanding religion Hick has moved a stage further in his thought, in a logical development of his thinking, to what has been termed a 'soteriocentric' view of religion. We have already demonstrated that the experience of salvation is central to his understanding of post-axial religion, indeed in a popular exposition of his thought he says quite simply "salvation is what religion is all about".[32] Attempting to take the phenomenology of religion seriously he recognises that his earlier thinking has been too theocentric and failed to take sufficient account of the non-theistic experience of salvation-liberation. In order to correct this bias Hick adopts the Hindu distinction between *Saguna Brahman*, that is ultimate Reality as experienced in different ways by humanity, and *Nirguna Brahman*, Reality beyond human knowing and experience, utterly transcendent. Saguna Reality is experienced as both personal and impersonal, in much the same way that physicists describe light in terms of both waves and particles. Such talk is convenient and essential but fails to capture the full reality of which it speaks. Similarly, the Real is experienced and must be articulated in these various ways, but none is adequate to do full justice to the infinity of Nirguna Reality, the God beyond human grasp. Hick develops the Kantian distinction between noumenon and phenomenon to illustrate his argument at this point, suggesting that the noumenous is experienced humanly in both personal

---

30 Hick, *Myth*, p181.

31 "The Jesus who is for the world is not the property of the human organisation called the Christian Church, nor is he to be confined within its theoretical constructions", Hick, *Myth*, pp182-3.

32 J. Hick, *The Second Christianity* (SCM, London, 3rd Ed., 1983) p79.

and impersonal phenomena.[33] Kant did not believe that God could be experienced, even phenomenologically, but Hick's extension of the idea does not seem unreasonable, and for some provides weight for his argument.[34]

Hick's clear and repeated advocacy of a 'Copernican revolution' in the theology of religions has won many supporters during the last decade or more of debate, notably Paul Knitter, Alan Race and Hick's original mentor Wilfred Cantwell Smith. But there are those who have opposed this sort of move on a number of grounds, one of the earliest being Duncan Forrester. Like the more recent and detailed criticism of Gavin D'Costa, Forrester begins his response by questioning the picture of the so-called 'Ptolemaic' theology that Hick presents. In fact, argues Forrester, the Christian theological tradition in relation to other faiths is much more varied than Hick would have us believe.[35]

D'Costa agrees and in a careful analysis of the development of the well-known doctrine of *extra ecclesiam nulla sallus* (outside the Church no salvation) suggests that Hick has both misinterpreted the doctrine and is insensitive to the preoccupations and the context of those Fathers who developed and applied it.[36] In fact the doctrine evolved over a lengthy time-period in response to pastoral concerns of the Church, which did not include encounter with the great world faiths. The contemporary responses, such as those of Rahner and Küng – labelled by Hick as 'epicycles' – could well be regarded as legitimate developments of the traditional doctrine in response to the new situation now facing the Church. This not only draws on Newman's concept of the development of doctrine, but also could be paralleled in Christological doctrine as, for example, C.F.D. Moule has argued.[37] Chester Gillis too, has suggested that it is perfectly reasonable to come to an understanding of historical and historic events after the fact. Some events can only be understood properly with hindsight, indeed this may be the distinguishing feature of genuinely revelatory experience. There is of course the contemporary flash of insight into 'the Real', but this is followed by ongoing reflection and development of its significance within new and differing situations. It is unfair to caricature all this as illegitimate epicycle. Thus, if Hick has not presented an entirely fair picture of what he calls 'Ptolemaic' theology, then his 'Copernican revolution' may be unnecessary.

Even so conservative an apologist as Michael Green is not prepared to concede that traditional doctrine required *explicit* knowledge of the person and work of Christ as essential to salvation. Rather wherever people rely on "the Great God" to accept them irrespective of their merits, they are indeed accepted as children of Abraham, the archetypal believer.[38] However, Green and others who hold what is actually an

---

33 Hick, *Interpretation of Religion*, pp233-49, and chapters 15 and 16 respectively.

34 E.g. Race, *Christianity and Religious Pluralism*, p86.

35 D. Forrester, 'Professor Hick and the Universe of Faiths', *Scottish Journal of Theology* 29 (1976) pp65-72.

36 G. D'Costa, *John Hick's Theology of Religions* (UPA, New York, 1987) p80.

37 C.F.D. Moule, *The Origin of Christology* (CUP, Cambridge, 1977) pp1-10.

38 M. Green (ed), *The Truth of God Incarnate* (Hodder & Stoughton, London, 1977) pp118-9.

'inclusivist' position, still maintain that such salvation is through Jesus Christ. Hick's rejection of this position requires a jump in the argument. This was first noted by Duncan Forrester when he points to "a quiet transition" from the rejection of 'no salvation outside the church', to the setting aside of 'salvation through Christ alone' as if the two can be directly equated. By labelling attempts at a Christocentric theology of religions as 'epicycle', Hick identifies them as identical to ecclesiocentric theologies and therefore moves on to his initial theocentric model without adequate argument.[39]

Hick's initial thesis was widely criticised for removing Christ from the centre of the universe of faiths, only to replace him with the Christian God. For example, in his consideration of the identity and role of Jesus, Hick was perfectly happy to talk of God's agape, but if Christ is removed from the central point of God's self-communication, how does Hick know that God is love? Gillis and others point out that this assumption about the nature of the divine is a fundamentally Christian concept.[40] Moreover, as Lesslie Newbigin suggests, the Copernican analogy does not provide an exact parallel to what Hick is trying to do. Copernicus replaced one objective reality, the earth, by another, the sun. But in putting God at the centre of his new map of the universe of faiths Hick focuses on that which is not capable of objective investigation; God and the religions are not in the same class.

Because we do not have, and cannot have, any frame of reference for comparing 'God as God really is' with 'God as conceived by the various religions', we are left with the claim that: "one theologian's conception of God is the reality which is the central essence of all things ... Hick's conception of God simply is the truth and there is no possibility that one of the world's religions can challenge it".[41] Newbigin also recognises that, at this stage of the debate at least, the God at the centre of Hick's Copernican revolution is not unknown but that as "infinite and inexhaustible love" it is a profoundly Christian understanding of God.[42] D'Costa concurs that it is impossible to separate Hick's theocentrism from Christological assumptions.[43] He argues that Hick holds covertly to a 'decisive' status for the revelation of God in Christ, and points out the difficulty inherent in trying to relativize the events by which God is disclosed without relativizing the disclosure itself. D'Costa suggests that for the Judaeo-Christian-Islamic religious tradition there is an intrinsic relationship to historical contexts and particulars, "which if taken seriously should cause certain apprehension in adopting Hick's possible *non-particularist* theocentrism".[44] This is an important issue to which we shall return.

Hick wants at all costs to avoid the 'scandal of particularity' because for him it contains the assumption that those who do not come into direct relationship with that particular revelation will be outside the sphere of salvation. However, many of

---

39 D. Forrester, *Scottish Journal of Theology*, 29 (1976), p68.

40 C. Gillis, *A Question of Final Belief* (Macmillan, London, 1989) p170.

41 L. Newbigin, *The Open Secret* (Eerdmans, Grand Rapids, 1978) p185.

42 L. Newbigin, 'The Christian Faith and the World Religions', p317.

43 D'Costa, *Theology and Religious Pluralism*, p31.

44 D'Costa, *John Hick's Theology of Religions*, p113.

his critics not only challenge the validity of that assumption but also argue that revelation *must* take concrete and particular form if it is to reach concrete and particular human beings. Hick, of course recognises this in his arguments about cultural conditioning, but he then goes on to suggest that all concrete and particular religious expressions of the 'Real' might be valid within their historico-cultural limitations. Anything which turns people from self-centredness to 'reality-centredness' can be viewed in this light.[45]

Theologians such as Brian Hebblethwaite have seen no contradiction between a unique incarnation of God in Christ, and God's will for universal salvation: "The particularity of the incarnation – the fact that if God was to come to us in person it would have to be at a particular time and place in history – certainly involves seeing the whole creation and the whole of human history pivoting upon a brief slice of space-time in the history of the ancient Middle East".[46] In the same volume Stephen Neill suggests that this may be seen as unitary and inclusive rather than divisive and exclusive, for if the human race really is one, then history may well have a 'central point'.[47] But Hick is as reluctant to be tied to history as he is to any doctrine of creation, and this means that he is hard put to anchor his soteriology. Hick seems to suggest that in the axial period, 'the Real' was at work throughout the world in various revelatory experiences. In that case, argues D'Costa, "If it is acknowledged freely that God has acted throughout human history in various and particular ways, there is no a priori reason why one act within the complex series of acts should not be viewed as the climax and high-point of all the rest".[48]

Hebblethwaite makes precisely this point about the Incarnation in his various responses to Hick. He argues that it is a 'total interpretative key', which illustrates and transforms all other knowledge of God, "just because it is God's own particular act in time and for eternity".[49] Kenneth Cragg has adopted this procedure in his major discussion *The Christ and the Faiths*,[50] searching out 'the Christic', which, he suggests, may be found in all the great religious traditions. But, as he noted in an earlier excursion into this field, and in relation to Hick, this does not free us from the ties of history, for "Christian faith in Christ as 'Son of God' has first been faith in a historic actuality in order to be, also, as Hick rightly stresses the Christian's proceeding upon his image of God".[51]

The justification for the use of Christ as the measure or criterion, by which other claims to revelation have been judged, has been for most Christian thinkers, the

---

45 See the discussion in Hick's essay 'On Grading Religions' in *Problems of Religious Pluralism*, pp67-87.

46 B. Hebblethwaite in Green (ed), *The Truth of God Incarnate*, p104.

47 S. Neill in Green (ed), *The Truth of God Incarnate*, p80.

48 D'Costa, *John Hick's Theology of Religions*, p140.

49 B. Hebblethwaite, 'The Moral and Religious Value of the Incarnation' in M. Goulder (ed), *Incarnation and Myth* (SCM, London, 1979) p190; see also his discussion in Green (ed), *The Truth of God Incarnate*, pp101-6.

50 SPCK, London, 1986.

51 Cragg, *The Christian and Other Religion*, p76, see also chapter 6 below.

Resurrection. As we have seen above, Hick pays all too brief attention to this particular, but it cannot be ignored for it is the basis for all the claims to uniqueness of the Christian faith. Gillis writes:

> The argument from the resurrection as a *sui generis* event that validates the life and ministry of Jesus and the Christian community's claim that he was divine as well as human is an appeal to history that indeed is difficult to verify. However, there are many theologians and exegetes who would claim this as the central revelatory event of Christianity that gives credibility to the credal statements about Jesus.[52]

Moreover, Hick's analysis of the biblical material is weak, distinguishing too sharply between the Hebraic and Greek thought-forms in the hybrid milieu of the New Testament. There is no reason to suppose that the New Testament affirmations about Jesus as the Christ or as the Son of God, are all entirely functional. Many may well have had ontological implications.[53] Frank Whaling notes that even those who have argued the case for 'degree Christologies' do not necessarily assume a relativistic view of Christ.[54]

Although Hick is reluctant to tie revelation too closely to the particulars of creation or history, he does argue from the particular experience of prayer and worship, especially within the mystical strands of the various religious traditions, that there is in fact an underlying unity which supports his position. Here he builds too much on slender grounds and one is often forced to wonder whether he would ever actually admit to the possibility of contradictory truth-claims. He always seems to believe that in the end all such differences are due to history or geography or culture. D'Costa makes a telling point in his comment that Hick "tends to make truth a function of birth".[55] Gillis argues that Hick *expects* to find areas of agreement, the process of dialogue is entered with this specific purpose, and when this is so it may be difficult to appreciate a lack of convergence of thought when it is encountered.[56]

Hick stresses the importance of 'truth-seeking' dialogue, but one often has the impression that Hick already knows the truth that partners in dialogue are really in fundamental agreement, which, if they are open and honest enough with each other they will eventually discover. That is why he has difficulty with Newbigin's 'confessional dialogue' for he believes it will be a barrier to discovery of the truth. Partners in dialogue must be prepared to leave behind the cultural baggage of their own tradition, even cherished doctrines such as the Incarnation.[57] Newbigin points out that such a view cannot legitimately suppose a 'neutral' starting point, for there

---

52 Gillis, *A Question of Final Belief*, p92.
53 See the remarks by Gillis, *A Question of Final Belief*, p95.
54 F. Whaling, *Christian Theology and World Religions* (Marshall Morgan & Scott, London, 1986) pp97-8. A good example would be J.A.T. Robinson.
55 D'Costa, *Theology and Religious Pluralism*, p41.
56 Gillis, *A Question of Final Belief*, p163.
57 J. Hick, *God has Many Names* (Macmillan, London, 1980) pp82-3, 85-6.

is no such place. We can only start from where we are, and, for the Christian, Jesus Christ is the given, the *a priori*. Newbigin clearly shows that any framework which we adopt to facilitate agreement will become our ultimate commitment. Thus Hick's starting point has become the notion of 'transcendent being' (the 'Real'), linked with his belief about the nature of revelation and the pattern of human religious development. This is Hick's truth claim and it must defend itself against rival positions.[58] It cannot, however, claim the evidence of religious experience in its support. The pioneering phenomenologist Ninian Smart will have none of it and says in a collection of essays (edited by Hick!), "From a phenomenological point of view it is not possible to base the judgement that all religions point to the same truth upon religious experience".[59]

Kenneth Cragg comments that Hick's examples of doctrinal compatibilities are "subtle and remote from actual religion".[60] Again Hick's supporting argument about cultural isolation is made to bear too much weight, and a number of critics have pointed to the evidence of the interaction and interdependence of various religious traditions, in fact Cragg argues that "hardly any are explicable without reference to another",[61] and even Hick's supporter Alan Race makes the same point.[62]

In response to his critics Hick has moved further and tried to clarify his position. (Gavin D'Costa suggests he is developing his own epicycle!) His redrawn map of the universe of faiths is no longer theocentric but soteriocentric. In other words, he has recognised that his earlier version of the theory was still too dominated by the Judaeo-Christian theistic tradition in which he stands and failed to do sufficient justice to the non-theistic paths to salvation-liberation. D'Costa suggests the label 'transcendental agnosticism' for this new position, in which Hick argues that 'the Real' can be equally validly represented in human cultures by theistic or non-theistic models.

This still leaves a number of areas of difficulty, particularly the question as to how we can know whether there is *any* correspondence between the 'Real' and any particular *personae* or *impersonae* of it. At this point do we not reach the stage of total scepticism and we may begin to wonder whether Feuerbach was correct in his suggestion that all talk of the divine is nothing more than human projection onto a universal screen.[63] Secondly, is not a soteriological position equally dependent on some form of specific doctrine to give it positive content? Does not the notion of salvation-liberation, however it may be conceived, actually presuppose something about the nature of 'the Real'? Hick may have removed both Christ and the Christian

---

58 Newbigin, *Open Secret*, pp188-9.

59 N. Smart, 'Truth and Religions' in *Truth and Dialogue* (ed) J. Hick, (Sheldon Press, London, 1974) p50.

60 Cragg, *The Christian and Other Religion*, p75.

61 Cragg, *The Christian and Other Religion*, p76.

62 Race, *Christians and Religious Pluralism*, p83; where he cites the examples of Hinduism and Buddhism, and Judaism and Christianity.

63 P. Byrne makes the same point in his article, 'John Hick's Philosophy of World Religions', *Scottish Journal of Theology*, 35 (1982), pp289-301.

Father from the centre of his map, but we may still detect traces of the One who saves, and Hick must address the question of who he saves, how he saves and what form/s such salvation might take.[64]

Having examined in some detail perhaps the most influential contributor to the discussion of religious pluralism, in the next chapter we will consider the development of pluralistic approaches and consider some of the more significant theological responses.

---

64 Gillis concurs, *A Question of Final Belief*, p171.

CHAPTER 4

Religious Pluralism in Western Culture and Some Christian Responses

4.1 Modernity and Post-modernity[1]

Much of the current debate about the relationship of the religions centres on the issue of modernity and post-modernity. In the sociological disciplines, modernity refers to life in advanced industrial societies and the contrast is drawn with pre-modern existence. This is a development of the original talk of modernity in the seventeenth century as a word of contrast with all that was feudal or medieval. In contemporary philosophical usage, modernity and modernism have acquired a moral dimension with reference to the problems and tensions of life in the industrialised world. Andrew Walker has characterised it thus:

> Modernity is a historical process that began in the eighteenth century with the philosophical Enlightenment. It accelerated in the nineteenth century as industrialisation took place, and increased even more rapidly in the twentieth century under the impact of advanced technology and science. Modernity is a radical break, both socially and philosophically, with feudalism.[2]

Modernity and subsequently post-modernity are the outcome of a whole series of revolutions in European and world history and society. Not simply intellectual, these radical movements took scientific, political, industrial, socio-economic and cultural forms. Even before the intellectual revolution of the eighteenth century, the scientific revolution of the previous century, with its developments in mapping and time keeping, provided the basis for a socio-economic revolution, as Professor David Harvey has demonstrated. Since experiences of space and time are the primary vehicles for the coding and reproduction of social relationships, "the Renaissance revolution in concepts of space and time laid the conceptual foundations in many respects for the Enlightenment project".[3] Harvey argues that after capitalism's first crisis (during the recession of 1846-7), modernism developed an essentially urban

---

1 A version of this discussion appears in my chapter 'Inculturating Christianity in Postmodern Britain' in P.S. Fiddes (ed), *Faith in the Centre: Christianity and Culture* (Smyth & Helwys, Macon, Ga, 2001) pp235-56.

2 A. Walker, *Enemy Territory: The Christian Struggle for the Modern World* (Hodder, London, 1987) p71.

3 See David Harvey, *The Condition of Postmodernity* (Blackwell, Oxford, 1989) p249.

form, existing "in a restless but intricate relationship with the experience of explosive urban growth, strong rural-urban migration, industrialization, mechanization" and the massive reordering of landscape and built environment,[4] but that it remained a fundamentally Enlightenment project until the radical transformations of the period 1910-1915 with its "rampant confusions" in social and cultural thought,[5] an associated loss of faith in notions of progress, together with alienation, anarchy and "the discovery of the irrational self".[6]

This confusion and incoherence in social and political life coincided with the development of what Harvey terms "Fordism", that is mass-production and the necessary mass-consumption to sustain it, (in uneven but fundamentally stable ways until the oil-crisis recession of 1973 onwards) based on a triangular relationship between large corporations, unionised labour and western governments. But after 1945 the culture of modernism, reflected in art and architecture, literature and the new media of film and television, was increasingly "taken over" by the establishment, especially in the United States where there was "absorption of a particular kind of modernist aesthetic into official and establishment ideology".[7] This led to the anti-materialistic revolutionary and counter-cultural movements of the 1960s and the beginnings of talk of postmodernism.

Through this historical process of modernity, the philosophy of the Enlightenment became a functional rationality increasingly characterised by secularization.[8] Owen Chadwick draws attention to a number of factors in this process in his definitive study *The Secularization of the European Mind in the Nineteenth Century*.[9] One was the emergence of religious toleration for the English Dissenters, which bore two significant consequences: "Religion being what it is, the right to religious opinion must include the right to religious practice. And freedom of religious opinion is impossible without freedom of opinion"[10] in general. The rise of historical consciousness and the development of scientific and critical methods of discourse were thus given free reign in this more open climate. Chadwick suggests that the name of Darwin became synonymous with this new approach, although "the secularizing force was not Darwin the author of the book [Origin of Species] or of several books. It was Darwin the symbol, Darwin the name which stood for a process...[11] Similarly Marx applied critical methods to the analysis of early modern capitalist society and the place of religion within it. He believed that just as the failing socio-economic structure of capitalism would be swept away by the relentless tide of history, so too must religion collapse in its wake.[12]

---

4 Harvey, *Postmodernity*, p25.
5 Harvey,.*Postmodernity*, p270.
6 Harvey, *Postmodernity*, pp29-30.
7 Harvey, *Postmodernity*, pp37-8.
8 See Walker, *Enemy Territory*, pp110-20.
9 CUP, Cambridge, 1975, 1990 reprint.
10 Chadwick, *Secularization*, pp26-7.
11 Chadwick, *Secularization*, p174.
12 Chadwick, *Secularization*, p59.

Chadwick also notes the emergence of a secular teaching profession and the almost entirely new profession of journalism in the same decade of the nineteenth century,[13] and argues that, "It is possible that the coming of the press weakened (more than the coming of modern science) the established moral agreements upon which the consensus of European society rested; and with these moral agreements was integrated religion. It is possible that the coming of the press pushed ordinary readers towards a feeling of the relativity of all opinion and especially the relativity of moral standards".[14] Indeed the press, and later the development of other means of mass communication, helped to give shape and expression to the "mass of tensions, contradictions, opinions" which characterised western society, but which were previously only half-formed, and therefore partly hidden.[15] A number of writers in this field refer to Peter Berger's notion of the "sacred canopy",[16] by which he refers to the sense of a shared culture or shared roots, both spiritual and social. The combination of socio-economic, technological and intellectual processes has destroyed the pre-modern cultural consensus, resulting in a world where there is no appeal to common tradition.[17]

Many aspects of communal life, family, marriage, the place of the elderly, have been radically reshaped, (Walker suggests destroyed[18]) by the privatisation inherent in these processes. As David Tracy comments:

> The effects of all scientistic models remain powerful, even pervasive, forces in the culture at large despite the intellectual bankruptcy of its reigning ideology. Consider the radical privatisation of all claims to truth in art, religion, ethics, and historical actions. Consider the modern scientistic narrowing of the classical notions of reason. Consider how pluralism can collapse into a repressive tolerance.[19]

The sociologist Zygmunt Bauman discusses the notion of postmodernism as "living with ambivalence",[20] while Harvey refers to the impossibility of universals, "of any global project"[21] as typical of the postmodern society in which many now find themselves. Similarly, the French philosopher J. F. Lyotard has famously defined postmodernism as "incredulity towards meta-narratives".[22] Postmodernity is,

---

13 Chadwick, *Secularization*, p42.
14 Chadwick, *Secularization*, p40.
15 Chadwick, *Secularization*, p38.
16 P. Berger, *The Sacred Canopy: Elements of a Sociological Theory of Religion* (Doubleday, New York, 1967).
17 Walker, *Enemy Territory*, p188.
18 Walker, *Enemy Territory*, pp120-30.
19 D. Tracy, *Plurality and Ambiguity* (SCM, London, 1987) p31.
20 Z. Bauman, *Modernity and Ambivalence* (Polity Press, Cambridge, 1991) Chapter 7.
21 Harvey, *Postmodernity*, p52.
22 J.F. Lyotard, *The Postmodern Condition* (MUP, Manchester, 1986) pXXIV.

for Harvey, a crisis in human experience of space and time;[23] its prevailing mood, reflected in architecture and urban design, is that of "fiction, fragmentation, collage and eclecticism, all suffused with a sense of ephemerality and chaos".[24] For Walker too, the pluralism characteristic of postmodernity has to do with the culmination of this historical process in the arrival of mass communication, travel, new patterns of emigration and immigration and wider access to education,[25] in sum, in the jargon of the age, with the arrival of "the global village".

In postmodern thought there is widespread recognition of these many worlds that co-exist within the time-space continuum, a willingness to recognise their "otherness" and difference, and an acceptance of the need of the voices from these worlds to find their authentic self-expression as part of the legitimate pluralism of our culture. But Harvey argues that by its willingness, in some forms, to ally itself with neoconservative entrepreneurialism, by its ignoring of the realities of global economic forces,[26] and by its deconstruction of all forms of argument and meta-narrative, postmodernism destroys not only itself, but also disempowers the very minority voices it claims to acknowledge.[27] The last three decades, since 1973, have been an intense period of space-time compression. In almost any city in the world:

> The whole world's cuisine is now assembled in one place in almost exactly the same way that the world's geographical complexity is reduced to a series of images on a static television screen ... The general implication is that through the experience of everything from food, to culinary habits, music, television, entertainment and cinema, it is now possible to experience the world's geography vicariously, as a simulacrum. The interweaving of simulacra in daily life brings together different worlds in the same space and time.[28]

The throwaway society engendered and required by the consumer culture of late capitalism, has engendered also the throwing away of values, lifestyles, stable relationships and all manner of attachments.[29] If, for Chadwick, Darwin is the symbol of the processes of modernism, President Ronald Reagan symbolizes for Harvey the postmodern triumph of image over substance, aesthetics over ethics.[30] We are, in Tracy's words, self-consciously "linguistic, historical, social beings struggling for some new interpretations of ourselves, our language, history, society and culture".[31]

Some would see postmodernism as an entirely new phase in western cultural development, but a number of commentators agree with David Harvey that it is a

---

23 Harvey, *Postmodernity*, p201.
24 Harvey, *Postmodernity*, p98.
25 Walker, *Enemy Territory*, p136.
26 Harvey, *Postmodernity*, px
27 Harvey, *Postmodernity*, pp116-8.
28 Harvey, *Postmodernity*, p300.
29 Harvey, *Postmodernity*, p286.
30 Harvey, *Postmodernity*, pp329-30.
31 Tracy, *Plurality and Ambiguity*, p50.

particular stage within the evolving modernism of the last two hundred years, "there is much more continuity than difference between the broad history of modernism and the movement called postmodernism. It seems more sensible to me to see the latter as a particular kind of crisis within the former..."[32] He argues that one of the missions of modernism is "the production of new meanings for space and time in a world of ephemerality and fragmentation",[33] as a reaction to the Enlightenment rationalization of time and space. Seen as a whole movement in history, modernism "explored the dialectic of place versus space, of present versus past," and offered multiple possibilities in which the many "other" worlds can flourish together.[34] This is surely the key feature of the contemporary experience. For pre-modern consciousness there was, at best, a sense of two worlds, the material and the spiritual. For the modern and the postmodern, with the space-time "compression" of which Harvey speaks, within our global village there is consciousness of incredible diversity and therefore of choice,[35] in every area of life, including that of religion.

With this diversity of experience has come the recognition of the limitations on human knowledge, more a feature of postmodernism than the modernist confidence of earlier generations. This is not to deny any possibility of truth, but simply to acknowledge that we know with *relative* adequacy, within the boundaries of language, history and society.[36] Any coherence within postmodern culture "will be a rough coherence: interrupted, obscure, often confused, self-conscious of its own language use and, above all, aware of the ambiguities of all histories and traditions".[37] Tracy argues that the religions, of all aspects of culture, out of their understanding of sin and ignorance, should be least surprised or frightened by this. Indeed the religions should resist attempts at too easy coherence and refusals to face up to "the radical plurality and ambiguity" of all traditions, including their own. But the religions can also resist the postmodern characteristic of being able to see the problem but not able to act.[38]

Religious pluralism is thus one aspect of a wider plural culture with roots in the whole experience of modern life over two hundred years or more, characterised by a developing historical consciousness, the rise of scientific method within an increasingly technological society, and the first-hand encounter with other cultures in the rapid western expansion of the nineteenth and twentieth centuries. Within Christianity, the rise of biblical criticism and the widespread adoption of the historical-critical method were particular expressions of this movement, and created a climate in which pluralistic approaches to other faiths could develop. Arguably, however, these intellectual developments were less important than the disintegration

---

32 Harvey, *Postmodernity*, p116.
33 Harvey, *Postmodernity*, p216.
34 Harvey, *Postmodernity*, p127.
35 "Eclecticism is the natural evolution of a culture with choice". C. Jenks, *The Language of Post-Modern Architecture* (Academy Editions, London, 1984) p127.
36 Cf. D. Tracy, *Plurality and Ambiguity,* pp61ff.
37 Tracy, *Plurality and Ambiguity*, p83.
38 Tracy, *Plurality and Ambiguity*, pp83-4.

of the "sacred canopy" as a whole, and the increasingly rapid "space-time compression", of which the missionary movement, with its direct encounter with the "other worlds" of religions and cultures, ironically and unwittingly, was a part. As Owen Chadwick has observed in a similar context, "The sacredness of an object was not caused by rational thinking. Therefore the end of that sacredness could not be caused only by rational thinking".[39] Equally pluralism is not solely a matter of the ·intellect, but of the whole human experience. Religion, like morality, is not simply a matter of mind, but "is founded in the affections ... the mere assent of the mind is not enough".[40]

We have already seen something of the Christian response to this experience in the earlier chapters, where we examined the shape of the debate about Christian relationships with people of other faiths against the background of, predominantly European, Protestant thinking since the World Missionary Conference of Edinburgh 1910. This is of course the most relevant background for the activity and writing both of Kenneth Cragg and Lesslie Newbigin as British, Protestant, missionary theologians. However, the wider debate on cultural and religious pluralism, and their own distinctive contributions, has been increasingly influenced by Roman Catholic and worldwide reflection on these issues over the last thirty years. We must now review briefly these further responses. We begin with the work of Rahner and other Catholic theologians, since this work has been influential far beyond the boundaries of the Roman Church, and Rahner in particular has found an admirer and defender in Gavin D'Costa, and in a qualified way in Maurice Wiles. We shall then note the importance of Christian pluralistic positions, often taking their cue from the important work of Hick already discussed, before describing the growing dissatisfaction with thoroughgoing pluralism as an adequate Christian response.

4.2 Developments in Catholic Thought

Karl Rahner (1904-1984), the German Jesuit theologian, was a powerful influence behind the scenes at the Second Vatican Council, in his position as adviser to the German bishops. His published work since then in his *Theological Investigations*, and in *The Foundations of Christian Faith*, has provided the most significant Roman Catholic treatment of the whole question of a Christian theology of religions. Rahner is always conscious that he writes as a dogmatic theologian and not as an historian or philosopher of religion. In this capacity he believes that "pluralism is a greater threat and a reason for greater unrest in Christianity than any other religion. For no other religion – not even Islam – maintains so absolutely that it is *the* religion, the one and only valid revelation of the living God, as does the Christian religion".[41]

---

39 Chadwick, *Secularization*, p6.
40 Chadwick, *Secularization*, p238.
41 Rahner, *Theological Investigations*, Vol. 5, (DLT, London, 1964) p116.

At the same time Rahner maintains the doctrine of the universal salvific will of God. This is not to suppose that all will in the end be saved, but that if God seriously wills the salvation of all, as scripture and tradition affirm, then he must provide effective means of such salvation for all who respond to him in repentance and faith. For Rahner this must be understood not only Christologically but also ecclesiologically, not only as an abstract or logical possibility, but also as a real and historically concrete opportunity.[42]

The strength of Rahner's position is found in its integration of this question within his whole theology. It shares the same foundations as his whole systematic programme, namely, a Christian anthropology which (like Brunner and unlike Barth[43]) argues for the receptivity of man to the transcendentality of his experience in the world. Thus, he argues, "If man really is a subject, that is a transcendent, responsible and free being who as subject is both entrusted into his own hands and always in the hands of what is beyond his control, then basically this has already said that man is a being oriented towards God".[44]

Such an inner direction inevitably leads to a form of expectancy and anticipation within the human spirit, which Rahner calls the "searching memory", by which human beings recognize and interpret transcendence when it is encountered in . concrete human living. For Rahner such experience is always concrete, grounded in the realities of time and place, history and culture. Humanity is not held in deterministic chains because there is always the possibility of shaping the experience through the response that it evokes within the human spirit.

Equally, such moments of illumination are not simply unaided self-discovery, but are enabled only through God's gracious self-revelation. There is an inescapable element of paradox here, since in such experiences the finite subject is not overwhelmed nor extinguished, but reaches fulfilment and fullest autonomy precisely as subject. This notion of the "human as subject" being the "event" of God's self-communication expresses an existential of all people without exception.[45] Only through divine grace is humanity so constituted. Christian revelation is distinctive in that it allows immediate and direct access to the divine self-giving, which is revealed in ultimacy and absoluteness in the life, death and resurrection of the man Jesus. There is no escaping the particularity of Jesus as "absolute Saviour", upon whom the salvation of all times and all people hinges.[46] This is demonstrated for Rahner in the decisive events of Christ's Passion and Resurrection in which the man Jesus is revealed as the "Son of the Father", the absolute meeting point of the human search and the divine self-offering.

Christ thus becomes "the clearly unique 'specifically' distinct perfection" of the relationship between God and the created order, in which all other realities of this

---

42 Cf. *Theological Investigations*, Vol. 6 p391.
43 See the discussion in chapter 2 above.
44 Rahner, *The Foundations of Christian Faith* (DLT, London, 1978) p45.
45 Rahner, *Foundations*, p127.
46 Rahner, *Foundations*, p232.

nature are "deficient modes of this primary Christological relationship".[47] The Incarnation is not so much a causal link in a chain of temporal events, but the primary expression of the universal salvific will of God. As such it has an absoluteness which he often describes as "irrevocable" or "irreversible", especially in connection with the cross and resurrection. All this reveals an eternal verity that, "Jesus is now and for all eternity the permanent openness of our finite being to the living God of infinite eternal life".[48]

From the Christian perspective the Incarnation, and especially the cross and resurrection, provide the definitive "existential moment", but Rahner recognizes that there is a question as to whether all peoples and all cultures share the same moment. His answer is that all look to the events of the Incarnation, but that the existential moment occurs in temporally varying ways because of the pattern of human history. It occurs for each culture when it is confronted with the Christian gospel in a culturally meaningful and accessible manner. Until that moment the non-Christian religions are responses to the common experience of transcendence, which may be to a greater or lesser extent true or false responses. A true response is made only through the grace of God in Christ, even where a person may never have heard his name, and this is what Rahner terms, "anonymous faith". He argues that, "There can exist an 'anonymous faith' which carries with it an intrinsic dynamism and therefore an obligation to find full realisation in explicit faith, but which is nonetheless sufficient for salvation even if a man does not achieve this fulfilment during his lifetime, as long as he is not to blame for this".[49] By 'explicit faith' of course he means Christian faith, but there is a clear recognition that this is not an historically or culturally viable option for much of humanity, which may nevertheless be saved, not through assent to dogma, but by an attitude of trust in response to transcendental experience.

Because for many people their "transcendental experience" is mediated through their non-Christian religion, these religions are in this limited sense vehicles of salvation. Even where debased and corrupt, they may still bear witness to humanity's essential transcendence, and mediate a genuine and grace-given transcendentality.[50] Within any particular historical, social and cultural setting, humanity is not only capable of hearing the Word of God, but positively expects it, and the expressly Christian revelation that is Christ, "becomes the explicit statement of the revelation of grace which man always experiences implicitly within the depths of his being".[51] All who accept this experience of inner grace are "anonymous Christians": Christians because they have really encountered and responded in faith to the grace of God in Christ, but anonymous because they have no means of recognizing or naming the Christ whom they have met. What then are we to say of the mission of the Church? Rahner argues that "anonymous Christianity" should be regarded as the

47 Rahner, *Theological Investigations*, Vol. 1, pp163-5.
48 Rahner, *Theological Investigations*, Vol. 3, p44.
49 Rahner, *Theological Investigations*, Vol. 16, p54.
50 Rahner, *Theological Investigations*, Vol. 18, pp293-4.
51 Rahner, *Theological Investigations*, Vol. 6, p394.

"enabling condition" for the preaching of Christian faith, a necessary prior condition in fact. There can be no response to the preaching of the Gospel unless the Holy Spirit has already been active. The "anonymous Christian" is thus the one whom the Spirit has been preparing to receive the message of Christ. In Rahner's scheme Christian mission is not primarily about the salvation of people who would otherwise have been lost; rather it becomes a fresh embodiment of God in Christ in new historical and cultural settings, "actively contributing to the incarnational dynamic of grace".[52]

The result of this fresh 'incarnation' is of course the same as the definitive one, namely salvation. But this does not necessarily involve a change of status from "lost" to "saved". Just as Jesus claimed a certain continuity between the Law and the prophets and the fulfilment which he brought, so too the mission of the Church is to bring to fruition the seeds of faith already in existence. This in no way undermines the centrality of Christian mission, but may well have vital implications for missionary methods, as the irenic approach of Vatican II begins to recognize. Rahner is also conscious of the risk implicit in this understanding of the missionary task. If the anonymous Christian rejects the call to explicit faith with its inherent challenge to radical discipleship, s/he thereby becomes culpable before God. The very seriousness of this situation underlines the importance of the missionary task of the Church.

The primary strength of Rahner's thesis lies in the completeness and coherence of his system. It is an integral part of his whole theological enterprise, quarried and built from the same "raw material" of Christian tradition as the rest of his dogmatic scheme: he argues "from the heart and not the margins of Christian revelation".[53] It rests on a clear understanding on the relationship between God and creation and of the nature of humanity within the purposes of God. Through his emphasis on the universal salvific will of God, Rahner is able to give due weight to the *missio dei* in creation and redemption, and to integrate the Church within this divine mission. From the point of view of traditional Christian doctrine Rahner's scheme vitally preserves the saving significance of Christ, especially the centrality of the cross and resurrection. He insists therefore, that he is talking about "anonymous *Christianity*", not simply a universal *theism*.[54]

A further strength lies in the realism with which Rahner deals with the human situation, recognizing as he does, the historical, social and cultural boundaries to which Hick and others have drawn attention. Within Rahner's scheme divine grace is mediated within communities, historically and culturally shaped, and inextricably bound up with human fallibility and corruption. Still, he argues, God is present

---

52 Rahner, *Theological Investigations*, Vol. 12, pp168-76.

53 David Wright, 'The Watershed of Vatican II' in A.D. Clarke and B.W. Winter (eds), *One God, One Lord in a World of Religious Pluralism* (Tyndale House, Cambridge, 1991) p171.

54 Cf. D'Costa, *Theology and Religious Pluralism*, p74.

through and not *despite* the non-Christian religions.[55] In this he reflects Catholicism's innate understanding of human religiosity, which Protestant critics rarely achieve,[56] and Catholicism's view that grace operates by the perfecting of nature rather than its destruction.

Despite these strengths Rahner's argument is vulnerable on a number of grounds, and has been subject to intense scrutiny and criticism. What, for example, might constitute "culpable rejection" of the divine self-offering? Given that in his theory no one, except Jesus, ever fully responds to that offer, can anyone totally reject it? If not, then we are left with differing degrees of trustful response and on such a sliding scale where is the point of acceptance or rejection? Even from day to day, or moment to moment, some of us find ourselves oscillating between trust and doubt, faith and disbelief. What sense can we make of "culpable rejection" in the light of this experience? Moreover, given the reality of historical, cultural and social circumstances, we might argue that these factors fundamentally condition our response of faith and love, or even actually determine it, at least within a range of possible options. This all raises difficult questions for a theory of culpable rejection.

Further objection has been made to the whole scheme, not least as we shall see, by both Cragg and Newbigin,[57] on the grounds that it is nothing short of imperialism, or at the very least chauvinistic and patronising; thus it provides no real basis for encounter or dialogue of any sort. Of course Rahner is not attempting to define a mutually acceptable basis for inter-faith dialogue but to provide an account of the religions within the limits of specifically Christian doctrine. In which case the notorious reversibility of the process, in which an Indian could regard a Christian as an "anonymous Hindu" for example, does not matter. In fact Rahner accepted that this might well be the case. Nevertheless, at times, Rahner's tone is paternalistic, not to say arrogant as George Lindbeck asserts:

> There is something arrogant about supposing that Christians know what non-believers experience and believe in the depths of their beings better than they know themselves, and that therefore the task of dialogue or evangelism is to increase their self-awareness. The communication of the gospel is not a form of psycho-therapy, but rather the offer and the act of sharing one's own beloved language – the language that speaks of Jesus Christ – with all those who are interested, in the full awareness that God does not call all to be part of the witnessing people.[58]

But we must note that even Lindbeck assumes that Christians are in some implicitly special way *the witnessing people* of God. Lindbeck has a more substantial point to make about the nature of religion in his argument that myth, ritual and belief are not

---

55 But see, for example, the very negative assessment of religion in Peter Cotterell, *Mission and Meaninglessness* (SPCK, London, 1990) p51; and Andrew Kirk, *Loosing the Chains* (Hodder and Stoughton, London, 1992) Chapter 6.

56 As David Wright notes, 'The Watershed of Vatican II', p171.

57 See below Parts 2 and 3.

58 Lindbeck, *The Nature of Doctrine*, (Westminster Press, Philadelphia, 1984) p61.

outward culturally determined expressions of a common transcendental experience, but actually constitute and form that experience. Religion, says Lindbeck, *shapes* the subjectivities of individuals, and therefore is a significant factor in determining the content of the experience. In which case, differing outward expressions signify different inner realities. There is no, or a very limited, underlying unity to the religious experience of the human race. Maurice Wiles suggests that this is to make too much of the point; it implies that religions (and other culturally coherent communities?) are impervious to one another in such a way as to make communication impossible. This is clearly not the case. Whatever the difficulties of mutual comprehension presented by different socio-linguistic groups, they are not "totally opaque" to one another.[59] Nor does such a theory of religious grammar remove the referential element in speaking of the transcendent. Dialogue between such groups is not simply a matter "of negotiating a better relation between two ways of speaking and living religiously, which are at our disposal to do whatever we like with; it is a shared search for truth".[60]

Wiles, also makes another significant point. Rahner's theological method is correct, but his Christological criterion is wrong. The criticism of the theory of "anonymous Christians" serves for Wiles to illustrate the fundamental tension in Rahner's thought. This is inevitable in trying to hold together belief in salvation only through Christ with the affirmation of the universal salvific will of God. But how can the Christ-event be uniquely salvific if all history truly is "salvation-history"? Wiles concurs with Bruce Marshall's opinion that Rahner's basic theological method is not just in tension, but "radically inconsistent" with his commitment to the particularity of Jesus as the only redeemer.[61] Whereas Marshall adopts Rahner's Christological conviction and abandons the theological method, Wiles opts for the theological method and modifies the Christological conviction. Wiles, like Hick, remains to be convinced that there are sufficient grounds for the sort of affirmations about Jesus that Rahner wants to make. We are back here to the familiar arguments about the significance of the cross and resurrection of Christ as events in history. But there is a further point worth making in relation to Wiles' critique of Rahner. If the fundamental theological method is correct, how can we know that all history contains the divine self-offer? Christian tradition affirms the universal salvific will of God on the basis of what has been revealed in Christ, especially in the cross and resurrection, and the proof text underlying this doctrine has a specifically Christological content (1 Timothy 2:3-6).

For many Christian thinkers theological method depends upon Christological conviction, and therefore, according to Monsignor Pietro Rossano, secretary of the Vatican Secretariat for Non-Christian Religions, "every theological evaluation of the

59 Wiles, *Christian Theology and Inter-religious Dialogue* (SCM, London, 1992) p37..

60 Wiles, *Christian Theology and Inter-religious Dialogue*, p39.

61 Marshall, *Christologies in Conflict* (Blackwell, Oxford, 1987) p106; Wiles, *Christian Theology and Inter-religious Dialogue*, p58.

human religious phenomenon is based on this image of Christ".[62] This does not make it impossible to recognize the various colours of human religiosity as part of the spectrum of response to the illumination of the same divine Word, which no human language or culture is fully adequate to express.[63]   Gavin D'Costa in championing Rahner's cause, makes a spirited defence of the notion of "anonymous Christians", first of all on the grounds that this is primarily Christian theological reflection. What Rahner is articulating is a Christian theology of religions, which will inevitably reflect Christian assumptions, it can do no other. There are links here with what Newbigin has to say about *a priori* starting points. D'Costa concedes that the term "anonymous Christian" may be unhelpful and even misleading, but the fundamental point is that when a person is saved it is through the grace of God, and by that he means the grace of God revealed in Christ,[64] even though a particular individual may not be consciously aware of this.

In fact D'Costa goes on to suggest that such a theory actually facilitates dialogue in recognizing the possibility of divine grace in our partner's life and religion, which for example, exclusivism could not do. It also provides adequate theological grounds for the pluralistic presumption of the activity of God in the non-Christian religions, "which is never properly substantiated [by pluralists, and is] surely as paternalistic" as inclusive positions are accused of being by pluralists and exclusivists alike.[65] For Rahner and D'Costa, as for Cragg and Newbigin, in the end there can be no escape from the Christological criterion. To discern the Spirit at work throughout history, requires the presence of the Spirit of Christ in the Church. But this Catholic form of fulfilment theology also struggles to contain the tensions of continuity and discontinuity within itself. As Gerald Anderson has noted, if the emphasis before Vatican II was on discontinuity, since the Council and in the work of Rahner and many other Catholic thinkers, the stress has been with continuity.[66] Most important of all we must question whether Christology refers primarily to ecclesiology, or whether its primary reference is to the doctrine of God. In other words, the life, death and resurrection of Jesus is about the Kingdom rather than the Church,[67] as Küng and some other recent Catholic theologians affirm.

Catholic thinkers are more likely to view the religions as a positive *preparatio evangelica* than Protestants like Barth, Brunner or Kraemer and contemporary Evangelical theologians like John Stott and Peter Cotterell. Newbigin's sympathies are clearly of this type. Cragg's emphasis, like that of other Anglican missionary theologians such as Max Warren and John V. Taylor, shares the Catholic respect for

---

62 P. Rossano, 'A Roman Catholic Perspective' in G.H. Anderson and T.F. Stransky (ed), *Christ's Lordship and Religious Pluralism* (Orbis, Maryknoll, NY, 1981) p101.

63 Rossano, 'A Roman Catholic Perspective', p102.

64 D'Costa, *Theology and Religious Pluralism*, p90.

65 D'Costa, *Theology and Religious Pluralism*, p90.

66 See Anderson's response to Rossano's paper, in Anderson and Stransky (ed), *Christ's Lordship and Religious Pluralism*, p114.

67 See the discussion by Paul Knitter in *No Other Name?*, pp131-4.

the spiritual depths found in people of other faiths, whilst retaining a firm commitment to the Christological criterion.

4.3 Developments in Pluralistic Theology

Despite the protests of neo-orthodoxy, the liberal theological tradition has continued to flourish and to pose important questions which have been answered with increasing seriousness by more conservative theologians.[68] Hick in particular, has forced the wider theological community to take the quest for a more adequate Christian theology of religions with due seriousness. This is reflected in the growing number of theologians who are advocating pluralistic positions. Alan Race would be typical of other Anglicans in seeing pluralism as "the most positive response to the encounter between Christianity and the world faiths".[69] Other examples of Anglicans who have moved this way would be Maurice Wiles and Keith Ward.[70] Paul Knitter may stand for a Catholicism moving from a Christological to a theocentric model under the influence of liberation theologies from Asia and Latin America.[71] We have already noted the significance of Raimondo Pannikar, and also influential from an Asian context is the work of the Jesuit, Aloysius Pieris.

Perhaps the most significant movement has been that of the World Council of Churches which, under the direction of its then General Secretary Willem Visser t'Hooft, until 1961 retained a conservative approach to this issue, but which has developed a much more open attitude largely through the work of Dr Stanley J. Samartha and his successor Dr Wesley Ariarajah. This may be seen as a parallel development to the Second Vatican Council. Samartha may be regarded as the guiding hand for the World Council as Rahner was for Vatican II. Samartha, a presbyter in the Church of South India and former Principal of Serampore College, was Director of the WCC Unit for Dialogue with People of Living Faiths and Ideologies from 1968-80. He is suspicious of the neat theological categories to which the discussion is often reduced and to which "the delicate complex web of religious relationships does not lend itself".[72] Samartha argues that the starting point for inter-religious relationships must be the mutual recognition that humanity is bound together in the bundle of life, and there is no ignoring the pattern of "power relationships" which history has thrown up and of which Christianity and the other

---

68 Note for example the dialogue between John Stott and David Edwards in *Essentials: A Liberal-Evangelical Dialogue* (Hodder and Stoughton, London, 1988).

69 Race, *Christians and Religious Pluralism*, p135.

70 For Wiles see *Christian Theology and Inter-religious Dialogue*; for Ward see *A Vision to Pursue* (SCM, London, 1993) and *Religion and Revelation* (T&T Clark, Edinburgh, 1994).

71 Knitter, *No Other Name*, chapters 9 and 10; and his essay 'Toward a Liberation Theology of Religions' in *The Myth of Christian Uniqueness*, pp178-200.

72 See his essay 'The Lordship of Jesus Christ and Religious Pluralism' in *Courage for Dialogue* (WCC, Geneva, 1981) p97. (Also published in Anderson and Stransky (ed), *Christ's Lordship and Religious Pluralism*.)

religions are a part. For this reason he believes that the language of "mission" must be abandoned by the Church because of its threatening associations with the era of Western colonial power.[73] He goes on to suggest that in the incarnation, God relativizes himself in history, and Christian theologians are wrong to absolutise that which God has relativised.[74] He recognizes that, "without a disclosure of meaning at particular points in history or in human consciousness, there can be no human response to Mystery".[75] The religions are to be understood as different responses to that experience. Traditional exclusivist claims for Jesus are all too often tainted with "ideological assumptions based on economic influence and political power". Therefore, he appeals to a theocentric Christology, centred on the experience of "Mystery", rather than the Jesuology or the Christomonism so often found in Christian tradition. It will be a critical reflection on the God-human encounter in Jesus Christ "in a situation where new perceptions of religious pluralism cannot be ignored any more".[76] This will lead to the abandonment of "helicopter" model Christologies in favour of the "bullock-cart" model of Christology from below, rooted in history and culture, and therefore as relative as everything else historical and cultural.

The exclusive claim that only in Jesus Christ has God been revealed once-for-all to redeem the human race "is not integral to the Gospel or Christian faith in God through Jesus Christ or to the content and practice of Christian mission today".[77] This is not to argue for the abandonment of Christian mission, but a re-thinking of the kind of mission and manner of mission appropriate in a religiously plural world. Christian mission will continue to derive its inspiration from the life and ministry of Jesus, serving the poor in Christ's name, struggling for justice and righteousness in society, even to the point of death as witness to "the liberating truth and all-embracing love of God in Christ".[78] Such mission has its basis in the congregational and worshipping life of Christian communities secure in their Christian identity and commitment, but reconciled to their neighbours of other faiths with whom they share in the divine task to bring wholeness to creation. Samartha's appeal to the legacy of colonial history must be taken with all seriousness, as we have already been concerned to do. We shall come back to his disclosure of the "power-struggles" which sometimes underlie the language of exclusivism and to the nature of Christian mission in the final section of this volume. It is clear that his understanding of religion has much in common with the positions of Rahner and Hick with their emphasis on differing historically and culturally conditioned responses to the Mystery of Transcendent Being or the Ultimately Real.

---

73 Samartha, *Courage for Dialogue*, p102.

74 In his essay 'The Cross and the Rainbow' in *The Myth of Christian Uniqueness*, p69; subsequently published as Chapter 6 'Christ in a Multi-religious Culture' *One Christ – Many Religions* (Orbis, Maryknoll, NY, 1991).

75 Samartha, 'The Cross and the Rainbow', p76.

76 Samartha, *One Christ – Many Religions*, pp96 and 98.

77 Samartha, *One Christ – Many Religions*, p118.

78 Samartha, *One Christ – Many Religions*, pp150-4.

Once again we see the issue of Christology at the heart of the discussion and we must question whether what Samartha regards as God's self-relativizing in the incarnation necessarily implies what he suggests it does. Might it not be more accurate to describe the incarnation as the particularizing of God's being in human history and culture, through which the divine self-offering is made absolute and therefore of universal significance and appeal, as the Christ-hymn of Philippians 2:5-11 suggests? Such an approach would in fact reinforce the weight of Samartha's argument about the nature and manner of the Christian mission in service and sacrifice, but retain the sort of cosmic Christology he seems intent on abandoning. Nevertheless, his emphasis on witness rather than judgement in relationships to people of other faiths is in line with the approach of both Cragg and Newbigin, although both would argue that the cross of Christ exposes an inherent judgement which is inescapable. Christ is not simply interpreting the true nature of the world and its relationship to God, but redeeming it at great personal cost.

4.4 Reactions to the Pluralistic Trend

It is a measure of the strength and cogency of the pluralist argument that it has begun to provoke a serious response from those who remain unpersuaded that this approach can provide a fully Christian theology of religions. The forms and patterns of response indicate that pluralism is being recognized as a significant issue, and that it simply will not do to write off the faith, culture and traditions of the vast majority of humanity, past and present, in any dismissive way. It would still be true to say that many self-consciously Evangelical writers are suspicious of religion and human religiosity. Andrew Kirk provides a typical (if rather lurid) warning when he comments that, "religion forever walks on the precipice overhanging the abyss of idolatry".[79] Peter Cotterell, in conceding the significant point that salvation may indeed be found by adherents of religions other than Christianity while they are still in them, nevertheless argues that such salvation "will be found not because of them, but in spite of them".[80] Waldron Scott accepts that God may well be reflected in greater or lesser degree in the religions of humanity, but suggests that people tend use this religiosity "to escape from God".[81] He admits this "low" view of religion as means of revelation may seem indistinguishable from that of Kraemer's "radical discontinuity", but suggests that this does not preclude an increasing number of Evangelicals from appreciating the world's religions as "cultural expressions of humankind's drives", and therefore providing a more positive engagement in the processes of inter-religious encounter and dialogue.

The Lausanne Covenant (1974) is typical of this sort of position in its careful protection of the uniqueness of Christ, and its rejection of syncretism, yet in its attempt to reckon positively with the need for "that kind of dialogue whose purpose

---

79 A. Kirk, *Loosing the Chains*, p50.

80 P. Cotterell, *Mission and Meaninglessness*, p51.

81 W. Scott, '"No Other Name" – An Evangelical Conviction', in Anderson and Stransky (ed), *Christ's Lordship and Religious Pluralism*, p66.

is to listen sensitively in order to understand".[82] *The Manila Manifesto* (1989) following-up Lausanne after fifteen years reflects an increasing openness among Evangelicals to "elements of truth and beauty" within the religions, while still rejecting relativism and syncretism. We find also a recognition of, and repentance for, past attitudes "of ignorance, arrogance, disrespect and even hostility", and a commitment to bear positive witness to Christ which would include inter-faith ·dialogue.[83] However, we must ask whether this reflects a fundamental affirmation of and commitment to dialogue, or merely the adoption of a convenient strategic device?

One of the most substantial discussions of the pluralist theology of religions written from an avowedly Evangelical position is Harold A. Netland who in two volumes *Dissonant Voices*[84] and *Encountering Religious Pluralism,*[85] seeks to address the arguments of Hick in particular with "the question of truth". He argues the case for a Christian exclusivism which maintains the person and work of Christ as "unique, definitive and normative".[86] However, such a position does not entail the denial of any truth in other religions, nor imply that there is no value in other religions. In fact, claims Netland, all religions are to some extent exclusive in their assertions of truth. After an overview of key elements in Hindu, Buddhist, Muslim and Shinto thought, Netland concludes that, "rather than regarding the various religions as providing different answers to certain common questions...it is perhaps best to think of them as responding to certain issues that arise within our particular historical and cultural contexts. And while there may be some overlap in issues addressed, there is also considerable diversity, both in terms of questions posed and answers given".[87] Clearly not all such differences necessarily imply opposition of doctrine or understanding, but there are instances in which the various religions do seem to make mutually incompatible claims about the nature of reality, which lead in turn to differing ethical standpoints. All this, he urges, make the looser claims of pluralism about common understandings conveyed in culturally diverse ways, untenable.

In response to the argument that no judgement about the truth or falsity of such religious world-views can be made since religious truth is personal, Netland makes a trenchant defence of truth as both personal and propositional. He argues, for example, that in a personal revelation to humanity, God inevitably reveals information about the divine nature. The personal and the propositional belong together. Indeed, Netland is persuaded that the propositional element is more basic than the personal, for it is presupposed in all other uses of "truth". In any case, whatever philosophers and theologians may think, religious believers commonly accept their faith as true in the sense of corresponding to reality. Clearly religious

---

82 *Lausanne Covenant* (LCWE, Pasadena, 1974) Para.4.
83 *Manila Manifesto* (LCWE, Pasadena, 1989) Para.3.
84 H.A. Netland, *Dissonant Voices* (Apollos, Leicester, 1991).
85 H.A. Netland *Encountering Religious Pluralism* (Apollos, Leicester, 2001).
86 Netland, *Dissonant Voices,* p34.
87 Netland, *Dissonant Voices,* p110.

discourse differs from scientific or political discourse, for example, and obviously involves an existential involvement with the object of faith; "But none of this should obscure the fact that even in religion the notion of propositional truth is ineradicable".[88] Ultimately Netland cannot escape the cautious conclusion that "at least some of the central tenets of some religions must be false",[89] and from the Christian position he affirms the sort of Christological criteria we will see in both Cragg and Newbigin. Neither what Netland terms Hick's 'Inspiration Christology', nor Knitter's 'Theocentric Christology', will do from his Evangelical perspective, and he reaffirms the traditional claims of orthodox Christian belief in relation to Jesus as "the definitive self-revelation of God" and the "one and only Saviour" of humankind.[90]

There is considerable confusion among those who advocate such exclusivism about what it really means. One problem seems to be that the term 'exclusivist' is used both to describe statements about Christ and to refer to the soteriological question about who will find themselves 'excluded' from salvation. Many such writers are beginning to see that it might be possible to retain an "exclusivist Christology" whilst remaining open to the cosmic effects of the salvation achieved in Christ. We have already noted, in the discussion of Hick's work, that even such a conservative and orthodox writer as Michael Green effectively argues for a form of 'inclusivism'. In addition to the discussion to which Netland draws attention,[91] a good illustration of the sort of position which many leading Evangelicals are beginning to take is articulated by Peter Cotterell, former missionary and sometime Principal of the then London Bible College (now the London School of Theology), "The stark exclusivism of a salvation that is offered only to those who are of the privileged few who overtly hear the proclamation of the Good News would appear to be not a biblical exclusivism".[92] Instead he argues (like Michael Green) that, "Salvation comes to us exclusively through Christ, but an overt knowledge of Christ or the work of Christ was not a condition of salvation under the Old Covenant and is not a condition of salvation under the New Covenant".[93]

Similarly, Christopher Sugden, then Director of the Oxford Centre for Mission Studies, writing on "*Evangelicals and Religious Pluralism*" describes Jesus as the climax of God's redeeming activity in history and argues that such exclusive claims as Christians will want to make for Christ must be proposed with "proper sensitivity". This will avoid pretensions to superior religious experience, be aware of the dangers of cultural imperialism and pay due attention to the witness of the Christian community as a whole rather than concentrating on Western individualism. Within such witness the voice of the poor and the powerless will be particularly significant. He too concludes by recognising the possibility of a salvation beyond

---

88 Netland, *Dissonant Voices*, pp126-33.
89 Netland, *Dissonant Voices*, p233.
90 Netland, *Dissonant Voices*, p261.
91 Netland, *Dissonant Voices*, pp262-77.
92 Cotterell, *Mission and Meaninglessness*, p78.
93 Cotterell, *Mission and Meaninglessness*, pp80-1.

the Church, which nevertheless remains *in Christ*.[94] All of which suggests that the agenda has subtly changed for many Evangelicals. While retaining a high or "exclusive" Christology, the soteriological question remains more open. Timothy Bradshaw draws attention to this in his contribution to a Cambridge symposium by pointing out the sharpness of the issue of particularity at the point of the cross. To what extent is salvation in Christ "primarily cosmological or primarily moral and spiritual"?[95] The issues of revelation, Christology and soteriology are closely bound together.

It should not be thought, however, that the reappraisal of the pluralist approach is restricted to a predictable backlash from the conservative wing of the Church. While admitting the cogency and even the attractiveness of much of the pluralist argument, there are many who feel that in the end it simply does not do justice to the historic Christian faith nor to the witness of Christian experience both past and present. Pluralism may be a significant and coherent theology of religions, but is it a *Christian* perspective, or that of a secularised postmodern society? Kenneth Surin offers what he terms "a materialist critique" of the Hick and Cantwell Smith variety of religious pluralism, (for pluralist thought is of necessity diverse) in which he argues, like Newbigin, that the whole notion of "religious pluralism" as a philosophy or theology of religions is part of the intellectual legacy of western modernity.[96] Such arguments assume a "common human history" which simply cannot exist within the current economic and political world order. It is no surprise therefore, that "global theology" matches the relentless march of "global capitalism".

Like Harvey's critique of postmodernism, Surin argues that the pluralist theology of Hick and others, with its stress on myth and cultural relativism, serves as a distancing device in which the genuine differences between the faiths are smoothed away.[97] In this process the "otherness" of the Other is traduced, and any possibility of fundamental confrontation between religions is eliminated. The result is that the great faiths of the world are reduced to the status of commodities available for consumption at the whim of the individual consumer: "'Pluralism' thus conceived, shamelessly reinforces the reification and privatisation of life in advanced capitalist society".[98] This disguised form of Idealism leads in practice to assimilation and homogenisation, although obscured "by the pluralists' loud disavowal of 'exclusivism'".[99] As we have already noted this method is as 'exclusivist' as any other.

---

94 C. Sugden, 'Evangelicals and Religious Pluralism' in I. Hamnett (ed), *Religious Pluralism and Unbelief* (Routledge, London, 1990) pp148-65.

95 T. Bradshaw, 'Grace and Mercy: Protestant Approaches to Religious Pluralism', in Clarke and Winter (eds), *One God, One Lord in a World of Religious Pluralism*, p179.

96 K. Surin, 'Towards a "materialist" critique of "religious pluralism"', Hamnett (ed), *Religious Pluralism and Unbelief*, p116.

97 Cf. David Harvey's critique of postmodernism noted above.

98 Surin, 'Towards a "materialist" critique', p123.

99 Surin, 'Towards a "materialist" critique', p125.

Christian Uniqueness Reconsidered,[100] the collection of essays written in response to Hick and Knitter's volume *The Myth of Christian Uniqueness,* is probably the most significant indication of dissatisfaction with pluralist theology within mainstream Christian thought. A distinguished group of theologians such as Rowan Williams, John Cobb, Wolfhart Pannenberg and Jürgen Moltmann take issue with the reigning orthodoxy of pluralism in academic theology. Many of these writers have considerable experience of multi-cultural and inter-faith encounter, but still wish to reiterate the distinctiveness of the Christian faith. In this symposium Newbigin launches a characteristic attack on the sheer self-centredness of the pluralist position. Like Surin, Newbigin sees here the religious expression of the ethos of the consumer society where the individual is free to choose the image of God found most congenial, with no objective reality against which subjective choice must be measured. It belongs to "the world of the supermarket, where the customer is king".[101] Of course Newbigin is aware that Hick and others provide a criterion of movement from self-centredness to "Reality"-centredness, measurable by the achievement of salvation-liberation, as a fixed point in the sea of relativism. But the replacement of concrete and particular references like the person of Jesus or the Torah or the Vedanta with abstract nouns is no simple solution to the problems. For Newbigin this simply underlines the point that the central reference of pluralist theology is the human self, for who is to define these concepts of salvation and liberation? As Alasdair MacIntyre has posed the questions: *Which Rationality? Whose Justice?*[102] Market forces are not adequate to such questions, at least in the light of the cross from which Christian perspectives on salvation, judgement and justice are derived. Newbigin is clear that the pluralists' position undercuts the very freedom and justice they claim to espouse. The move from self-centredness can only be achieved through the cross of Christ which shifts attention from "me and my need of salvation" to "God and his glory".[103]

Similarly Paul J. Griffiths characterises pluralism as the new form of Christian imperialism, since by implication most of the religions will be required radically to revise their traditional self-understanding and reassess their salvific value in order to enter the brave new world of pluralism.[104] A purely functionalist analysis of religious doctrine is inadequate for the task of inter-religious dialogue. What is required is not reductionism to reach a lowest common denominator, but a deeper understanding of the faith enshrined in the doctrines which can be brought to the place of meeting and encounter. Such a confessional approach is neither obscurantist nor obstructive, it is simply an honest recognition of our inevitable particularity and

---

100 G. D'Costa (ed.), *Christian Uniqueness Reconsidered* (Orbis, Maryknoll, NY, 1989).

101 Newbigin, 'Religion of the Marketplace', in D'Costa (ed), *Christian Uniqueness Reconsidered*, p138.

102 A. MacIntyre, 'Whose Justice? Which Rationality' (Duckworth, London, 1988).

103 Newbigin, 'Religion of the Marketplace', p139.

104 Paul J. Griffiths, 'The Uniqueness of Christian Doctrine Defended', in D'Costa (ed), *Christian Uniqueness Reconsidered*, pp157-73.

specificity: "an openness which is essential for serious theological work and indeed for any serious intellectual work that is not in thrall to the myth of the disembodied and unlocated scholarly intellect".[105]

This recognition of the inevitable particularity of Christianity, and indeed the other faiths of the world, is one of the features of this important collection of essays,[106] but there is also an attempt to hold this in tension with the universal aspect of the faith, especially through the setting of Christology within its Trinitarian context. Notably Gavin D'Costa expresses the importance of Trinitarian doctrine through five theses in which he suggests that it guards against the extremes of 'exclusivism' and 'pluralism', and relates the particularity of Christ to the universal purposes of God by the work of the Holy Spirit. An adequate Trinitarian theology reveals love as the normative mode of relationship, identifiable in the Christ-event as sacrificial love, by which measure the whole world including the Christian Church is judged by the Spirit.[107] Like Newbigin's suggestion of "committed pluralism", such an approach, argues D'Costa, is both committed and open; committed to the Triune God of Christian faith and to the Good News of Christ entrusted to the Church, open in refusing to make a priori assumptions about the religions, and open to the possibility of hearing testimony to the work of the living God beyond the bounds of the Christian world. Moreover, such commitment is, as Rowan Williams puts it, fundamental to "being Christian", enabling positive response to the God who is revealed as source of both logos and spirit, impelling dialogue and practical action with those of other faith traditions.[108]

---

105 Griffiths, 'The Uniqueness of Christian Doctrine Defended', p169.

106 See, for example, ch. 13 by John Milbank 'The End of Dialogue,' and ch.14 by Ken Surin, 'The Politics of Speech' in D'Costa (ed), *Christian Uniqueness Reconsidered*.

107 G. D'Costa, 'Christ, the Trinity and Religious Plurality' in D'Costa (ed), *Christian Uniqueness Reconsidered*, pp16-29.

108 R. Williams, 'Trinity and Pluralism', in D'Costa (ed), pp3-15.

Conclusion to Part 1:
Rediscovering a Missiological Perspective

This initial discussion has highlighted some of the main issues in the debate during the twentieth century. It has shown just how much the preoccupations of the Western Church and Western culture as a whole have dominated the whole pattern of relationships between Christianity and other faiths, and how the context of the discussion has shifted from an internal debate as to the basis and method of the Christian mission, to the secular question as to the relative value of the various religious traditions. This shift is seen in the move of the main centre of debate from mission circles to secular academic institutions. However, some of the key questions recur within this new context, for the encounter between faiths happens as much within the newly plural societies of the West as in the older religious ferment of Asia. Can there be any absolute standard by which human history, culture and religion may be assessed? Must such a standard be objective, or can human subjectivity be significant in any absolute way? To what extent is the relationship of Christian faith to other faiths one of continuity or discontinuity, and if the former how valid is any discussion of 'fulfilment'?

In the central chapters of this volume the intention is to examine two of the most significant contributions to the on-going discussion which have retained a missiological perspective on inter-faith encounter. The work of Bishops Cragg and Newbigin is distinctive in engaging not only with the reality of other faiths, but also with the contemporary secular debate, from their conviction of the truth and significance of the 'Christ-event', and from long experience in the missionary encounter with other cultures and faiths. As we shall see they bring differing emphases to the discussion standing as they do in different streams of the missiological tradition, and having worked in differing cultural settings. I will argue that Cragg represents a development of a position such as Farquhar's, which assumes fundamental continuity between Christianity and other religions and for which 'fulfilment' would still be the appropriate term. Newbigin, however, is more akin to Kraemer with an emphasis on discontinuity. Both represent refinements of these positions which bring them closer to each other, and the final questions to be asked are whether this convergence creates a coherent missiological perspective on the relationship of Christianity and other faiths.

Part 2

Kenneth Cragg's Theology of Encounter

CHAPTER 5

Engaging Islam

Albert Kenneth Cragg was born in the seaside town of Blackpool in Lancashire, England on 8th March 1913. He was raised in an evangelical Anglican family, schooled locally and, at the age of 17, went up to the University of Oxford to read history at Jesus College. He then studied for the Anglican ministry at Clifton (now Trinity) College, Bristol, a theological and missionary college.[1]

He was ordained deacon in the Church of England on his 23rd birthday in 1936 and to the priesthood the following year, and served as curate of St Catherine's Church in Tranmere (near Liverpool) for three years. However, Cragg already had a sense of vocation to the service of the church overseas, and having served his curacy he took up the opportunity for work with the Anglican community in the Middle East, to which in various roles he would regularly return over the next half-century.

From 1942-1947 he was Chaplain and adjunct professor of philosophy at the American University of Beirut, which gave him the opportunity for his first sustained encounter with Islam. He then returned to Britain as Rector of Longworth in Oxfordshire for four years, during which period he completed his Oxford Doctor of Philosophy thesis under the supervision of Dr Ernest Payne, the distinguished Baptist scholar. (E.A. Payne went on to become General Secretary of the Baptist Union of Great Britain, vice-President of the Baptist World Alliance and vice-Chairman and later President of the World Council of Churches; at this stage Payne was the Senior Tutor of Regent's Park College.) At his initial meeting with Kenneth Cragg to discuss the proposal for the doctoral research, Dr Payne, who was also Oxford University Lecturer in Comparative Religion, commented: "Mr. Cragg, you already know more about this subject than I ever will – I suggest you get on with it!"[2]

On completion of his dissertation, Dr Cragg then spent five years in the United States as Professor of Arabic and Islamic Studies at Hartford Seminary, Connecticut, during which time he became editor of the journal 'Muslim World'. He returned to the Middle East in 1956 as a Canon of St George's Cathedral, Jerusalem and study secretary to the Near East Council of Churches. In 1959 he took up an appointment ˙

---

1 Cragg offers some profound reflections on his life experience in his autobiographical study *Faith and Life Negotiate* (Canterbury Press, Norwich, 1994). A brief account of his life is found in the opening chapter of Christopher Lamb's important study of Cragg *The Call to Retrieval* (Grey Seal, London, 1997).

2 Bishop Cragg reported the incident to the present author in a personal conversation.

at the Central College of the Anglican Communion in Canterbury, of which he became Warden in 1961. Dr Cragg held this appointment until the enforced closure of the Central College in 1967 at the instigation of Archbishop Ramsey.[3] During the next few unsettled years Dr Cragg moved between various university appointments in the United States (at Union Theological Seminary, New York), Nigeria (University of Ibadan) and Cambridge, where he was Bye-fellow of Gonville and Caius College. In 1970 he returned to Jerusalem following his consecration as Assistant Bishop in the Jerusalem Archdiocese, based in Cairo. He maintained his close links with the area when he took up his final (full-time) post as Reader in Religious Studies at the University of Sussex from 1973-78, for he remained Honorary Assistant Bishop to the Presiding Bishop of the Jerusalem Province from 1976-86.

Retirement found him active as assistant bishop and community relations' adviser to the diocese of Wakefield and incumbent of Helme, Yorkshire. Currently Dr Cragg lives in retirement in Oxford, where he has been senior member at Wycliffe Hall and lectured for the Faculty of Theology of Oxford University. He was also an honorary assistant bishop in the large Oxford diocese. During this very active life he has found time to write not only prolifically, but with considerable insight and sensitivity, not to mention elegance, on Islam, on the whole area of inter-faith relationships and on the specific issue of Christian-Muslim relations. Christopher Lamb notes that, "he not only produces words but plays with them, feeling for their richness and ambiguity".[4] This has meant that he is frequently misunderstood, although such is his integrity and scholarship that he has also been characterised as *the Christian Imam*.[5] This was confirmed to the present writer by Bishop Lesslie Newbigin who told how, on a visit to the Christian community of Madras many years ago, Bishop Cragg was taken over by the Muslims of that city.[6]

The aim of this chapter will be to examine Cragg's contribution to Muslim-Christian dialogue and to illustrate his characteristic method within this area of specialist expertise. This will provide the basis for an examination of his wider application of this approach in the next chapter. The basis for this analysis will be those works that concentrate most specifically on Islam itself or the relationship between Islam and Christianity. Those books which seek to tackle the wider issue of inter-faith relations will be discussed in detail in the following chapter.

---

3 The story of the Central College has been told by Dr Cragg in *Anglican & Episcopal History*, Vol. LIX, no. 2 (June 1990) pp224-42.

4 Lamb, *Call to Retrieval*, p5.

5 By the late Edwin Robertson in a chapter on Cragg's work in his little book *Breakthrough* (Christian Journals, Belfast, 1976). This was a fulsome tribute from one energetic 'retired' cleric to another!

6 Although it is probably fair to note that Cragg's work has been better received by Indian Muslims that others. See the helpful discussion by Lamb, *Call to Retrieval*, pp123-30.

5.1 Meeting at the Mosque

Kenneth Cragg's whole career has been devoted to encounter, to dialogue or meeting, not just (or even mainly) of systems or ideas, but also of people in their whole range of being, physical and emotional, mental and spiritual. In his early work this was reflected by titles such as *The Call of the Minaret*[7] and *Sandals at the Mosque*,[8] but it has been his constant concern to explore the possibilities of meeting, in which human situation, he believes, rests the integrity and relevance of the worlds of faith.

The *muezzin's* call represents this summons to meet, and the rows of sandals at the mosque door symbolise such a moment of encounter in the Muslim world.[9] Cragg always attempts to convey the atmosphere of Islam, wanting to distil its essence and communicate its spirit of devotion, piety and practice, and not only its articles of belief. Thus he begins the opening section of *Sandals at the Mosque* by going *In Quest of Islam* and vividly describes a typical New Year celebration, and in his Jerusalem studies in Islam for Christians, *The Dome and the Rock*,[10] he not only expounds Islam's five great pillars, but includes parallel chapters giving examples of Muslim prayer and devotion during the annual fast of *Ramadan* and the great pilgrimage to Mecca.[11] He is fully aware of the demands that such encounter makes on those who are prepared to face it, but he is convinced not only of the value of such an enterprise, but that it is a real possibility. To those who question both the value and even the possibility of any such mutual interpretation and understanding, he refuses to concede any ground. Such approaches tend to assume an isolation and imply a despair which is contrary to his whole understanding of the human situation, and which is a denial of that universality which is central to both Muslim and Christian self-understanding.

Cragg remains a keen advocate of what he described as "Frontier Theology",[12] in his own metaphor: ever ready to sail into open waters, rather than content to hug familiar shorelines. Such a venture requires a true mutuality in which "Mosques ... are for meeting in the ultimate, as well as the immediate, sense".[13] This means that no neutral ground is available, whether that of impartial scholarship or crude

---

7 OUP 1956; reprinted with corrections 1964; 2nd Edn, Orbis, Maryknoll, NY, 1985, Collins, London 1986. All references to the latter.

8 First volume of the 'Christian Presence Series' edited by M.A.C. Warren (SCM, London, 1959).

9 See Cragg's apologia for such an enterprise in the Foreword to *Sandals at the Mosque*, pp17-21.

10 SPCK, London, 1964.

11 Chapter 4 'The Prayer of Ramadan' pp31-46, and chapter 7 'A Pilgrim's Prayer Manual' pp67-79. As Lamb notes this reflects the influence and approach of Constance Padwick e.g. *Muslim Devotions: A Study of Prayer Manuals in Common Use* (SPCK, London, 1961), see also Lamb *Call to Retrieval*, pp100-1.

12 *Sandals at the Mosque*, p20. See also the preface to *The Christ and the Faiths* (SPCK, London, 1986), where, with characteristic insight and courtesy, he questions the narrowly domestic concerns of much contemporary Christian theology, ppix-xii.

13 Cragg, *The Call of the Minaret*, p162.

utilitarianism, rather the muezzin's cry re-echoes from faith to faith, in order to evoke a faith response: "we must bring, in all honest openness, that faith by which we live and understand".[14] What Cragg characterises as "studied vacancy of mind" will not suffice, impartiality is, in the end, impossible:

> Can we in fact dispossess our minds of all criteria of approach even if they be
> ·   supposedly merely those of scholarship? Will it not be sounder, not to say more
> feasible, if we confess our interests, take conscious control of our 'prejudices', and
> by discipline and hope release their potential assets of affinity, humility,
> perception and involvement?[15]

Marshall G.S. Hodgson, a fellow Islamicist, agrees that there will always be what he terms "scholarly precommitments" which cannot be eradicated but which can be guarded against. The answer: "cannot finally be to divest ourselves of all commitments, but to learn to profit by the concerns and insights they permit, while avoiding their pitfalls".[16] Despite what he terms the "sensitive and suggestive studies" of Cragg and others, Hodgson feels that "the ultimate judgements such approaches presuppose are suspect".[17]

Hodgson does recognise, however, that an approach from within another great tradition may be just as informed as that from within the tradition in question and Cragg argues persuasively that the attempt, at least, must be made to gain 'an inside view' of the faith, respecting the autonomy of Islamic criteria, recognising the Muslim frame of reference and decision, and refusing to 'Christianise' Islam by reading into it that which it does not accept.[18] Cragg notes that his approach has been misinterpreted in this way, albeit by Western scholars rather than by Muslims! For example, Charles Adams characterises Cragg's approach as "irenic" and comments that "Cragg has penned some of the most evocative and appealing work on Islam as a religion that has ever been done in English",[19] but Adams goes on to argue that his method is inherently flawed since its seeks to find Christian meaning within Islamic experience and doctrine. He even accuses Cragg of "doing extreme violence ... to the historical reality of Islamic tradition" and refusing to accept the *sui generis* character of the faith.[20]

---

14 Cragg, *The Call of the Minaret*, p159.

15 Cragg, *The Dome and the Rock*, p6.

16 M.G.S. Hodgson, *The Venture of Islam*, Vol. 1 (Chicago University Press, Chicago, 1974) p27.

17 Hodgson, *The Venture of Islam*, Vol. 1 p29.

18 This is the charge of Charles Adams in L Binder (ed.), *The Study of the Middle East* (John Wiley, New York, 1976) p39.

19 C. Adams in Binder (ed.), *The Study of the Middle East*, p39.

20 Cf. Charles Adams' chapter 'Islamic Religious Tradition' in Binder (ed), *The Study of the Middle East*; see also Marshall Hodgson, *The Venture of Islam*, Vol. 1 pp27-30; see Cragg, *Muhammad and the Christian* (DLT, London, 1984) pp12-3.

Cragg refuses to admit that there can be no communication between faiths, and suggests that the alternative leads to "wholly isolationist" conclusions.[21] By abandoning any attempt at mediation: "we legitimise all religious decisions simply because they have been historically taken. Doing so would effectively terminate all relationship. Each would then be left in impenetrable self-congratulation or delusion."[22] Therefore, investigation and exposition are only half the task, the necessary preliminaries before attempting to relate or mediate within and between conviction and commitment. On the other hand, as Cragg noted early on: "ideas of universal hospitality ... contain within themselves seeds of an exclusivism as complete as that asserted by the plainly intolerant", and moreover they frequently exhibit a "sharp intolerance of those that claim the ultimate truth of one".[23] If faiths are not permeable to each other, they must remain incomprehensible to the believer also, especially any faith, like both Islam and Christianity, in which there is a claim to finality and culmination. But most Muslims in the world are non-Arab and non-Arabic speaking, and this very fact indicates the reality of cross-cultural meeting in which the Qur'an and Islam prove their capacity to give "authentic religious existence".[24]

The value of Cragg's method was appreciated by Stuart E. Brown, of the World Council of Churches Commission for Dialogue with People of Other Faiths, when he wrote:

> ... this careful balance between the rigours of external history and the reverence of inner conviction, and his genuine sensitivity to the inherent disparities between Christianity and Islam provide an articulate and sensitive rejoinder to those of his critics for whom Muslim-Christian relations can never reach beyond an austere if respectful aloofness.[25]

It is inevitably a difficult process of dialogue between 'absolutes', but for religions there is no other choice since the 'absolute' is precisely what religion is about. Thus partners in dialogue: "must live with a situation in which the one holds to criteria which the other either excludes or believes to have been already fully satisfied. Both must be gentle and honest with the manifest dispute about the criteria themselves."[26]

Privacy is not an option for a universal faith. However, there are, within any faith community, various opinions as to what the authentic expression of the faith might be. Within Islam the well-known division lies between the majority *Sunni* 'orthodox' tradition and the minority *Shi'ah* expression, each containing numerous

---

21 Christopher Lamb is right in his assertion that for Cragg, "mission depends on the possibility of communication, which itself assumes a relationship and at least a potential kinship." *Call to Retrieval*, p119.

22 Cragg, *Muhammad and the Christian*, p13.

23 Cragg, *Sandals at the Mosque*, p68.

24 Cragg, *The Mind of the Qur'an* (Allen & Unwin, London, 1973) pp15 and 18.

25 S.E. Brown, *Ecumenical Review*, Vol. 37 No. 4 (October 1985) pp515-7.

26 Cragg, *Muhammad and the Christian*, p2.

sub-groupings. Beyond all these are the various mystical groups commonly known as *Sufism*. Much of this diversity is related to the rapid expansion of early Islam into different cultural, religious and ethnic communities, but Dr Cragg is reluctant to attribute all variation to external influence, and retains a significant place for the inner dynamic of the sturdy young faith. In any case, limitations on diversity were found in the speedily accepted definitive text of the Qur'an, and the unitary confession of faith, the *Shahadah*: "There is no god but God: Muhammad is the *Rasul* (Prophet, Messenger, Apostle) of God". Much of Cragg's work has been devoted to an exploration of the origins of Islam as the vital clue to understanding its inner life, particularly the relationship between the Holy Qur'an, the content of the revelation, the Prophet Muhammad, the means of the revelation, and the Muslim community, the receivers of the revelation.

The next section will attempt an overview of Bishop Cragg's extensive work in this area, always bearing in mind that for him, "the goal of study is an open country of relationship".[27]

5.2 Islamic Origins in Christian Perspective

Although Islam belongs within the 'Western' tradition, from Abraham to Aristotle, nevertheless it retains a self-conscious 'otherness' as a unique community of belief and culture. This is true not only *vis-à-vis* Judaic and Christian culture, but the creation of Pakistan is a clear indication of this distinction in relation to Indian culture and patterns of belief.[28] For Christians in particular there has been a profound difficulty in any recognition of Muhammad because of his post-dating the events of the gospel records, and for reasons of the Muslim claim to a fulfilment which Christian faith suggests is not required. When Muslims point to the reverence of the Qur'an for both Jesus and his mother, Christians must call attention to the inadequacy of the Qur'anic portrayal of Jesus, not only by its omission of most of his teaching, but also by its exclusion of what Cragg characterises as "the divine meaning of the Cross and the Resurrection".

As we shall see, Cragg believes that in two significant senses the cross of Christ is indeed present in Muslim understanding, but this "implicit 'cross' achieves no historical redemption of the evil" and is incapable of acceptance as a divine act.[29] Despite these inherent 'dissuasives' (Cragg's term for the negative factors in Christian-Muslim relations), in a number of places and with varying emphases Cragg seeks to explore the origins of Islam and its on-going significance as a community of faith.

27 Cragg, *The Event of the Qur'an* (Allen & Unwin, London, 1971) p187.

28 Cragg, *The Call of the Minaret*, pp175 and 178.

29 See *Muhammad and the Christian*, p10, and further development of this theme in *Jesus and the Muslim*, chapter 6, pp166-88; cf also the introduction to his translation of M. K. Hussein's *Qarayah Zalimah, City of Wrong* (N.V. Djambatan, Amsterdam, 1959).

5.2.1 The Prophet and the Book

There is no doubt of the supreme importance in Muslim history and faith of the figure of the Prophet Muhammad, even though his career as an Apostle began relatively late at the age of forty. His generally accepted dates are 570-632 CE, the earliest revelations starting in the year 610 CE.[30] The identification of Muhammad as the Apostle of God is the indispensable second clause of the Muslim statement of faith, the *Shahadah*, and in several widely spaced works Dr Cragg has discussed his life and teaching.[31] The Islamic faith was born in the dual encounter of the man Muhammad with the reality of God, and of the word of God through Muhammad with contemporary Meccan society. Cragg rejects the rather mechanistic theories of inspiration given by much of orthodox Islam, in favour of a more personal account, which, he argues, is no less divine. Indeed a major difficulty of extremely passive understandings of *Wahy* or revelation is the implication "that the more an activity is divine the less it is human".[32] The Qur'an in many places clearly reflects the life situation of the Prophet, but Cragg argues that this does not detract from its divine qualities; rather in grounding it in one historical location, it makes it accessible to other times and places. In any case, even if the thought forms of the Messenger are not consciously employed in the process of *Tanzil* or descent of the revelation from God, they are inescapably present in the hearing community to whom the message is addressed. If this is not the case there could be no communication, and hence no revelation, at all.[33]

The traditional view of the role of Muhammad in this process is frequently upheld by the Qur'anic description of Muhammad as *ummi*, often translated as 'illiterate' in the 'literal' sense of the word. This seems inherently unlikely in view of Muhammad's profession as a merchant, and Western scholars suggest it should be understood as 'uneducated'. But Cragg regularly argues that the word should really be translated as 'unscriptured'. Muhammad is thus the agent of God in bringing the 'Book' to a previously unscriptured people. This is not to deny what Muslims call the *i'jaz* or matchless character of the Qur'an, nor to diminish the mystery of *Wahy*, "To say and believe, as with Muslims we surely must, that he did not 'have it from himself', nor of himself, is not to have to believe that Muhammad was the recipient of a heavenly dictation which by-passed all his yearnings of heart or processes of mind and virtually ignored both the stress of his environment and the travail of his personality."[34]

Attempts to isolate and immunize the Qur'an from the context in which it was given and received are fundamentally misconceived, for "one cannot proceed *to* the

---

30 The common dating practice will be followed throughout, i.e. CE = Common (Christian) Era; BCE = Before Common (Christian) Era.

31 Notably in *The Call of the Minaret*, Chapter 3; *The Event of the Qur'an, passim*; *The Mind of the Qur'an*, especially chs 1-5; and in most detail, *Muhammad and the Christian*.

32 Cragg, *Muhammad and the Christian*, p84.

33 See, for example, *Muhammad and the Christian*, pp84-6.

34 Cragg, *Muhammad and the Christian*, p87; cf. *The Call of the Minaret*, pp66-7.

abidingness of the Qur'an, in word and meaning, unless one proceeds *from* its historical ground and circumstance."[35] Indeed the great mass of the *Hadith* or tradition about Muhammad and Islam's historical origins is witness to the inherent significance of the original context and environment. Within this environment were not only the range of contemporary Arab belief, which already included the concept of a high god named *Allah*, but also the influence of both Jewish and Christian tradition. The precise impact of such influence is a matter of some controversy and is now impossible to gauge from this distance, but Cragg suggests that it might at least have provided the framework of 'people and book' as a concept within which to work:

> All that can be said with certainty is that Muhammad knew of Jews and Christians and something of their history; ...[This gave Muhammad] the most fundamental concepts in his vocation and in subsequent Islam: a sure monotheism and a prophetic mission in which a divine relationship of revelation, through scripture, created a community of faith. It was a tremendous step when Muhammad became assured of himself as a new and final term in prophetic continuity, making a new book, and thence a new faith.[36]

Another major factor in the development of early Islam and the strategy of Muhammad was the generally negative reception given to his message by his fellow-citizens in Mecca. However, the response is interpreted by Muhammad and his followers as not merely a response to the prophet himself; it is by implication the answer of Meccan society to the God on whose behalf Muhammad claimed to speak. "Public and personal reaction to the prophet then emerges as the explicit form of reaction to the God whom he serves and for whom he speaks. Thus his reception in the world becomes a test case of the human relation to the divine will."[37] As such in a sense this reaction was not unexpected, since Muhammad was sufficiently aware of the Judaeo-Christian tradition to realise that God's messengers frequently met with opposition. But Cragg identifies Muhammad's response to this situation as determinative for the future development of Islam. Such a response was perhaps inevitable given the circumstances of time and place into which Muhammad was called to speak. Whatever influence from Jewish or Christian tradition we may detect, the formative experience "is the primary and ultimate encounter of Muhammad with Arabian pluralism of both belief and tribe".[38]

The hostility of Mecca, the most potent expression of this plurality, made for a situation with an inner logic of political action: "The devotion of the prophet required to be achieved in the resources of the ruler".[39] Thus, it is not surprising to

---

35 Cragg, *The Event of the Qur'an*, p114.
36 Cragg, *The Call of the Minaret*, p67.
37 Cragg, *The Mind of the Qur'an*, pp88-9
38 Cragg, *The Event of the Qur'an*, p10.
39 Cragg, *The Event of the Qur'an*, p66; cf. also *The Mind of the Qur'an*: "... with Muhammad above all, prophecy emerged into power and witness into statehood", p87

see the Islamic emphasis on group solidarity and organic unity, develop in the subsequent life of the community. The power structures of Arab society were a real factor in this development, and were incorporated into the Muslim understanding of the totalitarian nature of faith: "On every count, then, it seems fair to conclude that Muhammad's *Sitz im Leben* was such as to teach and require a lively source of the power equation in human affairs and scarcely to generate the sort of power-repudiation by which faith inauguration proceeded elsewhere."[40]

Cragg suggests that Islam celebrates and participates in that stream of prophetic-activism which includes Abraham, Moses and David; but it knows little or nothing of that complementary figure, the prophet-poet, who suffers with and for his message, which is exemplified in Hosea, deutero-Isaiah, and, supremely, Jeremiah.[41] Given both this understanding of the prophetic role, and the circumstances that obtained in seventh century Mecca, the choices made by the embryonic Islamic community and their leader are understandable and perhaps inevitable.

The vital clue, to which Cragg repeatedly returns, is the *Hijrah*, the migration of the small and persecuted Muslim community, from Mecca to the neighbouring town of Yathrib, later to be named *Madinat al-Nabi*, the city of the Prophet, or Medina. The significance of this event is symbolised by the dating of the Muslim calendar from this point as years 'after the *Hijrah*',[42] and by the division of the Qur'an into *Surahs* delivered either at Mecca or Medina. After the move the *Qiblah* or direction of prayer, was re-oriented from Jerusalem to the ancient temple of the *Ka'bah* in Mecca, a clear indication that the *Hijrah* had not stifled Muhammad's ambitions for his native city.[43] Cragg believes therefore, that the *Hijrah* provides the central interpretative clue to the understanding of Muslim society:

> The counting of the years by the Muslim calendar from the point of the *Hijrah* is, then, a proper symbol and a sure instinct. The event which more than any other defines Islam is critical both for what it concludes and what it inaugurates. It has to be seen as the epic of a religion requiring by its inner quality to become political. It discloses in retrospect the inherently self-ordering nature of the Islamic society, its impulse ... to engender ... a state.[44]

Note that although Cragg believes the circumstances of Arab society are significant in influencing the shape of the Muslim community, he also wishes to stress the internal factors at work in the process, hence his reference to the *inner quality* of the religion in its *inherently self-ordering nature*. This "marriage of religion and state", however implicit in Muslim thinking, was reinforced and made explicit by the

---

40 Cragg, *Muhammad and the Christian*, p42.
41 Cragg, *Muhammad and the Christian*, pp43-5.
42 The year was 622 CE.
43 Mecca remained 'the desire of his mission': "Muhammad's purpose turned on a vigorous marriage of Medina's occasion with Mecca's ultimacy", Cragg, *Muhammad and the Christian*, p24.
44 Cragg, *The Mind of the Qur'an*, pp131-2.

experience of the *Hijrah* and has remained "elemental to Islamic genius and Muslim history" ever since.[45] At a recent conference Cragg even suggested that, in relation to the years in Medina, "Muhammad was his own Constantine".[46]

The return of Arab lands to Arab self-determination following the Second World War has raised this question in a new and powerful way. For Cragg the orientation of the *Qiblah* towards Mecca symbolises Muslim commitment to the doctrine and demands of the faith. Islam continues to determine the axis of the Muslim's whole existence in a way that other faiths have long ceased to do.[47] Islam also retains a fundamental confidence in the capacity of the state to achieve a right order in society; a confidence which other philosophies either have never shared, or now feel is misplaced.[48] Cragg correctly perceives that such issues raise important theological questions about human nature in relation to the divine will. As we shall see, he believes that Muhammad's choice of political power and the use of force provides one of the central contrasts and disagreements with Christian faith, but before leaving this aspect of the discussion we should note one further significant point.

Despite common assumptions to the contrary, both Christian and Muslim, Cragg indicates that, according to the Qur'an, allegiance to the community of faith, and faith in God are not identical. The word *islam* has a double edge, which indicates both personal religious submission to God and visible political submission to the Islamic community. The Qur'an is alive to the issue that force may not only ensure survival; it may in turn corrupt religion and bring hypocrisy. Cragg illustrates this point with a reference to *Surah* 49.14, where, in response to the claim of certain Bedouin to be believers, the rejoinder is: "Believers you are not. Rather say 'We profess Islam,' for faith has not yet found its way into your hearts".[49] However:

> It is not suggested here that multitudes do not combine genuine believing participation with such 'accidents' of birth and blood. Nor is it meant to disqualify founding of corporate continuity in the things of faith. But the fact remains that these criteria tend to diminish and even to exclude the truth that faith demands a personal rediscovery in every generation. Nobody is validly either Christian or Muslim merely since his father was or because he was born into that community.[50]

---

45 Cragg, *Sandals at the Mosque*, p61.

46 *Presence and Witness among Muslims* February 2004, IBTS Prague; see DVD and book Peter F. Penner (ed.), *Christian Presence and Witness among Muslims* (Neufeld-Verlag, Germany, 2005).

47 See Cragg's helpful discussion of this issue in *Sandals at the Mosque*, pp61-3, and pp82-5; and his more up-to-date remarks in the revised edition of *The Call of the Minaret*, Ch. 1 'Islam at the New Century', pp3-26.

48 See his discussion in *The Call of the Minaret*, pp127-156; *The Dome and the Rock*, pp184-196; and *Muhammad and the Christian*, pp31-52.

49 *The Koran*, Revised translation by N.J. Dawood (Penguin Classics, London, 1990) p364; see discussion by Cragg, *Muhammad and the Christian*, pp46-8.

50 Cragg, *The Dome and the Rock*, p221.

5.2.2 *The Community and the Book*

The final comment in the previous section reveals not only Cragg's deeply evangelical up-bringing, but also his profound understanding of the nature of religious community, and the subtle inter-play between that community and the authority to which it submits. Much of his estimate of the significance of Islamic origins has been formulated by his own study of the Qur'an in relationship to the Muslim community which it has engendered and whose identity it determines. In addition to his own translation and selection from the Qur'an,[51] he has published two major books on its origins[52] and interpretation[53], and his wide knowledge of the Scripture and associated Arabic studies informs all his work. He himself notes in this context:

> Every religious authority, in the end, turns on the terms of obedience of those who receive it with authority. Even where the authority is unquestioned, it is because acceptance is unquestioning. The guidance is always a receiving by the guided and the quality of the one will hinge upon the temper of other.[54]

Equally at home with abstruse and technical Qur'anic commentaries, in all his studies Cragg never loses sight of the powerful aural dimension of the book in the faith of the ordinary believer. The word *Qur'an* means 'recital' and in an anthology which he co-edited, typically en-titled *Islam from Within*,[55] he underlines the reverence and devotion with which the Qur'an is received in its recitation. Elsewhere he notes the significance of the practice of *hifz* by which the entire Qur'an is committed to memory, so that its contents and ideas imbue all other thinking. In this way it becomes "the theme by which the believer is articulate, like the singer in the song".[56] This fits with the logic of *tanzil*, the process by which the Scripture is revealed through the mouth, rather than the mind, of the Prophet: "As a *verbatim* Scripture it must live *verbatim* on the tongues of its community."[57] Although his own rendition is a selection in order to introduce the great themes of the Qur'an to an alien, and sometimes unreceptive, audience in a readily 'digestible' form, Cragg recognises that the elimination of the reiteration of the Qur'an would exclude not only some third of its volume, but also mean a loss of its "existential quality and its cumulative force".[58] We might note, however, the observation of Christopher Lamb

---

51 *Readings in the Qur'an*, selected and translated with an Introductory Essay by Kenneth Cragg (Collins, London, 1988).

52 Cragg, *The Event of the Qur'an*.

53 Cragg, *The Mind of the Qur'an*.

54 Cragg, *The Mind of the Qur'an*, p182.

55 *Islam from Within* (ed) K. Cragg and R. M. Speight, (Wadsworth, Belmont, CA, 1980), see especially pp14-17, with its citation of the well-known Muslim commentator, Muhammad Ali (1878-1931).

56 Cragg, *The Mind of the Qur'an*, p30.

57 Cragg, *Readings in the Qur'an*, p30.

58 Cragg, *The Mind of the Qur'an*, p33.

that one sometimes detects in Cragg "an over-spiritual approach to scripture",[59] or perhaps it is more truly characterised as Cragg's poetic temperament.[60]

Dr Cragg is also concerned to explore the relationship between fact and meaning, word and truth, the implicit and explicit dimensions of the text which must be studied with care and imagination, although with a proper caution in allegorical interpretation. Clearly its wide readership will receive it in different circumstances and variety of mood; a mystical apprehension of the Scripture must not be ruled out, especially since this must be akin to the experience of the Prophet in receiving it. However, the implicit must always be subject to the test of the explicit.[61] Attention must also be paid to the exegetical tradition of Islam itself, for "it is *this* exegesis which represents the faith-community's scholarly and authoritative possession of its document of revelation".[62] This existential facet of the Qur'an's authority is never far from his exposition of it, for it is emphatically *event* as much as document, the vehicle of both divine demand and human surrender.[63] Its fundamental challenge is to the pagan arena of seventh century Arabia, and the encounter with Judaeo-Christian tradition, although providing the model of a 'Scripture-centred community', was undoubtedly secondary. The revelation must be understood and interpreted in terms of this historical context, for any attempt at 'disengagement' would, "jeopardize, indeed disqualify, the whole possibility of revelation itself".[64]

A significant aspect of that context is the linguistic and literary form of the completed book. The notion of the 'unlettered Prophet' carries, in addition to the point already made, a distinction from mere 'versifying' and a distancing from "the habituations of the mere functionary".[65] But both language and letter are crucial to the whole concept of revelation, especially for the Muslim where the understanding of the Qur'an is that of a perfect uncorrupted human copy of the heavenly book. "For revelation itself, an utterance and a recital, there must needs be a, b, c. Its very inflexion must be treasured. The sense enters into them by the sequences of syntax, as shape is given to the pliant clay. The vessel hardens to hold what is given."[66]

Part of the necessary engagement of any revelation must be the grappling with the limitations of human language and the concepts to which our words give expression. Thus a prerequisite of true understanding must be a willingness to enter into the Islamic world through language and literature in Arabic, for "the bearers of the Word of God must everywhere be students and users of human words".[67] This is

59 Lamb, *Call to Retrieval* p143.
60 Lamb, *Call to Retrieval* p143, also notes Cragg's preference for the poetic over the prosaic.
61 See his discussion of such matters in ch. 3 of *The Mind of the Qur'an*, especially pp51-3.
62 Cragg, *The Mind of the Qur'an*, p69.
63 Cragg, *The Event of the Qur'an*, p13.
64 Cragg, *The Event of the Qur'an*, p17.
65 Cragg, *The Event of the Qur'an*, pp41-3.
66 Cragg, *The Event of the Qur'an*, p52.
67 Cragg, *The Call of the Minaret*, p185.

especially true of Qur'anic study. It is part of that reckoning with history which understands and appreciates 'the past in the present', which is, in Cragg's comprehension, at the heart of Islam's inner dynamic; although, like all things human, Islam itself is in flux.

The semantic question is part of the context which cannot be ignored, and from which 'historical religions' can never escape. The Islamic tradition bears witness to the on-going struggle to banish pagan, non-Muslim elements from the Arabic culture into which Muhammad spoke, and which continued to be reflected in greetings, the choice of names, and the taking of oaths.[68] For exactly the same reasons of communication, there must be a degree of continuity in which old language is stretched and filled with new meaning: "Beliefs cannot be challenged or changed without continuing vocabulary".[69] Indeed, where an old world is being challenged, usurped or even destroyed, there is all the more need for continuity and security. Cragg notes this tension also of communication between faiths. The language of belief marks the boundaries, "but it does not only divide. We are not always sure where it runs. At points we lose it altogether, only to find it again as a formidable thing. The map itself reads differently for the native and for the traveller."[70]

But it is the inter-play between Scripture and community which creates the Islamic distinctive: "Response to the book's meaning creates the *Ummah*, or household of belief, the society of the Scripture and the scriptured in their mutuality, the one definitive and the other derivative." [71] The balance can be alternatively stated, as Cragg himself has put it: "Qur'an-consistency will always be the criterion of the Islamic. But the criterion of the consistency will always be a Muslim decision".[72] Dr Cragg returned to this question in a series of lectures in the University of Oxford,[73] where he suggested that Islam arose in response to the clannishness and exclusivity of the Judaic tradition. Like Judaism, obedience to the divine law is central, but with Christianity, Islam shares the "will to universality". Muhammad was aware of 'the People of the Book', and the cohesion and identity that this 'enscripturing' brought. There is thus a triangular relationship between Book, Prophet and People. How can there be a people without a book, and how can there be a book without a prophet?[74] This leads, for Muhammad, to the more pressing personal question, could it be me? Cragg does not suggest that this was a deliberate, self-generated, response by Muhammad to 'fill the gap', rather his call to prophethood was to satisfy this yearning and the evident vacancy, but at a sub-conscious level.[75]

---

68 Cragg, *The Event of the Qur'an*, p149.

69 Cragg, *The Event of the Qur'an*, p139.

70 Cragg, *The Event of the Qur'an*, p187.

71 Cragg, *The Mind of the Qur'an*, p14.

72 Cragg, *The Event of the Qur'an*, p184.

73 *Judeo-Christian-Islamic Theology: Issues in Relation*, Michaelmas Term 1990.

74 This is reminiscent of Paul's argument in Romans 10:14-21.

75 Dr Cragg discussed these issues in his third lecture, *Islam: God, Prophet and Qur'an*, 24.10.90.

5.2.3 The Prophet and the Community

A final comment in this section must address the role of Muhammad in contemporary Muslim thought. He is not merely a figure of history, but continues as a vital factor in the cohesion of the community of faith. Muhammad's legacy is not only the 'Book' of which he was the instrument, for he remains the norm of Muslim behaviour enshrined in the *Hadith* and enjoined upon the Muslim as *Sunnah*, the second source of Islamic law, the *Shari'ah*. This is reflected in the characteristic understanding of the status of Man as *abd* or servant of God. Islam's most basic concern is with deed rather than doctrine: "Though this does not obviate theology, it means that Islam is finally, and more characteristically, concerned with what the Lord requires in moral deed."[76]

The Qur'an, however authoritative, is not exhaustive; in particular it contains no comprehensive code of behaviour, whether personal or social. It was therefore natural to turn to Muhammad as the exemplar of faith, giving to his *Sirah* or life-story an implicit legislative quality.[77] Cragg suggests that by this process a considerable volume of the customary law and practice of the lands conquered by the expanding faith was incorporated and legitimised as 'Islamic', the Prophet being credited with attitudes and actions compatible with Islam, but already common in the newly absorbed areas.[78] What is more this continues in current debate as modern historians and apologists for Islam validate their arguments by reference to Muhammad, and appeal to the implications or anticipations of his policy.[79] Thus it is not just the 'historical Muhammad' with which we must reckon, but also the Muhammad of Muslim faith and interpretation. Cragg recognises that this may well be a legitimate process, with some Qur'anic justification,[80] but he is keen to illustrate the way in which Muhammad is a central figure in Muslim self-understanding, in order to create a bridge between the rigorous Islamic view of monotheism, and the Christian doctrine of the Incarnation.

> The immediate point is to realize that the Muhammad with whom the Christian mind has to reckon is ... the paragon of ideals, of ideologies, of 'interests' philosophical and economic, which invoke him as their champion or symbol ... He is the mirror of Muslim self-understanding, the crucible of the contemporary value judgements of Islam.[81]

---

76 Cragg, *The Call of the Minaret*, p130.

77 Cragg, *The Call of the Minaret*, p89.

78 Cragg, *The Call of the Minaret*, p90

79 Cragg, *Muhammad and the Christian*, p67.

80 See his references to *Surah* 6.161-3 and *Surah* 39.11-12 in *Muhammad and the Christian*, pp68-9.

81 Cragg, *Muhammad and the Christian*, p68; cf. the examples of this procedure adduced by Cragg in the rest of this chapter on 'Muhammad the Definitive Muslim', pp70-8.

All this happens not just on a moral or socio-political scale, but has also a spiritual dimension, particularly in the realm of popular devotion and Islamic mysticism in which Muhammad becomes "the *Qiblah* of the soul".[82] Within the *Sufi* tradition are numerous examples of ecstatic writing in which divine grace is mediated to the faithful soul through the prophetic personality. Despite the orthodox rejections of any sense of mediation on the part of the Prophet, at a popular level the *Maulid* or birthday festivals of Muhammad provide a setting for a cult of loving devotion.

In the light of the controversy over the portrayal of Muhammad during the early months of 2006, it might be helpful to address a particular comment on this question. A series of twelve cartoons of the Prophet Muhammad, originally published in a Danish newspaper, were republished in newspapers in several European countries. This triggered outraged and sometimes violent protests across the Islamic world, where, especially for the majority Sunni tradition, the depiction of the Prophet is seen as scandalous and blasphemous. This in turn provoked strong reactions around Europe in relation to freedom of speech and in defence of a free press. Does all this simply confirm the thesis of the influential American political scientist Samuel Huntington[83] of an inevitable "clash of civilisations" in the 21st century, as one headline in the London *Times*, "Cartoon wars and the clash of civilisations",[84] seemed to suggest?

Perhaps we might better understand this clash of values as a conflict which reveals a yawning culture gap, a chasm that runs not simply between so-called 'civilisations' but within them – as some Christian reactions to the production of *Jerry Springer – the Opera* underlined. In relation to this particular episode we need to recall that the fundamental sin of Islam is that of *shirk* or 'association', or more popularly idolatry. No representation of God or his prophets, or indeed any living creature, is generally permitted. Protestants might well be able to understand this concern; much of the history of the Reformation was one of iconoclasm, the destruction of images, which our forebears, like today's Muslims, thought dangerous and blasphemous.

Alongside this is a deep respect and reverence in Islam for the person of the Prophet, whether Muhammad or Jesus, Abraham or Moses. All are seen not simply as bringers of a divine message, but as models to be followed, exemplary human beings whose own lives illustrate the message that they bring. An attack on the Prophet is for a Muslim tantamount to an attack on God. In the third place, the history between the Islamic world and the West has been characterised all too often by misunderstanding, antipathy and aggression. This is by no means the whole story of Muslim relationships with other cultures. There have been many examples, from St Francis to Akbar's India to modern Malaysia, of mutual toleration, co-operation and peaceful coexistence. But the folk memories of European and Islamic cultures are

---

82 Cragg, *Muhammad and the Christian*, p56.
83 S.P. Huntington, *The Clash of Civilizations and the Remaking of World Order* (Simon & Schuster, New York, 1996).
84 *The Times*, London, Friday 3 February 2006.

full of suspicion and mistrust; old anxieties and sensitivities are easily reawakened, especially where people feel threatened and vulnerable.

For centuries, until the oil crisis of 1973, the West seemed to be dominant. Muslims felt oppressed and under pressure. For the last thirty years, the West has been sensitive to a renewed confidence in the Islamic world and the growth of Islamic communities in the West. From a Muslim perspective, the West's liberal values are widely promoted through global communications and are exemplified in excessive drinking, indecency and pornography, and moral degeneracy – a judgement with which many Christians might concur! From a Western perspective, the hard won values of liberty and toleration are under threat. While this might explain, it is certainly not to excuse either the initial provocation or the more extreme responses.

However, it is too simplistic to see this only as a clash of values between Islam and the West. It is rather that most difficult of moral problems, a conflict of values, both of which are good, and both of which, incidentally, have an honourable history among Baptists and other historic dissenters: freedom of religion and freedom of expression. Normally we might expect the two to go hand in hand. What happens when they appear to conflict?

Context might help us here. How does it affect our perspective if we know that the cartoons in question were deliberately commissioned to test the boundaries by a right-of-centre Danish newspaper? That Muslims in Denmark are a minority who feel under pressure with a right-wing coalition government with anti-immigration policies? That many well-educated Muslims in Denmark are unable to find jobs commensurate with their education and qualifications? Might we then consider that slogans about 'freedom of the press' may well be a disguise for an attack on a minority population? Of course we might equally question the policies of some Islamist governments in relation to their own minority populations, and to reflect on how Christians and Jews are portrayed in some of the more extreme Islamist literature. Sadly this controversy has mainly served the cause of Islamists on the one hand and Islamophobes on the other.

Cragg suggests that a clue to the proper understanding of this aspect of Muslim faith may be found in the Qur'anic term *Tasliyah*, which means, "to call down blessings upon". God, the angels and believers alike are said to bless and salute the Prophet in *Surah* 33.56.[85] This is but the devotional expression of the fundamental article of Muslim belief, the *Shahadah*, which links in one conviction the Lordship of God and the Prophethood of Muhammad.[86] For Cragg this aspect of Muslim thought and practice provides a genuine point of contact with Christian theology, and he notes that such areas of controversy *between* faiths often reveal issues *within* them. Nevertheless, "there is hope that the very celebration of Muhammad may suggest a clue to the New Testament recognition of Jesus. For what but a *Tasliyah*,

---

85 It reads: "The Prophet is blessed by God and His angels. Bless him then, you that are true believers, and greet him with a worthy salutation." Dawood's translation, p298.

86 Cragg, *Muhammad and the Christian*, pp54-56, and the whole chapter 'Muhammad in the Soul', pp53-65.

'a divine salutation', is the familiar New Testament cry: 'This is My Son, my beloved, hear him'?"[87]

What then are we to say of Cragg's lifetime of study of Islam in Christian perspective? As he notes himself "Summary is always a precarious venture. But are not these two, the divine Lordship and the prophetic service robust for that Lordship, the core of the Muslim witness in any ecumene of faiths?"[88] It is in these two central areas of the nature of the divine and the understanding of prophethood that he finds both the points of closest contact and the greatest barriers in mutual acceptance. To these issues we must now turn.

5.3 Islam and Incarnation

Such an association of the notion of incarnation with Islam seems quite astonishing, but it was made by Kenneth Cragg in a splendid contribution entitled 'Islam and Incarnation' to the symposium *Truth and Dialogue* held at Birmingham University in 1970 of which he was a corresponding member.[89] Bishop Michael Nazir-Ali has pointed out the originality and daring of this line of thinking and suggests that the article, subsequently developed in *Jesus and the Muslim* and elsewhere, has been unduly neglected.[90] Cragg recognises the apparently hopeless task of any form of Christology within a Muslim setting, but suggests that such a negative outcome is not the only possibility in the meeting of the two traditions: "is there not a Christian sense of God in Christ truly compatible with the Islamic awareness of the divine unity?".[91]

What Cragg suggests is that some degree of convergence might be found in the notion of *rasuliyyah* or 'sentness': the Christian witness is to the 'sentness' of Jesus Christ, developed in the preaching of the Acts and the Epistles from the testimony of the gospel itself. It is also recognised in the fundamental Islamic term *Rasul*, the 'sent one', fulfilled pre-eminently in Muhammad himself, but as the culmination of a long sequence of prophets 'sent' by God as his messengers. It is this relationship between God and his messengers that Cragg suggests can be termed a true 'association' between God and the human. Such use of language he recognises as 'dangerous',[92] for 'association' is the normal English translation of the basic Muslim sin *Shirk*, otherwise denoted as 'idolatry'. But for God to be freed from false

---

87 Cragg, *Muhammad and the Christian*, p65. This same quotation is made in a similar context by Norman Anderson, *Islam in the Modern World. A Christian Perspective* (Apollos/IVP, Leicester, 1990) p116.

88 Cragg, *The Mind of the Qur'an*, p195.

89 Published in *Truth and Dialogue* (ed.) John Hick, (Sheldon Press, London, 1974) pp126-39.

90 M. Nazir-Ali, *Frontiers in Muslim-Christian Encounter* (Regnum Books, Oxford, 1987) p31.

91 Cragg, *Islam and Incarnation*, p126.

92 Cragg, *Islam and Incarnation*, p128; according to Nazir-Ali, it is 'deliberately provocative'! *Frontiers in Muslim-Christian Encounter*, p21.

association with idols, it requires his authentic association with humanity through his servants, the prophets: "We might almost say that there *are* prophets *because* there *are not*, and should not be, idols".[93] The same will that denies idolatry demands prophecy, and this is further underlined by the doctrines of creation, providence and law, all of which complement and reinforce the divine stake in the human; in all these ways God is committed to humanity. Thus he concludes that 'sentness': "presupposes a human aegis for divine purposes",[94] and is represented symbolically in the *Shahadah*, with its clear association of God *and* Muhammad.

Of course Cragg recognises the Islamic emphasis that Muhammad is *only* a prophet, nothing more, but this serves only to stress the divine origin of the revelation: it is not of Muhammad, but of God. The concern, identical with that of Christian doctrine in talk of the incarnation, is for the status of the revelation: "The status of prophet is identified in human texture that it may be known to be authoritatively God's doing".[95] This provides Cragg with a model of divine-human relationships into which the Christian witness can be fitted, although he admits that the criteria may have to be 'enlarged'. Nevertheless, all the essential presuppositions, divine sovereignty, creation and providence, history, law and prophecy, are there. There is a clear distinction between Islamic and Christian criteria about what might constitute a 'feasible association' between the human and the divine, but we are moving in the same realm of discourse, in which there is a fundamental continuity of thought. In this sense he suggests that all prophecy and revelation must be recognised as 'incarnational', locating, as they do, the divine command in the human arena: "To believe in the incarnation is not to exclusify that mystery. For it is relatively present everywhere in creation and without it this would not be the sort of world in which *the* incarnation could happen."[96]

Yet the Christian perception of God-in-Christ also serves to illumine all human instrumentality to God and gives the clue to all else in creation and history.[97] But Cragg argues that the fundamental concern of Christology in general and incarnational language in particular, is an 'instinctive solicitude' for the integrity and authenticity of the revelation. In other words they are the Christian equivalent of the *Shahadah*; they by no means say the same thing, but they serve the same function. Thus: "The present case is that, in 'association' itself, in 'sentness' with its divine

---

93 Cragg, *Islam and Incarnation*, p128.
94 Cragg, *Islam and Incarnation*, p131.
95 Cragg, *Islam and Incarnation*, p132.
96 Cragg, *Islam and Incarnation*, p134.
97 Cragg, *Islam and Incarnation*, p134. Cf. p138 n3, Cragg cites here as' an example of such a 'Christology in continuity', D. M. Baillie's *God was in Christ* (Faber & Faber, London, 1956). Ironically, in view of Hick's subsequent position, he also notes John Hick's critique of Baillie's work in his article 'Christology at the Crossroads' in *Prospect for Theology* 1967; cf. J. Hick, 'The Christology of D.M. Baillie' *Scottish Journal of Theology* (1958 No. 1) pp1-12.

fiat and its human aegis, we have a potentially recognizable affinity, beyond and beneath all else, however abiding and exacting the disparities."[98]

Even early Christian worship of Christ was not the *post facto* deification of a man, but a recognition of the divine *a priori* by Jews brought up with a clear understanding of the divine unity. The worship of Christ was not an affront to the divine majesty, but a "proceeding upon new and glorious criteria of that by which God was God indeed".[99]

In all this discussion Cragg has been careful to avoid what he terms the 'battlefield language' of 'sonship', wishing to gain a hearing for himself apart from such 'tyranny'. As Christopher Lamb astutely observes, "Cragg's theological aim is not to do away with controversy, but to refine it so that it focuses on the points he believes are ultimately at issue"[100] However, in closing he argues that the language of 'begetting' is equivalent to talk of 'sending', and used in a similarly analogous way. In fact he has argued this from his earliest attempts at Christian apologetics in a Muslim context, and he has been supported in the effort, even by so conservative a writer as Sir Norman Anderson,[101] in rejecting some Muslim interpretations of 'Father-Son' terminology as implying physical paternity. If there is paradox involved, it is no more than the paradox that speaks of God *and* his messenger, and already implicit in thinking of God *and* the world. All speak of the divine-human relationship, where we differ is in our understanding of how we recognise and confess that relatedness.

Michael Nazir-Ali, in recognising Cragg's original contribution to this debate, suggests that perhaps he has failed to allow a distinction between involvement *with* and involvement *in*. Qur'anic talk of God's nearness tends to stress his omniscience and willingness to hear prayer rather than his close involvement in the human situation. Even if Cragg is right to suggest that such talk implies exposure and involvement, Islam itself has refused to draw such a conclusion.[102] Moreover, Nazir-Ali is not convinced that Cragg has retained sufficient distance between God's revelation through his prophets and messengers and that unique revelation in his Son, in which "Divine involvement is complete ... the sender is also the one who is sent".[103] He implies that this paradox is of a different order to the general question of God's relation to the world. The argument of course hinges on recent discussions about the nature of Christology and distinctions of 'degree' or 'kind'. Cragg's commendation of Baillie suggests a leaning to the former, of· which it was an influential early example. We will return to the Christological debate in chapter 9 of this volume.

---

98 Cragg, *Islam and Incarnation*, p135.

99 Cragg, *Islam and Incarnation*, p136.

100 Lamb, *Call to retrieval*, p107.

101 See Cragg, *The Call of the Minaret*, pp285-7; cf. Norman Anderson *Islam in the Modern World*, pp117-27.

102 Nazir-Ali, *Frontiers in Muslim-Christian Encounter*, p21.

103 Nazir-Ali, *Frontiers in Muslim-Christian Encounter*, p31.

As we have seen, Cragg is all too aware of the differences in the 'criteria of the divine' between Christianity and Islam and he believes that these stem from a fundamental difference in the understanding of the nature of prophethood, and therefore a disagreement about the nature of the God whose messengers they are. "It is the insistent requirement of the concept of prophethood in Islam that it must exclude and negate the concept of incarnation, whereas, as Christians see it, prophethood deepens and climaxes into 'the Incarnate Word'."[104] For Cragg this is never clearer than in the comparison of Jesus' choice at Gethsemane and Muhammad's in the *Hijrah* and this crucial discussion will occupy our next section.

5.4 A Suffering Prophet?

In an Oxford lecture series[105] Dr Cragg cited with approval the aphorism of Tim Gorringe 'God engages!'[106] But the question at issue between Christianity and Islam is precisely *how* God engages, and what is revealed about the nature of God in that engagement. On the understanding of the sequel to the climax of hostility engendered by the ministry of Jesus, turns not just issues of historical fact, but "it also involves our ultimate understanding of God, our view of evil, of providence, of forgiveness and of divine power".[107] If God is personal, knowledge of the divine must come in a personal way, but for Islam, although revelation communicates God's law and will, God own self remains finally inscrutable.[108] The revelation comes by word and ear rather than by thought and experience, and in consequence "the Revealer remains unrevealed".[109] For Christianity, however, what is made known in the Gospel is not merely the divine will, but the divine nature, and therefore Christology is about the doctrine of God:

> The phrase [Son of God] means that Christ is God in divine self-revelation, an activity that begets or generates a historical personality, wherein what God is in revelatory love, God is also known to be in revelatory action. The Father begets the Son in the sense that the divine 'will' to reveal is translated into act. But all is of God and from God and by God. God is at once revealer and revealed – the Father and the Son. By this faith in Christ we recognise simply that when God reveals God, what he gives us is himself. Our faith in the divinity of Christ is not, as the Muslim has believed, an affront to God, an offense against the divine unity, the supreme doctrinal sin for Muslims. On the contrary it is the genesis and ground of our faith that the one living and eternal God has been self-revealed.[110]

---

104 Cragg, *Jesus and the Muslim*, p287.

105 Michaelmas Term 1990.

106 In his article 'Sacraments' in R. Morgan (ed), *The Religion of the Incarnation: Anglican Essays in Commemoration of Lux Mundi* (Bristol, Classical Press, 1989) p158.

107 Cragg, *Jesus and the Muslim*, p166.

108 Cragg, *The Call of the Minaret*, p42.

109 Cragg, *The Call of the Minaret*, p41.

110 Cragg, *The Call of the Minaret*, p262.

There is a further dimension to this issue of the self-revelation of God, to which Cragg repeatedly returns, namely exactly *what* is revealed about the divine nature through this process, and in particular the Muslim rejection of the possibility of the cross. It is a rejection based not so much on historic grounds, (although the evidence suggests that Muhammad's awareness of the Christian tradition may well have come through Gnostic channels), as on the dogmatic assertion that God cannot permit his servants, and thereby the divine cause, to suffer final humiliation. According to Muslim tradition, God intervenes to rescue Jesus and another is crucified in his place. This reflects for Cragg a *deus ex machina* notion of God, and poses a fundamental theological question: "What makes God God and glory glory?"[111] In any case, Cragg argues that even in its denial, the Qur'an affirms aspects of the facticity of the cross. He suggests that the cross can be viewed in three ways: as an act of wayward humanity, as a conscious choice on the part of Jesus himself, and as an act of God. The Muslim position recognises the first two of these; there is no doubt that people intended to kill Jesus, and he was himself willing to follow through his commitment to the bitter end. But, for the Muslim, the act of God is to be seen in the rescuing of Jesus from this fate, thereby confounding the enemies of God and his prophet.[112] Although the Qur'an is both radical and insistent in its denial of the cross as a divine act, it retains and admits within that very denial an affirmation of the first two aspects of its Christian significance.

Cragg suggests that behind *Surah* 4:157-9[113] lies the thought, essential to Islam, that no true prophet is actually done to death. If he is not rescued he is discredited.[114] Cragg provides a threefold analysis of the Muslim position: historically the cross did not happen, at least not to Jesus; redemptively it need not happen, and morally it should not happen.[115] If such a thing were to happen it would seem to the Muslim an unthinkable blasphemy against the greatness of God. What Cragg seems to be asking is how God relates to the suffering which the prophets' commitment to the divine commission inevitably entails. Both Muslim and Christian are agreed that God does not desert them, but simply to 'rescue' them leaves the evil encountered in the hostility unchanged, thwarted perhaps, but not overcome. Cragg gently but firmly proposes an alternative Christian view of this line of thinking:

> Adamantly to exclude the Cross of Jesus from the wisdom of God is not truly to believe *Allahu Akbar* [God is greater]. It is, rather, to withhold from this greatness what may well be its greatest measure and sign. We *may* be wrong to hold that it is,

---

111 Cragg, *The Call of the Minaret*, p268.

112 Cragg first suggests this line of argument in *The Call of the Minaret*, pp269-272; he develops it further in the introduction to his translation of M.K. Hussein's *City of Wrong*, and states it most fully in *Jesus and the Muslim,* chapter 6 'Gethsemane and Beyond', pp166ff.

113 Which reads in Cragg's translation: "They did not kill him, nor did they crucify him. They were under the illusion that they had." *Jesus and the Muslim*, p170.

114 Cragg, *Jesus and the Muslim*, pp171-2.

115 Cragg, *Jesus and the Muslim*, pp178-81.

but to exclude it essentially is to limit God no less – and perhaps more – than to believe the principle of the Cross to be indispensable.[116]

As we have already noted, Cragg believes that Islam is operating within just one stream of the prophetic tradition, and, that the Qur'anic Jesus is an 'emasculated' figure in need of deliverance from Muslim misconception.[117] It is not so much the issue as the Crusaders understood it, "the repossession of what Christendom has lost", as the "restoration to Muslims of the Christ whom they have missed".[118] The tense relationship between Christianity and Islam was reinforced by the Crusades and that legacy has yet to be outlived.[119] The Christian task is to enable the Muslim to come to a fuller understanding of the Jesus of the Gospels, if necessary by selected passages, which will not create immediate barriers to understanding. The encounter with this Jesus must be allowed to produce its own result and expression: there can be no requirement for 'orthodoxy' before and apart from faith, and such a process concurs with what must have happened for the first disciples and the evangelists themselves.[120] But Cragg warns that the manner of Christian affirmation is of vital importance, particularly in view of the history of strained relationships. Christian witness can never be about territorial expansion but the wider dissemination of Christ.[121] The underlying principle is clear: "we must affirm the fact of the Cross always in the same spirit in which Jesus himself suffered it".[122] Cragg is equally clear that 'the fact of the Cross' includes not just the witness to its historical reality for Jesus himself, but something, at least, of its interpretation within Christian tradition, for it has a central role in the Christian understanding of the divine-human relationship: "Christians read their harsh suffering as the index to a cosmic conflict between righteousness and wrong, between the Christ of God and the gathered *zulm* of the evil powers of society and state."[123]

The Christian experience is understood in the light of the experience of Jesus, and in this process the interests of faith and history meet. This does not threaten the history as such, for history is always a meeting of 'fact' and 'interpretation': "It has to do with what happened because of what what happened meant".[124] Jerusalem is thus the 'City of Wrong' and serves as a symbol for the human situation in all times and places. It is "a representative locus of the representative wrongness of the

---

116 Cragg, *Jesus and the Muslim,* p181.

117 Cragg, *The Call of the Minaret,* p235.

118 Cragg, *The Call of the Minaret,* p220; this is the key emphasis of Christopher Lamb's analysis of Cragg's theology in *The Call to Retrieval.*

119 Cragg, *The Call of the Minaret,* p240.

120 Cragg, *The Call of the Minaret,* pp259-60.

121 "It aims not to have the map more Christian, but Christ more widely known." *The Call of the Minaret,* p230.

122 Cragg, *The Call of the Minaret,* p265.

123 Cragg, *Jesus and the Muslim,* p105.

124 Cragg, *Jesus and the Muslim,* pp85-6.

world".[125] This develops further the contrast between the Christian understanding of the rebelliousness of human sin as something cosmic, and the Muslim awareness of sins as a symptom of human feebleness which can be corrected through sufficient discipline and the proper ordering of human society". This belief that the political expression and the rule of God can coincide has been the ruling characteristic of Muslim belief about society and the Muslim hope about history.

For Dr Cragg it is an assurance that no truly Christian diagnosis of the human condition could share.[126] It is perhaps this divergent understanding of the nature of sin, or more generally of the divine-human relationship, which lies behind the controversy over the cross. For Cragg the cross is as inevitable as it is impossible for the Muslim. There can be no 'artificial' rescue of the prophet-teacher who must live with the burden of his message, and face the 'Jerusalem' that has always murdered the prophets.[127] In fact, for Cragg, the Muslim reinterpretation of the cross "has made havoc of the manifest continuity between what Jesus taught and what Jesus suffered".[128] The cross "is what happens when a love like Christ's encounters a world like Jerusalem".[129] For the Christian the cross is paradoxically shown to be the greatest expression of the divine sovereignty of God in Christ: "The cross became his throne".[130] The essential difference between the Muslim conception of the exaltation of Christ through rescue and rapture, and the Christian understanding of exaltation through death and resurrection, is precisely this dimension of the love that suffers.[131] In the situations of the two prophets, Jesus and Muhammad, it is expressed in the choice Muhammad made in the *Hijrah* and Jesus in the darkness of Gethsemane. How were they to be accountable to God? "Islam has been confident that the Hijrah contains the pattern of being effectively accountable. With Jesus the pattern of accountability was 'the cup my Father has given me'. There will always be a profound if reverent contrast between the two."[132]

Thus the question of the interpretation of the cross is a vital issue in Christian-Muslim relations. It is vividly expressed by Cragg in his introduction to Muhammad Kamel Hussein's attempt at a new and imaginatively sympathetic Muslim perspective on the events of Good Friday: "What is this darkness in which the world is darkened during the three hours of a Friday afternoon? Is it, or is it not, a darkness in which love is redemptively at grips with sin? Or a darkness in which a mistake of identity works out its bitter way before an onlooking heaven? Only when the

---

125 Cragg, in 'Introduction' to M.K. Hussein's *City of Wrong*, pXVI.

126 Cragg, *Sandals at the Mosque*, pp122-4.

127 Cf. Luke 13:34-5.

128 Cragg, *The Call of the Minaret*, p268.

129 Cragg, *The Call of the Minaret*, p270.

130 Cragg, *The Call of the Minaret*, p274; cf. the comments of Kraemer and Newbigin in Part One above.

131 Cragg, *Jesus and the Muslim*, p183.

132 Cragg, *Muhammad and the Christian*, p52.

shadows that remain around this question are dispelled does the darkness itself become luminous."[133]

For Islam, faith in the finality of Muhammad as 'the seal of the prophets' is also a deep conviction about the adequacy of prophethood itself as the means of the divine education of humanity. It is the instrument of the divine imperative by which we have "'the words made Scripture', the Book;" whereas "in the Christian faith we have ·'the Word made flesh', the Christ who is Jesus".[134] Herein lies the heart of the contrast, because for Cragg, as for Christianity as a whole, the prophetic model, in the end is not enough. Islam cannot conceive of anything 'more than a prophet'[135] but this is precisely the truth about Jesus which the Gospel proclaims,[136] and is implied so graphically in the parable of the vineyard[137] where the relationship between 'owner' and 'tenants' is central, and in the comparison so simply stated by the writer to the Hebrews.[138] Cragg suggests that ultimately the 'prophetic model' for the divine-human relation fails to do justice both to the nature of God and the situation of Man:

> Is it not clear that the question whether prophecy is really final is also the question whether God's sovereignty is fully vindicated in 'prophetic' terms alone? Must we not also say that the question as to the adequacy of the prophetic is the question about the nature of man? May it not be that to see prophecy as the ultimate is to underestimate *both* the human situation and the divine competence? In that event, the meaning of *Allahu akbar* must be taken further.[139]

5.5 Cragg's Theological Model

In this chapter I have characterised Bishop Cragg's work as a theology of encounter, a true meeting which takes seriously the situation of both parties. It begins with the recognition that there is no neutral territory in the discussion, even if, as he clearly believes, there is common ground. From the Christian perspective, therefore, there are no other criteria than those provided by the Gospel. Nevertheless, he recognises that the Muslim is in a similar position, for the givenness of the Qur'an is the only starting point, with all that that implies for the ultimacy of prophethood as the means of the divine relationship to humanity. This is a genuine theology of encounter precisely because it takes seriously these issues in relationship, we meet and greet each other in common honesty.[140]

---

133 Cragg in 'Introduction' to *City of Wrong*, pXXIV.

134 Cragg, *Jesus and the Muslim*, p251.

135 Jesus' description of John the Baptist according to Matthew 11:9 and Luke 7:26.

136 Cragg, *Muhammad and the Christian*, pp126-7.

137 Mark 12:1-12, and parallels; cf. *Muhammad and the Christian*, p129.

138 "In many and various ways God spoke of old to our fathers by the prophets, but in these last days he has spoken to us by a Son." Hebrews 1:1-2a, RSV.

139 Cragg, *Muhammad and the Christian*, p128.

140 Cf. K. Cragg, *To Meet and to Greet* (Epworth Press, London, 1992).

For both faiths the crucial question is of convergence and divergence, continuity and discontinuity. Both stand within the Judaic tradition, and although this has not featured in this treatment, Cragg is clear that the relationship to Judaism is vital for Islam and Christianity, both independently and in their mutuality. The centrality of Jerusalem as a symbol in his writing points to this dimension which we will examine in the course of the following chapter. But it is on this issue of continuity and discontinuity that Cragg's work has been most closely questioned. As we noted in an earlier section, there are those who wonder whether his overtly Christian perspective allows Islam to be seen in its own right, not only in contrast to Christianity, but also in its own exclusivism.[141]

His own life and scholarship give the lie to any suggestion that Cragg is unwilling to take the world of other faith with anything other than utter seriousness. But he will not grant absolute autonomy to any religious tradition for two reasons. First, it would deny any possibility of meeting, and negate that common humanity which is such a central concern in all his thought.[142] In the second place, he is ever conscious that religion itself may become the agent of the fundamental human sin, idolatry or *shirk*. This is the "pride and perjury of all religion, its inherent vocation to possess and serve the absolute, and its inevitable temptation to forget that the absolute is not itself".[143] He continues in another context: "The claims of God must never be subordinated to claims on behalf of God".[144]

It is interesting to note that this same criticism can be made in the opposite direction, that is that Cragg fails to allow a sufficient distinctive for the Gospel. Michael Nazir-Ali draws attention to this issue in relation to the doctrine of God, and in the Christological context.[145] He contrasts the discontinuous approach of Kraemer and A. Rudvin, which denies any continuity between Christian revelation and human religious systems, with Cragg's recognition that while predicates may vary, the subject is still the same. Nazir-Ali wonders at what point disparity in predicates may indicate that the subject is not in fact the same.[146] The predicate is that which defines the subject, and often between religions the same subject is differently defined. If, in the end, the subject is not the same, the debate is meaningless. What is the balance between similarity and disparity? Nazir-Ali correctly identifies the Christological issue as crucial in this debate, for if God can be known more or less adequately in other ways, what need is there for the Incarnation? Thus he suggests that to speak of the divine involvement in the Incarnation requires "a totally different kind of model" from that of prophecy, with a difference of kind and not only of degree.[147]

---

141 So, for example, Marshall Hodgson, *The Venture of Islam*, Vol. 1, p29, see the discussion above, p66.

142 See for example Cragg's response to Hodgson and Adams in *Muhammad and the Christian*, pp12ff.

143 Cragg, *The Event of the Qur'an*, p37.

144 Cragg, *The Mind of the Qur'an*, p139.

145 Nazir-Ali, *Frontiers in Muslim-Christian Encounter*, chs 1 and 2 respectively.

146 Nazir-Ali, *Frontiers in Muslim-Christian Encounter*, pp18-20.

147 Nazir-Ali, *Frontiers in Muslim-Christian Encounter*, p31.

As we have seen, Cragg also believes that the prophetic model is, finally, inadequate for the self-revelation of the suffering God. But he is wary of talk of 'total' or 'absolute' distinction, for the reasons given above, and even more important in the Christian context, because if this were the case, there would be no grounds for an Incarnation at all. Cragg is surely correct here in his affirmation of the doctrines of creation and humanity, which mean that this world is the sort of place, and humanity is the type of being, in which Incarnation is possible. Nevertheless, his own commitment to the decisiveness of the revelation in Christ, as the place and the person in which the divine Incarnation actually does happen, and which reaches its climax in the cross and resurrection, is not in doubt. However great the common ground which Islam and Christianity shares, Cragg is ever conscious that "in truth the Cross has no parallel. It may be best to wait for those who are strangers to its meaning to see it by its own light"[148]. But this perception must come out of its own context, for Cragg is equally clear that "the purpose of the Christian mission is not cultural displacement. It is the presentation of Christ as saviour within every culture".[149] The outcome of this process is not displacement but fulfilment.[150]

This obligation to witness is neither unique to Christianity, nor does it stem from a determination to succeed at all possible costs. It is based rather in a will to universality which hopes to unite humanity, that is from religion's inner dynamic not any external pressure:

> The meeting of faiths is not to be seen as a prudent conformity to external necessity. It is rather the obligation of their nature and their ancient sense of the metaphysical oneness of humanity. For that must be the spring of guidance when physical forces impose an externally common predicament but do not of themselves illuminate its nature or undertake its burden.[151]

As the good bishop that he is, Kenneth Cragg remains confident of the power of the Gospel of Christ, when once it wins a hearing for itself. This may best be achieved, not by intellectual debate, but in response to the cry of the human heart:

> There is no reason within Islam why Muslims should be exempt from the appeal which reaches from Jesus even if it comes – if need be – in spite of, rather than in line with, the Christian Christology. Nor need the familiar Islamic dissuasives be more resistant to such attraction than the sundry motives of reluctance that derive from secular scepticism or indifference. Perhaps it is the lesson of the long centuries of *doctrinal* encounter between faiths, and in particular between Islam and Christianity, that we should let the poets of faith take over its commendation, as

---

148 Cragg, *The Call of the Minaret*, p273.
149 Cragg, *The Call of the Minaret*, p306.
150 Cragg, *Sandals at the Mosque*, p92.
151 Cragg, *The Call of the Minaret*, p166.

that for which the vigilance of dogma was always watchful when it was properly dogmatic.[152]

If at times Dr Cragg's style is so allusive as to be elusive, it is because he is not only a theologian, but also a 'poet of faith'.

152 Cragg, *Jesus and the Muslim*, p45.

CHAPTER 6

A Theology of Fulfilment?

In the previous chapter I provided a detailed survey and analysis of Kenneth Cragg's engagement with Islam, and underlined his characteristic approach, which takes the world of other faith with utter seriousness. This is seen in the careful listening which strains to catch the nuances of what the other is truly saying, and, in so doing, wins a willing hearing in its turn. This chapter will show how Bishop Cragg has developed this method into a full inter-faith theology, and how he has applied it in his wider studies of the whole religious field. It comes to fruition in his magisterial work *The Christ and the Faiths*,[1] but is anticipated in a number of other books in which he considers Christianity in its global setting.[2] Dr Cragg is acutely aware of the diverse cultural contexts in which the inter-religious relationships have developed and it is at this point we must begin.

6.1 Humanity, Culture and Mission

Cragg's fundamental assumption is our common humanity.[3] Within the huge range of historical situations and the enormous diversity of cultural settings there remains the sharing as human beings of our common life upon the globe. Hence the opening chapter of *The Christian and Other Religion* entitled 'This Earth, My Brother'.[4] All religions must begin with this human situation: "life as a personal dilemma, kinships in the flesh, constraints in society, puzzles in the soul, pressures in the will,"[5] and the meeting of the faiths must also take place upon this common ground. Cragg believes that human considerations can never be alien to the heart of God,

---

1 SPCK, London, 1986

2 *The Privilege of Man* (Athlone Press, London, 1968); *Christianity in World Perspective* (Lutterworth Press, London, 1968); *The Christian and Other Religion* (Mowbray, London, 1977).

3 It is interesting to note the links with M. K. Hussain again at this point, of whom Dr Cragg has written: "Truth and faith would have to be a sort of continuum, the one validating the other. Religious meaning could not be separated from religious believing and religious believing could only be grounded in human nature." in *The Pen and the Faith: Eight Modern Muslim Writers and the Qur'an* (Allen & Unwin, London, 1985) p129.

4 Mowbrays, Oxford, 1977, pp1-16.

5 Cragg, *The Christian and Other Religion*, p2.

whether he reveals himself through covenant or prophet or incarnation,[6] but to begin with theology or revelation is to exclude from the start: "whether or not we share the sense of divine grace, we certainly participate in the human condition. It is this alone which allows us the hope of finding ground where all our pluralisms meet."[7]

If objections to this approach are raised from the Kantian perspective of subjectivity and we attempt to rule humanity out of the question, then there remains no question to answer. For there is no meaning in any of these issues, whether deity, or reality, or transcendence, that is not meaning *for humanity*. We are driven to recognise that "Faith, and the faiths, have to do with the transcendent reference of self-consciousness."[8]

This self-conscious common humanity must be explored within its present context, although that will of course include what Cragg describes as "the compound interest of history", with its sharp dilemma between human competence and human confusion. In particular the context for the meeting of the faiths is two centuries of Christian mission and expansion. Cragg suggests that there are noticeable contrasts between the apostolic mission of the first century and nineteenth century Christian missions: "Not the least of these was the marked dominance of western cultural forms and assumptions in the whole context of Christian thought, worship, custom and practice among the nations of the Gospel's dispersion. The geographical universality of the Church, or nearly so, had been achieved only in the context of a deep cultural partiality."[9]

Cragg believes that the apostolic preaching attained a greater reciprocity between the preacher and the hearer, which is symbolised for him in the credal formulation "for us men and our salvation", an inclusive phrasing which avoids the patronising posture characteristic even in liberal condescension.[10] He recognises that such judgements are easily made with twentieth century hindsight, and he argues that the close juncture of 'the Flag and the Cross' assumed by western critics and accused in non-western thought, was actually a more involved and uncertain relationship. This assessment finds support in an important survey of protestant missions and British imperialism by the mission historian Brian Stanley. Dr Stanley notes that imperialism itself was not a monolithic movement and where missionary support for British policy was forthcoming, and this was by no means a foregone conclusion, "concern for national prestige was rarely uppermost in Christian minds".[11] He concludes that the missionaries' vision was frequently clouded by national and racial pride and distorted by a post-Enlightenment world-view which was over mechanistic. But:

---

6 See, e.g., Cragg, *Jesus and the Muslim*, pp202 and 253.
7 Cragg, *The Christian and Other Religion*, p3.
8 Cragg, *The Christian and Other Religion*, p5.
9 Cragg, *Christianity in World Perspective*, p9.
10 Cragg, *Christianity in World Perspective*, pp5-16.
11 B. Stanley, *The Bible and the Flag* (Apollos/IVP, Leicester, 1990) p182.

Their relationship to the diverse forces of British imperialism was complex and ambiguous. If it was fundamentally misguided, their error was not that they were indifferent to the cause of justice for the oppressed, but that their perceptions of the demands of justice were too easily moulded to fit the contours of prevailing Western ideologies. In this respect our predecessors reflect our own fallibility more closely than we care to admit.[12]

Like Stanley, Cragg recognises the sacrificial devotion which was the inspiration of many of the missionaries who were often 'zealous in their compassion', but, notwithstanding this in many ways admirable zeal, the colonial relationship was a 'power relationship' in which the colonizers enjoyed every advantage, and "the dissemination of Christian faith fell all too readily into the same pattern".[13] Cragg notes also a dimension of 'aloofness' and retention even in the giving, which amounted to "a withholding of humanity"; as the African statesman Kenneth Kaunda remarked: "They gave many things but they did not give themselves".[14] There was an absence even in the presence. Perhaps this was an anticipation of that loss of self which Cragg elsewhere identifies as characteristic of modern western man, in Kafka's phrase "I lack nothing except myself". Cragg believes that this contemporary sense of alienation is actually a measure of human vocation: "It comes only because over against a *whole* world of significance, we have forgotten our humility, or in a partial world of value we have been misled by our pretension."[15] This is the case not only for the individual, but a theme that haunts our whole culture, a culture which, according to Ionescu, "no longer contains ourselves". It seems to have no room for us, and we have no room for it. But for Cragg, such withdrawal can provide no ultimate answer or satisfaction, for, as the previous chapter already suggests, "to be is to meet".[16]

This failure of nerve and crisis of identity is not merely the lack of self-confidence of western people and western culture, but a loss of self due in part to the over-reaching of western sociology and psychology. When their proper explanations have been given due weight, the human reality remains, with what is for Cragg "a more final significance" by which religion lives.[17] Even the apparent nihilism of much contemporary art and literature inherently suggests a continuing belief in human value, as Cragg reiterates, "a literature of despair is a contradiction in terms".[18]

---

12 Stanley, *The Bible and the Flag*, p184.

13 Cragg, *Christianity in World Perspective*, p22.

14 Cragg, *Christianity in World Perspective*, p25.

15 Cragg, *The Privilege of Man*, p24.

16 Cragg, *The Christian and Other Religion*, p11; cf. Cragg's later book *To Meet and to Greet, passim*.

17 Cragg, *The Christian and Other Religion*, p12.

18 *The Christian and Other Religion*, p12. This is also true of the whole scientific enterprise which seeks to relate the partial to the whole: 'A science of irresponsibility, like a literature of despair, is plainly a contradiction in terms." *The Privilege of Man*, p23.

Indeed in our technological expertise contemporary humanity 'possesses the world', and if we are in danger of losing our soul it is not inevitably so:

> There is no reason to imagine that the capacity for poetry is somehow annulled by the competence of the machine, that there is wonder in the heavens for shepherds but not for astronauts. If the latter fail to find it, it is not its absence by which the former were deceived: it is rather the pride by which the last are blinded.[19]

Another aspect of this contemporary setting is a *conscious* pluralism.[20] Modern people are aware of choices which previously were not possible, for, historically, the faiths "have not, for the most part, been options freely chosen out of a feasible neutrality, but rather denominators of birth and culture, of language and geography".[21] Now, despite (or because of?) two centuries of modern missions, there is an increased optionality, which means that pluralism is not only the 'fact of life' it always was, but the 'condition and context' of Christian relationship to the world.[22] In addition to the fact of plurality of belief and practice, a philosophy of pluralism and relativism, undergirds the apparent tolerance of the secular society. Whilst tolerance is preferable to hostility, Cragg suggests that it easily degenerates into indifference and apathy; the real task is to move 'beyond tolerance' and how this may be achieved each faith must answer out of its own resources.[23] It is the wrestling with this question that occupies so much of Dr Cragg's life and work.

A significant consequence of this 'conscious pluralism' is that Christ and the Christ-event have gathered a wealth of meaning and interpretation not limited to the Church or even to Christian culture. All the great faiths of the world have their own characteristic version of Christ. Contemporary authors may well write about 'the unknown Christ',[24] or the 'anonymous Christ'[25] of other faiths, but "the paradox, rather, is not that he is unknown or anonymous. It is that they know him by their own naming".[26] An illustration of this experience may be found in Cragg's own work in Islamic-Christian relations where he draws attention to the profound Muslim respect and affection for Jesus, which yet disallows the Christian interpretation of him:

> Islam finds his nativity miraculous but his Incarnation impossible. His teaching entails suffering but the one is not perfected in the other. He is highly exalted, but by rescue rather than by victory. He is vindicated but not by resurrection. His

---

19 Cragg, *The Privilege of Man*, pp7-8.

20 This point, made originally by Cragg, is underlined in the standard surveys of religious pluralism, e.g., Race, 'Christians and Religious Pluralism', D'Costa, 'Theology and Religious Pluralism', Knitter, 'No Other Name?'

21 Cragg, *The Christian and Other Religion*, Preface, pxi.

22 Cragg, *The Christian and Other Religion*, p10.

23 Cragg, *The Christian and Other Religion*, p66.

24 So R. Pannikar, *The Unknown Christ of Hinduism* (DLT, London, 1964).

25 Famously K. Rahner *Theological Investigations*, Vol. 5 (DLT, London, 1966).

26 Cragg, *The Christ and the Faiths*, p5.

servanthood is understood to disclaim the sonship which is its secret ...it has for him a recognition moving within non-recognition, a rejectionism on behalf of a deep and reverent esteem.[27]

The Christian responsibility in this context is to bring the Christian 'version' of Christ into these existing indwellings within the other religions, to translate 'the Christ of the New Testament' into these 'prepossessions'. This is no easy task because it involves communication in the realm of the emotions, indeed the passions, as much as that of the intellect. People invest emotional security within their religious fidelities, which means that "to reckon duly with a passion may be as urgent as to wrestle squarely with a doctrine".[28]

In a series of Oxford lectures,[29] Cragg concluded that theology faces two temptations in this situation: the first is the tendency to hard dogmatism and censure, unwilling to listen and failing in courtesy. This he suggested could never reflect the way of the Incarnation where that *to* which God speaks, is that *in* which God speaks. By contrast the second danger is that of a soft sentimentalism and unthinking eclecticism unprepared for the rigours of interpretation and the recognition of real disparities between the faiths. What is required is what Max Warren termed 'a theology of attention' in which true communication can occur. Therefore, Cragg argues that in this context what is vital is a true human mutuality: "Meeting is more urgent than surmise. Pluralism does not primarily require of our theology hypotheses about its being so. It awaits a Christian fidelity of mind and will in the relationships it entails and offers".[30] Such encounter is an ongoing process, for religion "is not so much a closed pool of reflection as the retreating wake behind a moving thing".[31] The context for this meeting is this one earth where as never before in history man is "*neah-gebur*, neighbour, nigh and boor, near and an earth-dweller"; it is in such conscious neighbourhood that meeting takes place.[32]

6.2 Criteria for a Christian Theology of Religion

As we saw in the previous chapter, Dr Cragg is convinced that there is no neutral territory from which the world of culture and religion may be surveyed with dispassionate eyes. We meet only on the common ground of our mutual humanity. But this is always occupied with a particular stance which means that "only each faith of itself can define for itself a relation to the rest".[33] The ambivalence of Islam to Jesus outlined above, is ambivalence only by Christian criteria, but these are all

---

27 Crag,g *Jesus and the Muslim*, pp278-9.
28 Cragg, *The Christ and the Faiths*, p7.
29 *Issues in Judeo-Christian-Islamic Theology*, Oxford University, Michaelmas Term 1990; No. 8 'Christian Theological Vocation Now', 28 November 1990.
30 Cragg, *The Christ and the Faiths*, p10.
31 Cragg, *The Christian and Other Religion*, p16.
32 Cragg, *The Christian and Other Religion*, p16.
33 Cragg, *Christianity in World Perspective*, p71.

that the Christian theologian can bring and are essential for a mutuality which assumes an active responsibility rather than a quiescent or casual relationship.[34] It is also essential to reckon with the realities which the other faiths bring with them, the preconceptions and loyalties which already exist, for it is into these that the Christian must speak. If possible these must be recruited into the communication in order that what Christians proclaim as Good News may be recognised as such by the hearers, for as 'a joke's prosperity is in the ear of the hearer' so too with the Gospel.[35] In other words only the audience can determine whether the Christian proclamation of 'Gospel' is in fact good news for them.

In order to achieve real dialogue certain risks must be taken with language, testing its elasticity by adventurous and imaginative translation: "Communication between widely differing parties may be said to hinge on a certain ambivalence of terms through which growing equivalence may be ventured."[36] This might be· viewed as a process of conversion and baptism, not of individuals but of culture and language and understanding. For example Dr Cragg suggests that the African sense of 'the name' might be recruited for such a Christian understanding given that for the African a name is not what a person is *called* but expresses what they *are*. If for the African "name spells relationship" so too does baptism for the Christian. This is a good example of what Cragg means by "the measure of Christ" as the criterion of Christian inter-faith relationships. The constant effort is "to discover every 'in Christ' quality, or feature, or accent ... not possessively, and certainly not patronisingly, as if we were proprietors, but with a lively and generous hope".[37] But the measure of Christ or even more briefly *the Christic* requires closer definition.

What is crucial is not only the *fact* of Christ but the *manner* of Christ, not just for Jesus' own messianic vocation but also for the mission of the Church: "The delineation of the Christian relation to the world is to be sought and found in the understanding of Messianic decision on the part of Jesus Himself. For in that Christly decision the Christian and the Church are constituted."[38] For Cragg, Jesus' key decision, as we saw in relation to Islam in the last chapter, is that of Gethsemane. But this serves as a dramatic focus of that "free, courageous and steadfast choice" by which Jesus embraces the Kingdom of heaven,[39] and in which he is sustained throughout his ministry by a deep-rooted communion with God. That radical teaching in which Jesus opened doors and windows of hope for the despised and dispossessed of the world is "most perfectly exemplified and achieved" by the Cross.[40] (The significance of Christ's passion in Bishop Cragg's thought is frequently indicated by the capitalization of the word 'cross'.) The event of the cross is nothing strange, artificial or contrived, it is simply the dreadful disclosure of the

---

34 Cragg, *Jesus and the Muslim*, p279.
35 Cragg used this analogy in the lecture referred to above.
36 Cragg, *Christianity in World Perspective*, p144.
37 Cragg, *The Christian and Other Religion*, pp63-4.
38 Cragg, *Christianity in World Perspective*, p43.
39 Cragg, *The Privilege of Man*, pp128-9.
40 Cragg, *The Privilege on Man*, pp131 and 132.

reality of evil, and by the same token a revelation of the love that must meet with it and deal with it. The Cross is the measure of the enormity of the messianic task, a task "great enough to be, and need to be God's doing", and in Christian eyes God is "great enough to be the doer".[41]

The ministry and decision of Jesus thus shape the Christic; it is not so much a pattern to which he conforms, but rather one which emerges out of his vocation and ·the experience of being Messiah *in this way*. The measure of Christ is thus located in the decision of Christ, and it is a decision that means the Cross – the expression in reality of that willingness to suffer for and with his message implicit throughout his ministry. Cragg argues that this suffering was endured within the context of a filial relationship expressed in the passion prayers and sayings of Jesus. 'Sonship' was the context of his doing and therefore of his being: "If Jesus is 'Son of God' in the music of the *Te Deum* and in the confessions of Nicea and Chalcedon, it is because he was the Son of God beneath the olive branches of Gethsemane, and in the darkness of Golgotha."[42] The drama so graphically enacted on a dark Friday in Jerusalem is a form of 'cosmic theatre', which avails for a cosmic catharsis. In the New Testament this process is naturally described in the language of the cultic system which lay so readily to hand, but even here we find that language is being stretched in order to communicate the depth of the new experience. These rich metaphors are not finally adequate for "the reality of the Cross transcends these terms even as it fulfils them".[43] In Christian thought the passion of Christ is a universal reality, all-embracing in its scope, but Cragg believes that it cannot bring a salvation which is universally successful: that would entail an over-riding of humanity's precious freedom of soul and will. It is, however, "a universally accessible salvation, where accident of birth, in the ethnic sense of Sinai, or in the cultural sense of Aristotle, would not determine life in Christ."[44] The Cross of Christ provides a universal index to the nature of the God there perceived as love, and apprehended as such in the three 'realms' of Scripture, Church and Sacrament: the documentary, the institutional and the liturgical perpetuation of the Christ-event. Thus in meeting and sharing:

> The Christian takes other religion to a babe in a manger and a man on a cross, to a holy table where bread and wine invite to a fellowship in redemption. Our ambition is to have these always present to be the text of that search for expression which lies nearest to the heart of all human living, so that to feel, to suffer and to understand become one and the same thing.[45]

Through this process, which Cragg characterises with telling ambiguity as 'cross-reference', the Christian may bear *bona fide* witness to the Christ of Christian faith.

---

41 Cragg, *Jesus and the Muslim*, p197.
42 Cragg, *The Christian and Other Religion*, p56.
43 Cragg, *The Christian and Other Religion*, p57.
44 Cragg, *The Christian and Other Religion*, p57.
45 Cragg, *The Christian and Other Religion*, pp111-2.

If we are to take a religiously plural world at all seriously Cragg suggests that such cross-reference is the only possible theology.[46] The credential of this theology is "God in Christ – the disclosure in grace of the God of creation and history", seen within a nexus of relations and referents: Jesus as this Christ, the Christian to Christ, Christ to the custodian community of the Church, which is an inclusive community of faith comprehending all and excluding none, and all of this to the human heart.[47] This discussion begs the question of history, both in the sense of the relation of the Christ of faith to the Jesus of history, and that of the accessibility of this Jesus to contemporary discussion. As the analysis thus far makes clear, Cragg is convinced of the inner logic and consistency of the New Testament witness, which, for all its variety, presents a unity of theme, focused upon the Kingdom and the Messiah. It contains five elements to Cragg's mind: teaching, healing, communing, resolving and suffering; if the latter finally emerges as decisive it was implicitly present all the time.[48]

There is an inevitable link between the document of Scripture and the faith of the Church but this mutuality has to be trusted if revelatory history is to be possessed. The interests of history are not threatened by the interests of faith, at least no more so than for any other history, since history is always the result of the interaction between event and interpretation:

> All history, anywhere, hinges on these two 'interests'. It has to do with what happened because of what what happened meant. Its necessary selectivity turns on faith about significance since, without some sense of meaning, recording of it would have no point and would simply not occur. Oblivion overtakes what does not, somehow, somewhere, avail enough to be meaningful.[49]

Selectivity also means particularity, but this too is inevitable not only as a consequence of what it means to be human, but also as a prerequisite of any divine-human communication. The human side of such relationship is always located within the particulars of time and place and culture. If God is to be humanly accessible in his self-disclosure, particularity is essential: "The relation of God to all history is made clear in a particular history. A special history prepares and introduces that which illuminates and redeems all history."[50] That God has so revealed himself is the common assumption of the Judaeo-Christian-Islamic tradition,[51] but the problem is located in the variety of particulars in which God is said to be located. Particularity is not so much a problem in principle but in its specifics. It is *this*

---

46 Cragg, *The Christ and the Faiths*, p13.
47 Cragg, *The Christ and the Faiths*, p21.
48 Cragg, *Jesus and the Muslim*, p126.
49 Cragg, *Jesus and the Muslim*, pp85-6.
50 Cragg, *The Call of the Minaret*, p251.
51 So, for example: "God, we believe, undertakes the condition of being human, by taking the prerequisites of our knowing – humanity, time, place and history – and expressing his nature therein." *Christianity in World Perspective*, p140.

particularity which must justify itself. Cragg believes that this can only happen in the sequel. The point of departure must fulfil itself in where it leads: "to end authentically is to justify one's beginning".[52]

There is a real logic to this position, and the argument bears similarities to the more developed position of John Hick, which he calls 'eschatological verification'.[53] Hick takes the argument to its logical conclusion with the irrefutable point that ultimate questions will ultimately be answered in the ultimate! However, there is a degree of circularity to the argument that is somehow unsatisfactory: presuppositions are justified in the outcome, but outcomes are judged by the presuppositions. The Christic is defined by the Christ-event – but the Christ-event will only be revealed as such by its authentic conclusion, and authenticity is assessed by 'the measure of Christ.' Nevertheless a beginning must be made: assumptions as well as the superstructure built upon them will be tested in the dialogue and cross-reference that ensues. In the end a *Christian* theology can only begin with *Christ*, "the criterion of both truth and relationship",[54] and, as Cragg believes, one way or another, "our justification will wait for us".[55] As those who believe in the interaction of God and human history, Christians may be entitled to believe that the divine providence has not been entirely absent "in the long vicissitudes through which, via evangelists, believers, scribes, copyists and scholars, the New Testament literature gives dependable access to Jesus and how he was the Christ, and to the genesis and life of the community which believed itself constituted and chartered by his recognition".[56]

6.3 The Application of the Criteria

We saw in the previous chapter how Cragg's fundamental criterion of 'the measure of Christ' emerged out of his own encounter with Islam, and to a lesser extent Judaism, during his various responsibilities in the Middle East. In this section we aim to demonstrate how he applies it in a wider setting, which will also inevitably include Islam. It is not proposed to deal with the Islamic context for dialogue in detail since this has already been considered at some length in the earlier discussion. But we will begin with a brief consideration of his account of the Muslim-Christian relationship in the global perspective, before a more detailed analysis of his application of the criteria in other areas.

---

52 Cragg, *The Christian and Other Religion*, p51.

53 Hick outlines the argument in *Faith and Knowledge* (Macmillan, London, 2nd ed. 1967), pp169-199; see also 'Eschatological Verification Reconsidered', *Religious Studies* XIII (1977 No. 2) pp189-202

54 Cragg, *The Christian and Other Religion*, pxiii.

55 Cragg, *The Christian and Other Religion*, p54.

56 Cragg, *Jesus and the Muslim*, p120.

6.3.1 Islam

In *Christianity in World Perspective* Cragg identifies five areas within the 'arc of theology' which are crucial to Muslim-Christian relations, and which must be considered apart from resentments, "and beyond mere controversial tradition or competition";[57] these inter-acting spheres are: Scripture, Politics, Worship, Continuity-in-displacement, and Theology.[58] Issues arising out of these areas include the relation of faith-loyalty to state-interest; stress due to technological change which poses acute questions about true human submission (*islam*); and the problem of sin, where understandings of idolatry must be expanded: "Idols are relatively innocent compared with the concepts they embody and far less subtle than the unworthy notions of God that have no embodiment but only adjectival, credal or conceptual existence."[59]

Central to all of this is the question of the divine-human relationship. The last comment hints at a vulnerability in God not generally recognised by Islam. Cragg argues that it is present, at least in implicit fashion, for the divine demand turns upon human response and is therefore in jeopardy. This can be the starting point for Christian witness, understanding the divine vulnerability more openly and with less reserve, indeed as central for the restoration of human waywardness. This is not to diminish the greatness of God, but to understand that greatness differently,[60] to offer a different predicate of the same subject as we concluded in the last chapter. It is not surprising, therefore, to discover that Cragg begins his discussion of Islam in *The Christ and the Faiths* with what he terms 'Theologies of Magnificat'.

Although the iconoclastic achievements of Muhammad can hardly be over-estimated in the context of pagan Arabia, it has lead to the dominance in Muslim thought of an emphasis on divine unity conceived in terms of number, and a rigorous dissociation of God from the human realm. Cragg argues that this dominance has failed to pay heed to the other notes found in the Qur'an itself and clearly implied in the notions of creation, law and prophethood. Each of the religions that stand in the Judaic tradition also recognise the paradox that the only God requires loyalty and recognition from his creatures, which they are free to withhold. Whatever the external appearances and constraints, the reign of God in human life depends vitally on inner attitude, "the sovereignty of God is of a nature to be realized in human life only when it is inwardly loved and wanted".[61] The ultimate sin of *shirk* is the denial of this relationship and the rejection of this 'sacramental quality' of our human situation within the assumed creation theology of the Qur'an.[62] Acceptance of divine rule, submission to God, is expressed politically through submission to

---

57 Cragg, *Christianity in World Perspective*, p126.
58 Cragg, *Christianity in World Perspective*, p124.
59 Cragg, *Christianity in World Perspective*, p134.
60 Cragg, *Christianity in World Perspective*, pp136-7.
61 Cragg, *The Christ and the Faiths*, p36; see his full discussion of this point pp32-7.
62 Cragg, *The Christ and the Faiths*, p42.

the Prophet and to the community, as Cragg has often noted, and all of this comes together in the prostrations of *salat*:

> The human form may itself be taken as a reading of the human dignity. The erect posture takes in the horizons and commands the scene. Mobility is by two limbs, leaving two for the dexterity on which all skill and power to attain depend. The mind presides over this human 'engineering' through nerve, sense, faculty and will. So the mind, in the head, is brought in lowliness to the ground in the sequences of the *Salat*, affirming the tributariness to God of all that man is and man attains. But this posture alternates with the return to erectness, just as the erectness acknowledges its privilege and mystery in the prostration.[63]

In all this it is quite clear that a relationship does exist between God and the world, in particular with the human race. The divine address assumes at least the potential for human response, and in the end 'all theology is about relationship'.[64] What is at stake is the nature of the relationship. Islam has a strong instinct to divorce the divine attributes, which are accessible to man, from the divine nature which remains inscrutable. This has parallels in Christian thought, for example Barth's emphasis in the *Church Dogmatics* where nothing is *necessary* to God. Here too we see a wrestling with the relationship between the eternal and the contingent. Cragg understands the desire to guard the eternal from dependence upon the contingent, but suggests that in so doing the 'sovereignty of freedom' may violate the 'sovereignty of grace'.[65] He points up the irony that theologies which assert God's freedom and sovereignty, seem frequently to feel the need to defend this God and his cause, iconoclasm can actually idolise itself! What is required is an understanding of God as 'transcending his transcendence' in a similar relationship to the artist and his art.[66]

If Islam has traditionally been characterised by its jealous zeal *for* the Lord, Cragg wants to explore how it might understand the zeal *of* the Lord in his self-disclosure to mankind. Prophets provide a clear focus for such zeal – the 'pro-zeal' on behalf of God, and the 'contra-zeal' of resistance and rejection. The challenge of the prophet is the testing ground of these two forms of zeal, and in Christian understanding this is most clearly focused in the cross of Jesus. This is why the passion of Christ cannot be excluded from any consideration of his significance, and here is the crucial point of witness in Christian-Muslim relations.[67] For it raises the question of how God is to deal with the 'contra-zeal' that his own 'zeal of the Lord' inevitably generates. For Cragg, the cross demonstrates how the enmity of a perverse zeal is "mastered

---

63 Cragg, *The Christ and the Faiths*, p47.

64 Cragg, *The Christ and the Faiths*, p75.

65 Cragg, *The Christ and the Faiths*, p80.

66 See the full discussion of these points in Cragg, *The Christ and the Faiths*, pp79-82.

67 Cragg, *The Christ and the Faiths*, pp87-8.

worthily of God",[68] and we find ourselves back with the issues decided differently by Muhammad in the *hijrah* and by Jesus in Gethsemane.

Bishop Cragg believes that from this discussion a common faith emerges in the God whose purposes are centred on his relationship with humanity, a relationship which is more than judicial, which awaits human recognition and consent, which awaits 'man's will to love'. But, does he 'come running', as in the tradition of Al-Bukhari and the parable of the prodigal son?[69] The Christian experience of divine grace suggests that God indeed 'comes running' to meet his wayward children, and this leads not to a loss of dignity, but to the opening of the door to the true and proper worship of the Lord.

6.3.2 Judaism

The Christian relationship to Judaism is clearly the first and in many ways is still the most urgent question in Christian relations with other faiths. For some time in the earliest life of the Church to embrace the Messiahship of Jesus was a genuinely open option for Judaism. That it did not in the end do so, has remained according to Cragg: "a perpetual disclaimer, from the most vital source, of the Christian conviction about the Christ, and about the nations".[70] Following the Jewish uprising against Roman rule in 66-70 CE, there was a marked reversion of Jewish openness to the Gentile world.

The ministry and mission of Jesus precipitated another crisis for Judaism which history has shown to be equally far-reaching. It was, however, a crisis within and for Jewry rather than against it. Similarly, the early Church had to face the Jewish-Gentile question and in many ways, whether explicit or implicit, the issue is central to the New Testament. In fact the issue is but a local rendering of a universal question, but the Jewish context of the New Testament writing, with the Jews in the central role of protagonists to the emerging Christian community, tends to obscure this fact.[71]

At the heart of Judaism lies the notion of election. The divine association which underlies all the Semitic faiths, here centres on God and his people. Cragg suggests that this link is declarative of the divine nature and purpose: there can be no God without 'and', which suggests a paradoxical sense of the necessity of man to God, although his being is by no means exhausted in human encounter. In Judaism the relationship stems from creation, but is quickly translated into covenant. All humanity is embraced within the Adamic covenant of creaturehood, and the Noachic covenant of seedtime and harvest, but supreme in the Hebrew Scriptures is the covenant of Exodus and Sinai which included only Israel, in all her generations, proleptically gathered at the mountain of God. The universal questions of human

---

68 Cragg, *The Christ and the Faiths*, p89.

69. Cragg, *The Christ and the Faiths*, pp74 and 91-2.

70 Cragg, *Christianity in World Perspective*, p92.

71 Cragg, *Christianity in World Perspective*, pp95-8; this is central to the discussion on fulfilment in the conclusion to this volume.

identity, who, where and whence, (Who are we? Where have we come from? What is our destiny?) are 'exceptionalised' in the particular tribal history of the Hebrew people. Theology becomes an account of themselves in this relational sense: "I will be their God and they will be my people".[72]

Such an inherently particular and 'peculiar' faith could be accused as the mere annexation of God to tribal interest, but this is not how it is viewed in the retrospect of the Deuteronomic history. In its sure monotheism the universality of God is preserved from tribalism. Rather this election can be viewed as a 'test case', a focus of divine purpose,[73] a calling to service on behalf of all humanity. The harsh lesson of the Exile lead to a cherishing of 'peoplehood' because the land was no longer possessed; the hope of repossession was never forgotten but gave birth to the messianic hope, and later to modern Zionism. Through all this the Adamic and Noachic covenants persist in counter-point to the main theme; the rest of humanity can never be forgotten in the constant inter-play between the particular and the universal – it is impossible to be different on your own! But this sense of call is not easy to bear:

> In tragic irony the 'blessedness' of being on behalf of all mankind by such necessary exception from them has been a frequent travail of distress.[74]

The historic hostility of other communities towards the Jews arises out of this 'exceptionality'. For to be 'peculiar' requires others to be 'ordinary', and the world thus feels 'inferiorized'. To be Jewish requires the non-Semite, but produces the anti-Semite. This theme is constantly wrestled with: throughout Jewish history the Joseph story is reiterated. Benediction requires distinction; therefore loss of identity inevitably involves loss of blessing. But if the blessing is for all, what form can the blessing take if it does not involve incorporation and the inherent loss of distinction?

Cragg argues that Christianity is born out of an abandonment of exception. The Church is not a form of 'open Judaism' but a genuinely open community in which the two streams of Jewish covenant thought are brought together as the two 'pillars' of the new 'temple'. Sadly the Jewish element was swiftly lost and by the second century 'old' and 'new' covenant had become firmly separated. There are those who would argue that all this is part of the divine purpose, not as Paul argues in Romans 9-11, but as permanent features; one covenant for the Jew and another for the Gentile. For Cragg this is to destroy the Gospel, John 3:16 becomes 'For God so loved the Gentile', whereas in the New Testament the gates of the city of God are open to all points of the compass, the common denominator found in a common humanity rooted in the doctrine of creation. He suggests that this must be held in tension with the 'interior truth' of a personal experience of being loved and held in relationship. Clearly this is anticipated in the exilic and post-exilic prophets, but

---

72 Cragg, *The Christ and the Faiths*, pp121-24; also discussed by Cragg in an Oxford lecture series, Lecture 2, 'The Self-Understanding of Jewry', 17 October 1990.

73 Cragg, *Christianity in World Perspective*, p100.

74 Cragg, *The Christ and the Faiths*, p124.

Cragg believes there is a difference of thrust: the Old Testament is 'centripetal', the New Covenant is 'centrifugal'. Thus the fundamental question as "to what manner of people is consonant with the nature of God and the human situation,"[75] is given a radical answer in the New Testament. That same inclusivism, which recognised 'neither male nor female, slave nor free,' affirms that there is 'neither Jew nor Greek' (Galatians 3:28). However, this does not mean extinction for either community:

> Clearly the Church was no sexless society like a community of snails. Male and female blessedly persisted. The point of saying 'there is neither male nor female' is that in respect of the fellowship the distinction, still in being, is of no significance. Likewise with 'Jew and Gentile'. The Church understood itself as a body in which this most resolute of human distinctions had been quite transcended. Both were equally called into a bond with God and between themselves in which all their continuing identity would find a unity.[76]

Incorporation into Christ meant suspension for the old priorities of birth and land and an accessibility which was parallel to the inclusiveness of creation – as in 'Adam', so in 'Christ'. But what happened was that the Church borrowed from Judaism the nation-people model of divine community, developed its own style of chosen-ness, and in turn generated some of the most virulent strains of race-and-nation self-assertion. Cragg cites as a modern example the apartheid system in South Africa with its backward look to the Hebraic pattern, and equally significant was Abraham Lincoln's characterisation of Americans as 'the almost chosen people'. At least one strand in contemporary American religious life would no longer accept the qualification 'almost'.[77]

This leads on to the second issue raised for Christianity by the persistence of Judaism, which questions the whole Christian scheme of redemption in a world and with a Church so patently unredeemed. For much of contemporary Judaism the trauma of the Holocaust has meant the end of Christianity's messianic pretensions. Cragg sees the Holocaust as the outcome of the clash between rival notions of 'chosenness', Jewish and 'Aryan', behind which lay a history of Christian aggression and anti-Semitism sometimes derived from the Fourth Gospel, and achieved with the apparent connivance of elements of the Church. However, the Holocaust is but the extreme and ultimate example of the traditional Jewish response to the messianic claims of Christianity on behalf of Jesus, that is the unredeemedness of the world in general and the Church in particular. Even within Judaism the understanding of redemption was diverse, but always rooted in creation and in history. The messianic hope was shaped by the nation's experience of kingship and priesthood and prophecy. Whilst messianism remained a future dream it could encompass this diversity of

---

75 Cragg, *The Christ and the Faiths*, p126.

76 Cragg, *The Christ and the Faiths*, p129.

77 See Cragg's discussion of this pattern of thought in *The Christ and the Faiths*, pp128-38, and my McCandless Lecture for 2004 'Faith in the Future? Secularization and Society in Europe and the USA'.

expectation and even contradiction, but in actualisation this was impossible. Cragg sees the passion of Christ as the outcome of these inherent tensions and contradictions of expectation. He suggests that Jesus' adoption of the ambiguous 'son of man' terminology was an attempt to forestall the inevitable clash of expectations, and that Jesus' understanding of the nature and manner of Messiahship, which brought the Church to a particular view of his person, only succeeded in dissuading many Jews of the fact of his messiahship at all.[78]

For some contemporary Jewish thinkers messiahship is always a future hope whose realisation is impossible, for no single event can constitute the messianic hope. Cragg cites Buber's claim that "Realised Messiahship is a contradiction in terms". He also notes Leo Baeck's critique of Easter as sheer romanticism and escapism; a false dawn revealed for what it is in the persistence of evil. One solution to these difficulties has been to retreat into pietism and talk only of personal and individual salvation, but Cragg recognises that this will not do. He suggests rather that the true messianic question is not the temporal one of *when?* but the relational one of *who?* and the theological one of *how?*

Yet again the Christian response to these issues is focused by the cross, in which the Person is revealed by the policy, and the policy is that of redeeming love. This deals with evil in a *qualitative* way, in that:

> ... there has occurred, once for all and concretely, in our human history, the one perfect and inclusive sacrament of that power by which, in the end and in the whole, all evil is redeemed. The Cross does not exonerate in its redemption: rather it energises men to its own reproduction and all the more surely for their sense of its redeeming authority already within their souls.[79]

Christian faith requires a standing in the sort of transaction which is constituted in the Cross and identifying in that location the true nature of human sin and the reality of redeeming love in the focal point of human history. Here is disclosed, symbolically and representatively, but comprehensively, the whole human condition. The love which bears, bears away. The force of evil is spent in the travail of suffering, and forgiveness flows and is received and recapitulated within the community of the church.[80]

For Christianity (as for Judaism in the Exodus) the past provides a frame of reference for the present, and indeed the future. The 'happenedness' of the Exodus does not contradict its future dimension, but the reverse is the case: "There was hope ahead *because* there was fact behind".[81] So too with the passion and resurrection of Christ, God's great I AM is revealed only in the event, in the going forward of faith, as I WILL BE what I WILL BE.[82] But if hope has *only* a future dimension then

---

78 Cragg, *The Christ and the Faiths*, p106.
79 Cragg, *Christianity in World Perspective*, pp114-5.
80 In his Lecture 2 noted above, cf. *Christianity in World Perspective*, p116.
81 Cragg, *The Christ and the Faiths*, p117. My italics.
82 Exodus 3:14.

history can hold nothing decisive, and, as Gershom Scholem points out it compels 'a life lived in deferment'.[83] For Christianity the future hope is grounded and given substance by the reality of the 'exodus' accomplished by Jesus in Jerusalem,[84] and in this way faith may speak of 'Christ our Passover'.[85] This is how Cragg understands the actualised messiahship of Jesus.

6.3.3 Indian Perspectives

Bishop Cragg's main experience and responsibility has been in the Middle East and this has naturally provided the major focus for his work. Nevertheless, he is conscious that some account should be attempted of the relation of Christian faith to other world-views and in his published work he has touched on both African and contemporary secular understandings.[86] In this section we shall examine briefly his fuller discussion of Hindu and Buddhist perspectives which originate from the world-view of the Indian sub-continent. In an Oxford lecture series Cragg pointed out that contrast provides for deeper appreciation, and there could not be much greater contrast for the 'whole Semitic programme' than that afforded by the standpoint of Indian thought.[87] The most obvious contrast is the point of departure for theological reflection, typically the Self rather than God.[88] Inevitably such 'self-experience' is always in flux and the root of the Indian quest for that which is real and permanent is found in this transience and its accompanying dissatisfaction. The centrality of personhood in Semitic faith is absurd to this tradition which strives to recognise the self for the illusion that it is. Its religious response is a drive to self-abnegation and dispossession, extinguishing the 'fire' by with-holding the 'fuel' until that 'oceanic' state is attained in which neither 'me-ness' nor 'is-ness' any longer obtain. The self is not extinguished because the self never had true existence.

It is for this sort of teaching that the eastern world-view is often characterised as 'life-negating', and Cragg implicitly accepts this approach when he suggests that by contrast the Semitic faiths 'take the positive option' of the reality of the self. He recognises that both choices are a gamble in the face of ambiguous human experience. For Cragg the crucial point is that in this context the Christian Gospel is self-evidently 'foreign' in a way long forgotten in Europe. It seems to require nothing of the Indian cultural heritage and Cragg suggests that this raises the vital

---

83 G. Scholem, *The Messianic Idea in Israel and Other Essays* (Schocken Books, New York, 1971, 1995 ed) p35.

84 Luke 9:31.

85 1 Corinthians 5:7; cf. Cragg, *The Christ and the Faiths*, pp116-7.

86 See, e.g., Cragg, *Christianity in World Perspective*.

87 Lecture 7, 'Perspectives from Further East', 21 November 1990.

88 In passing Cragg noted the parallel with Descartes, although he questioned his use of 'thought' (cogito ergo sum) – why not feelings, suffering and so on? We might also raise the further question: does the influence of Cartesian and Kantian philosophy explain contemporary western appreciation of eastern philosophy and religion?

issue of whether the Gospel can be indifferent to that which forms and even defines human beings:

> Being Judaic-messianic in its vintage it had no need of the Vedas or any other treasured source in *your* heritage. It presents itself to you out of foreignness as if to imply that its only use for you is your acceptance.[89]

He ponders whether it is not possible to produce a valid 'Indian Christology' parallel to the Greek version developed by the Fathers and others[90] and discusses the attempts of C.F. Andrews, A.G. Hogg and Raimundo Pannikar to wrestle with this problem. In particular he notes Pannikar's distinction, in a Christological context, between 'identity' and 'identification'. As Cragg sums up this position "Christhood is an identity wider and larger than the identification of it which Christians find in Jesus".[91] Cragg argues that it would be better to reverse Pannikar's distinction and regard Christ-Jesus as the 'identity', and that 'identifications' of him may be perceived elsewhere.[92] In other words we have a version of Cragg's own criterion 'the Christic'. Such identifications would be valid, but not complete. From the Christian point of view Cragg's version has the merit of locating the 'decisive divine action' in the Incarnation ('God in Christ reconciling the world'), whilst opening the possibility of recognising this divine principle in action throughout human history. Thus "that which is personally denominated, as here, is never plural: its character may be plurally recognized".[93]

Pluralism tends to assume that the 'how' defines the 'who' in Christological terms, but Cragg suggests that this arbitrary order may be reversed. What matters is where these twin recognitions converge into conclusiveness – for Cragg in 'Jesus and the Cross'. This raises the issue of history, which, in eastern thought has usually lacked both intentionality and purpose. On this view there can be no eschatology, for even if the terminus of a *chronos* may be anticipated, no goal of a *kairos* can be imagined. All is governed by an inexorable sequence of *karmic* law, with no possibility of repentance and forgiveness, or the sort of divine involvement the doctrine of the Incarnation assumes.[94] To affirm the 'happenedness' of the Christ-event incurs all the difficulties of historical study, but nevertheless Cragg argues that "there *was* a history yielding the Jesus of the *kerygma*", and the latter remains the primary evidence for the former.[95] This is vital unless a Bultmannian position is adopted in which the real Christ is the preached Christ. But then history may be abandoned and any theme or fantasy or mystery may be 'Christ-ized'. This way lies that gnosticism rejected early on by the Church. However, the Church has been

---

89 Cragg, *The Christ and the Faiths*, p181.
90 Cragg, *The Christ and the Faiths*, p178.
91 Cragg, *The Christ and the Faiths*, p185.
92 Cragg, *The Christ and the Faiths*, pp192-3.
93 Cragg, *The Christ and the Faiths*, p193
94 In Lecture 7 see above.
95 Cragg, *The Christ and the Faiths*, p201

restricted in its theological expression by its origin in the Mediterranean basin, in a way long since transcended by the arts. It has allowed the essential particularity of the Incarnation to hide its universality:

> ... the Incarnation had its necessary historical incidence, speaking Aramaic, summoning fishermen, hallowing bread and wine. But by the nature of Incarnation itself, the accomplished cross and resurrection leave behind the incidental and circumstantial in the inclusiveness which cannot fail to characterize the one 'who was made man'. The Canon and much theology, however, have persisted too long and too timidly with the incidental as if it had not yielded the universal.[96]

Rahner's notion of 'anonymous Christians' has largely 'failed to make its case'.[97] Cragg, like others, notes its apparent condescension and its putative and reciprocal character. But he suggests that a more acceptable formulation might be 'associate Christians', overcoming both the anonymity and the forbidding 'foreign-ness' of European Christianity. It would allow the possibility of the work of grace outside formal Christianity to be subject to a 'messianic test' of authenticity without incorporation into institutional Christianity. This would be the test of 'the Name' of Acts 4:12, which in Cragg's view is a summary of 'the action-pattern of the Messiah'.[98] He paraphrases Peter's sermon for a multi-religious context in this way:

> There is no saving evil situations except through the love that takes and saves them at its own cost. There is no other way in this whole wide world whereby redemption happens than the action-pattern of Jesus who fulfilled the messianic hope, the hope which was the Hebraic form of the human yearning for the decisive answer to the wrongness of us all.[99]

Even if Cragg's interpretation is accepted, there remains to be answered his own earlier question as to whether the antecedent hopes which Christ is claimed to realize are in their definition and character only Judaic.[100] Can there be a universal fulfilment in the 'action-pattern of Messiah'? Cragg clearly believes that there is, indeed it is the very uniqueness of Christ-Jesus that makes the Christ-measure a universal criterion.[101] This Christological singularity is an expression not of exclusivism, but of the essential inclusivism inherent in the unity of God. The divine nature is disclosed as both singular and inclusive in the 'singularity of the cross of Jesus'.[102]

---

96 Cragg, *The Christ and the Faiths*, p213.
97 See Part One above.
98 Cragg, *The Christ and the Faiths*, p224.
99 Cragg, *The Christ and the Faiths*, p224.
100 Cragg, *The Christ and the Faiths*, p182.
101 Cragg, *The Christ and the Faiths*, p193.
102 Cragg, *The Christ and the Faiths*, p225.

6.3.4 Inclusive or Exclusive?

For Kenneth Cragg, the holder of the pastoral office of bishop within the Anglican communion, this drawing out of the Christ-principle from the Christ-event in order to identify 'the Christic' beyond the boundaries of institutional Christianity, poses sharp questions about the nature of the Church. The Church, with its incorporating rite of baptism, seems to suggest very firm boundaries which exclude the rest of the world: 'exclusifying truth' is matched by an 'exclusifying community'.[103] But the early Church taught its non-Jewish converts that Judaic history was their history, and they were thus enabled to own a past which was not originally their own. Cragg suggests that in like manner the Church must learn to own 'the past behind any access to it'. The Hebraic will always have special significance as the particularity essential to the Incarnation, but the crucial point is that the Word was made *flesh*, and in that sense all histories and all cultures stand in relation to Him.[104]

Out of such thinking emerges Cragg's consciousness of the geographical and cultural limitations within which the Christian Scriptures were formed. The canon became fixed while the Church was largely confined within the Mediterranean basin with the result that the Church has inherited what might be termed "a Mediterranean source-book for a world theology".[105] It is not possible or desirable to re-open the Canon at this late stage, indeed "the finality it symbolises – the completeness of the faith – has perennial quality",[106] but it does require sensitivity in handling the Old Testament and appropriate initiative from within the New. Cragg urges that serious consideration should be given to the inclusion within Christian liturgy of "extra-biblical antecedents of the incarnate Word". This is not to conclude that Marcion was right all along, but to suggest that historic Christianity has failed in its obligation to belong with the whole of humankind.[107] It would also be a recognition that, for all the distinctiveness of the Gospel, *total* discontinuity is not feasible: "the reception of the new always turns upon categories already present",[108] however much it may stretch and challenge them. Such an approach to the self-disclosure of God in Christ is commensurate with a Christian doctrine of creation in which the diversity of people and cultures, shaped by their various environments, is accepted as legitimate. But this does not mean,

> ... that we become sanguine about man in nature or oblivious of the perversities in all religion. But these, heinous as they are, have no final veto on the initiatives grace can arouse in its own direction through ministries that kindle expectations by being themselves expectant in their relationships.[109]

---

103 Cragg, *The Christ and the Faiths*, p226.
104 Cragg, *The Christ and the Faiths*, p228.
105 Cragg, *The Christ and the Faiths*, p335.
106 Cragg, *The Christ and the Faiths*, p336.
107 Cragg, *The Christ and the Faiths*, p329.
108 Cragg, *The Christ and the Faiths*, p326.
109 Cragg, *The Christ and the Faiths*, p327.

6.4 A Revived "Fulfilment" Theology of Religions?

By way of conclusion and initial response to Cragg's position as outlined in this chapter, we will briefly explore the parallels between his approach and the supposedly discredited fulfilment theology current in much missionary thinking at the turn of this century, and which has already been touched on in the earlier introductory discussion of Farquhar and Kraemer. The general attitude of the early Protestant missionaries to India was largely hostile, shaped by a legacy of violent Christian-Muslim relationships in the Crusades and the struggles of the Reformation in which the fight for religious truth was often characterised by militant thought and action. Often such thinking drew upon the Old Testament strand of thought which was contemptuous of 'foreign gods' and virulently antithetical to all idolatry. It was borne along also by the energetic tides of the Evangelical Revival which created a new sense of urgency and revived the 'eschatological pressure' of the early days of the Christian mission. The traditional attitude is typified in the words of the reformer William Wilberforce in the Asiatic Journal of 1823: "Our religion is sublime, pure and beneficent. Theirs is mean, licentious and cruel."

By the middle of the nineteenth century, this attitude was being challenged from a number of directions. Even before the publication of Darwin's *Origin of Species* in 1859, the notion of 'progress' was already current (it was Darwin's practical application of the idea which struck home so forcefully and encouraged its extension into many areas of scholarship including the newly developing discipline of 'Comparative Religion'). Max Mueller suggested that traditional attitudes, such as that of Wilberforce, were blasphemous in ascribing to the devil what was in reality the work of God.[110] The influential evangelical scholar, Sir Monier Monier-Williams, was the first to adopt the term 'fulfilment' and apply it both to Hinduism in particular, and in the more general sense to the religious instincts of humanity.[111] William Miller, the distinguished Principal of Madras Christian College in the late nineteenth century, argued that it was Christ rather than Christianity in which religious hopes and aspirations would be fulfilled, and this distinction was to prove significant in later discussions.[112] The noted evangelist T. E. Slater (1840-1912) recognised that the Gospel must be presented in such a way as to make it accessible to the hearers of the message.[113]

A crucial element in this process of change towards a more positive Christian evaluation of other faiths was the actual encounter of the missionaries with people of other faiths and cultures. The general climate of opinion was clearly significant, but most of the missionaries were by their own upbringing, education and selection by the various missionary societies, men of conservative outlook and orthodox theological views. It was only the strength of their experience of missionary work in

---

110 Max Mueller, *Life and Letters*, Vol. II (Longmans Green, London, 1902) p464; cf. the discussion by Eric Sharpe in *Not to Destroy*, pp45-7.

111 Sharpe, *Not to Destroy*, p52.

112 See the helpful treatment of this issue by Sharpe, *Not to Destroy*, pp85ff.

113 See the discussion in Part One.

the field that forced them to reconsider their position, and this difficult process is reflected in the many missionary conferences of the late nineteenth and early twentieth centuries.[114] For example, the Revd J. Wenger of the Baptist Missionary Society in an address on 'Vernacular Preaching' to the Bengal Missionary Conference of 1855 criticised those who were eager "to assail the vulnerable and sore points of Hinduism". In the ensuing discussion Dr Boaz argued that "satirical allusions to the gods and goddesses have long since been discontinued", but in a postscript to the conference the Revd W. Smith felt it necessary to urge that "any allusions to their religion should be such as are not likely to irritate but to conciliate".[115]

Thus the fulfilment theology of religions so typical of the 1910 Edinburgh Missionary Conference had its roots in a century or more of missionary experience in India and elsewhere. What was expressed so notably by John Nicol Farquhar was the culmination of this process whose chief characteristics may be summarised as: a) an understanding of non-Christian faiths grounded in practical missionary experience; b) a dual concept of fulfilment in which Christianity was believed to meet a human yearning for God which was a universal experience, *and* could be viewed as giving a more perfect expression of specific aspects of the divine truth implicit in other religions; c) the notion that it was Christ rather than Christianity as a system which provided such fulfilment.

It should be apparent from the discussion so far that Bishop Cragg's method stands firmly within this tradition, although it is refined by a sophistication in understanding and sensitivity of approach. All of the characteristics suggested above are typical of his work. Its basis in a life-time of genuine encounter with Muslims, Jews and many others is self-evident, but the other points are perhaps in need of drawing out and this we will briefly undertake.

Cragg is firm that the goal of Christian theological vocation is 'God in Christ', and that decision about him and indeed for him must be sought within the realities of our contemporary world. "Jesus came to be followed, not to be discussed, assessed or even admired".[116] However, the goal of God in Christ does not mean a total rejection of human culture and religion, for: "The nature of the Gospel is such that the impact of Christ is not totally to displace, but paradoxically to fulfil, what is there."[117] The object of the Christian mission is not somehow 'to gain the world' for Christ, but to allow the world to possess for itself the Christ whom it so frequently misses.[118] This is what Cragg terms 'the call to retrieval' and is central to his own life's work

---

114 For a fuller discussion see N.J. Wood, 'The Changing attitude of Protestant Christian Missionaries to Indian Religion' (unpublished MA dissertation, London University, 1982) pp9-13.

115 The address and subsequent discussion may be followed in *Proceedings of a General Conference of Missionaries in Bengal* (Calcutta, 1855); these citations are from pp47, 63 and 170.

116 *Christian Theological Vocation Now*, Lecture 8, 28 November 1990.

117 Cragg, *Sandals at the Mosque*, p92.

118 Cragg, *The Call of the Minaret*, p220.

in relation to Islam.[119] Thus baptism enchurches new believers, but does not and should not deculturalize them:

> All that is not incompatible with Christ goes with them into baptism. Conversion is not 'migration'; it is the personal discovery of the meaning of the universal Christ within the old framework of race, language and tradition.[120]

What is good for the convert is also important for the established believer in order to maintain an 'open posture' to people of other faith communities. Writing in a pastoral context to people in the religious ferment of the Middle East, Cragg urges: "discover, possess, and acknowledge to the utmost, all that, by your Christian criteria is valid elsewhere".[121] The Christian criterion is as we have seen 'the measure of Christ'. This 'action-pattern of the Messiah' is to be found elsewhere in human history, but: "the definitive, heavenly commissioned, incarnation of the pattern, in a once-for-all disclosure of its nature and its cost, could not be other than as singular as God is."[122] Yet again we note Cragg's typical focus on the cross of Christ as the measure of the cost of divine redemption within human history, and it is the centrality of the cross in his fulfilment theology that prevents his version carrying the overtones of superiority so characteristic of the nineteenth century. Christianity, and Christ himself, are not the climax of some process of development "from fear to faith".[123] Rather: "It is a faith about a Cross which leaves no room for pride because it pardons, no room for monopoly because it includes all, no room for anger because it is forgiving, no room for despair because it is in character and inclusion ultimate."[124]

Like the earlier fulfilment theology, Cragg recognises the vital role played by non-Christian faiths within their own cultures and societies: "it is by their faith that cultures have been historically determined and spiritually inspired".[125] But he is well aware that religion cannot always be taken at face value. He notes the well-known critique of Karl Barth (forcefully restated by Lesslie Newbigin[126]), which characterises religion as "unbelief", and he questions: "Is not history proof of the inherent depravity of religious forms where men elude reality itself in myths and

---

119 So Lamb, *The Call to Retrieval, passim.*

120 Cragg, *The Call of the Minaret*, p306.

121 Cragg, *The Dome and the Rock*, p225.

122 Cragg, *Jesus and the Muslim*, p206.

123 The title of a widely used textbook for schools Religious Education in the 1960s and 1970s.

124 Cragg, *Christianity in World Perspective*, pp46-7.

125 Cragg, *Christianity in World Perspective*, p65; cf. the comment of the nineteenth century missionary E.E. Jenkins: "Religion has touched every angle of their life: it has softened their afflictions, restrained their passions, and given them their friends; it has been the pride of their rank, and the foundation of their immortal hopes." from *The Proceedings of a General Conference of Foreign Missionaries*, Mildmay, 1878 (London, 1879) p167.

126 See Part Three below.

cults?"[127] In recognising the weight of such criticism Cragg suggests that it must not become an excuse for a blanket condemnation of religion in general or any specific faith. He wryly comments that Shaw's aphorism on France ("It is such a great country. What a pity to waste it on the French!"), might be readily transferred to the religious scene. He instances: "Christianity is so rich a faith: what a tragedy it is held by Christians".[128] His generosity of spirit always searches out the best in other faiths and gives due credit for what he would see (in Buddhist fashion?) as right intention. Thus he can say: "The Cross presents itself as the place the world's worship always meant".[129] Such intentionality is rooted in the Christian doctrines of creation, the Spirit and the Logos. Even man-made temples may be God-evoked. Religion is part of what it is to be human and Christians must beware of writing off that which God is wanting to redeem:

> There is in the Christian doctrine of the Holy Spirit every reason not to consign [other faiths] impatiently into a limbo of futility ... It is no true relationship in the Christ of the Incarnation to find in the Christian Gospel a secular competence for which other faiths are pathetically disqualified *in toto*. There is no loyalty in these terms to 'the light which lighteneth every man', nor to a Christian understanding of revelation that is open to nature and humanity.[130]

True to the Johannine tradition on which he here draws, Cragg constantly returns to the Incarnation of the light-giving Logos as that which is distinctively and uniquely Christian, but which is yet universal and therefore inclusive of all that is truly human. He concludes his study *The Privilege of Man*, in these words:

> The mystery of the Incarnation is no more, and no less, than the climax of all religious mystery, whether of creation, or revelation, or prophethood, or law. For in each and all of these, that of which in belief we say 'of God' is 'with men'. Part of the wonder of the Incarnation is that it so insistently and inclusively occupies the central point of all religious paradox.[131]

Out of the breadth and depth of his own inter-faith experience Bishop Cragg thus expresses his deep conviction that Christ is the true fulfilment of the human religious quest. It might be thought that so to label his theology is to dismiss it as outmoded. Certainly it is open to the criticisms aimed by Kraemer and others at earlier generations of fulfilment theologians. However, to find it restated so cogently, so carefully and with such sensitivity by someone of Dr Cragg's stature might suggest that there lie within this pattern of approach strengths that have been overlooked or too readily dismissed. It is certainly a theology of religion from a *Christian* perspective, but for Cragg, as for Newbigin, this is to begin from those

---

127 Cragg, *Christianity in World Perspective*, p84.
128 Cragg, in the Preface to *The House of Islam*, (Dickenson, Belmont CA, 1969).
129 Cragg, *Christianity in World Perspective*, p89.
130 Cragg, *Christianity in World Perspective*, p191.
131 Cragg, *The Privilege of Man*, p193.

ultimates which are not negotiable, whether "under popular pressures or in the pursuit of mutual relations".[132] If emotional allegiance and cultural sanction mean that it is difficult to bring such ultimates into mutual reckoning this only serves to highlight that 'theology of cross-reference' is essentially a pastoral task.[133] The success of such an approach will be measured by its sacrificial quality, for if the measure of Christ is fundamentally 'the cross', then the measure of Christian witness cannot be any the less.

In the paradigmatic encounter of Peter with Cornelius in Acts chapters ten and eleven, Cragg notes that Peter "went furthest in both discovery and effectiveness, when he was not on his own ground, securely set in his tradition".[134] Christian theology is a theology in trust in which authenticity "will be accessible first in the dimension of sacrifice which it plainly sustains in the believer's dealings with his fellows".[135] Christians need have no fear to lose the Christ of their faith if they will only be loyal to the Christ of the world,[136] indeed only in that going into the whole world will the true universality of the Christian gospel be revealed:

We have taken the words 'Into all the World' as intending much more than a physically global mobility. Rather the impulse within them is seen as a sense of relevance in and anticipation from, all human cultures, taking the Church as that which corresponds, in all meanings of the verb, with 'the desire of all nations'.[137]

The Church will only fulfil this global role when it too allows itself to be judged by "the measure of Christ".

---

132 Cragg, *The Christ and the Faiths*, p318; Cragg cites Newbigin on the whole question of 'fiduciary frameworks' at this point.
133 Cragg, *The Christ and the Faiths*, p319.
134 Cragg, *The Christ and the Faiths*, p328.
135 Cragg, *Christianity in World Perspective*, p215.
136 Cragg, *Christianity in World Perspective*, p218.
137 Cragg, *Christianity in World Perspective*, p170.

Part 3

Lesslie Newbigin's Theology of Engagement

CHAPTER 7

Religious Pluralism in Newbigin's Theology

7.1 Introduction

The career of Bishop Lesslie Newbigin (1909-1998) is sufficiently well known to require only the briefest of introductions.[1] Brought up in a devout Presbyterian household in Newcastle-upon-Tyne and educated at the Quaker Leighton Park School in Berkshire, Newbigin read Geography at Queen's College, Cambridge, followed by theological education at Westminster College; he was ordained in the Church of Scotland for service as a missionary in India and sailed for the subcontinent in 1936. Except for six years with the International Missionary Council and its successor body in the World Council of Churches based in Geneva, India was to be Newbigin's sphere of service for nearly forty years. He became a founding bishop in the United Church of South India, first in Madurai and later in Madras. Following 'retirement' in 1974 there followed responsibility for teaching mission studies at the Selly Oak Colleges in Birmingham subsequently coupled with an active inner-city pastorate for the United Reformed Church of which he was elected national Moderator for 1978-79.[2]

Throughout this long and busy career in the service of the Church, Bishop Newbigin has maintained a steady flow of books and articles concerned with the nature of the Christian message and the life of the Church in the modern world. A recurring theme in the thought of Lesslie Newbigin is the question of the salvation of humanity. As he indicates in *Sin and Salvation*,[3] for him a crucial question is how the 'finished work of Christ' is related to the life of the believer and the believing community – "How does salvation become ours?"[4] This was the question which had been posed for him as a theological student in Cambridge, and the answer that he formulated then has remained true throughout his life and work. He expresses it in strongly Pauline terms, for it was in wrestling with the Epistle to the Romans that his convictions were formed, "This was a turning point in my theological journey. I began my study as a typical liberal. I ended it with a strong conviction

---

[1] See the useful biographical sketch in Paul Weston *Lesslie Newbigin Missionary Theologian* (SPCK, London, 2006) pp1-13 and the Introduction, 'A Man in Christ', to Geoffrey Wainwright's very full 'theological biography', *Lesslie Newbigin: A Theological Life* (OUP, Oxford, 2000) pp3-28.

2 See Bishop Newbigin's own account in his autobiography *Unfinished Agenda* (SPCK, London, 1985).

3 Written with the needs of village catechists in mind (SCM, London, 1956).

4 Newbigin, *Sin and Salvation*, p8.

about 'the finished work of Christ', about the centrality and objectivity of the atonement accomplished on Calvary."[5] Although he suggests that this new understanding "made me much more of an evangelical than a liberal",[6] he did not fall into the common evangelical trap of narrow individualism, but rather maintained a corporate and indeed cosmic sense of the work of Christ. It is precisely this awareness of the universality of the Christian proclamation, which poses the difficult question of how this salvation is to be manifested on such a scale. How can 'the finished work of Christ' be complete when so many communities and peoples are in ignorance of it and of the claim of the Church that 'Jesus is Lord'? Here we see something of the strength of the missionary imperative which runs throughout Newbigin's thinking. There is a necessary tension between 'the finished work of Christ' and the 'unfinished agenda' of the Church, a body that Newbigin repeatedly characterizes as "a community *in via*, on its way to the ends of the earth and to the end of time".

Newbigin expounds the human situation in terms of humanity's essential self-contradiction: we are at odds with each other, with the natural world, with our inner selves, and with God, which is "the basic contradiction on which all else rests".[7] This fundamental contradiction results in bondage to the hostile forces of the universe. Salvation therefore means release from this bondage and the resolution of these contradictions. It means 'wholeness' and the fulfilling of God's original purposes for humanity and the whole of creation. In his later writings Newbigin suggests that it is the denial of 'purpose' and the attempt to live without it, that is the particular expression of the human predicament for contemporary western humanity, "We all engage in purposeful activity, and we judge ourselves and others in terms of success in achieving the purposes that we set before ourselves. Yet we accept as the final product of this purposeful activity a picture of the world from which purpose has been eliminated."[8]

The modern scientific world-view is a mechanistic one, which can admit of no sense of purpose, yet in the realm of human relationships the whole discussion is dominated by concepts of 'the good' against which differing and contradictory accounts of purpose are assessed.[9] For Newbigin denial of purpose is tantamount to denial of God, and is therefore a contemporary expression of that fundamental disobedience to God traditionally called sin: "the essence of sin is unbelief, and the opposite of sin is faith".[10] Its inevitable result is seen in the human self-contradiction already outlined.

However, humanity is made in the image of God, and although sin causes us to contradict our true nature, it is not totally destroyed. Newbigin likens the image of God in humanity to the reflection of the moon in water, it may be distorted or even

5 Newbigin, *Unfinished Agenda*, p30.

6 Newbigin, *Unfinished Agenda*, p31.

7 Newbigin, *Sin and Salvation*, p13; cf. Wainwright *Theological Life*, pp38ff.

8 L. Newbigin, *Foolishness to the Greeks* (SPCK, London, 1986) p78.

9 Newbigin, *Foolishness to the Greeks*, p66 and pp78-9.

10 Newbigin, *Sin and Salvation*, p20.

totally hidden, it depends on the relationship between the two. Nor can the image be discovered in the individual, but only in relationship, especially in man-and-woman bound together in love. Humanity is made for love, but in failing to acknowledge and love God we are driven in upon ourselves. Sin thus comes to be self-love and idolatry, again expressed not just in the lives of individuals, but also in the lives of communities, of nations and of states. This idolatry is the result of the constant threat and anxiety experienced by the self which places itself at the centre of the universe, and which is expressed in the search for security. Idolatry is at the heart of much religious practice for this too is but an expression of the human search for certainty and security.[11]

The human situation produced by sin is real and terrible; its objectivity and inevitability are well conveyed by the traditional Indian concept of *karma*, although this fails to comprehend the corporate nature of sin and the collective guilt of the human race. There is no ultimate explanation for sin, but its reality as a "dark mystery of life"[12] is all too evident. It is impossible for humanity to save itself; for salvation requires a change of will and it is here that sin is at it most pervasive. God's wrath opposes sin and its destructive power and keeps all things in being, but only his mercy and grace bring salvation.[13] It is clear that all this reflects not just the opening chapters of Genesis, but also the Pauline interpretation of the human situation as outlined in the first chapter of Romans. Newbigin is convinced of the truth of John 3:16. God has acted in history for the salvation of the human race; it is God who is the source of salvation, springing from that eternal love which is expressed in the doctrine of the Trinity. As one reviewer put it: "Newbigin holds to and expounds those theological scandals which alienate other faiths – the Trinity and its expression in the cross, so that mission is seen as faith, hope and love in action."[14]

The doctrines of the Trinity and the Incarnation of the Son, the centre and climax of which is the Cross, stand at the heart of Newbigin's understanding of God and the divine action in the world. This influence can be traced in almost everything he writes. Newbigin retains a firm grasp of the link between being and relationship. The corporate element is central to his understanding not only of the human situation, but also to his understanding of the nature of God; relationship is therefore seen as an essential structure of salvation itself: "Interpersonal relatedness belongs to the very being of God. Therefore there can be no salvation for man except in relatedness."[15] Newbigin is equally clear that this salvation is focused in the person and work of Jesus of Nazareth: "Jesus was a man who lived among men in Palestine nineteen centuries ago; but he also spoke and acted as God's own representative with full power to claim the obedience which man owes to God".[16] At the heart of this

---

11 Newbigin, *Sin and Salvation*, pp26ff.
12 Newbigin, *Sin and Salvation*, p39.
13 Newbigin, *Sin and Salvation*, p42.
14 Cyril Davey, on 'The Open Secret', *Expository Times*, Vol. 91 (1979-80) p157.
15 Newbigin, *Open Secret*, p78.
16 Newbigin, *Sin and Salvation*, p59.

event stands the cross, although it cannot, and indeed must not, be separated from Jesus' life on the one hand, and his resurrection and ascension on the other. Although he recognises that no one theory of atonement is adequate, nevertheless the witness of Scripture and Tradition does allow some statements to be made. First that Jesus' death was both necessary and the will of the Father, for: "The holy love of God can only make terms with the sin of men at the cost of suffering and death".[17] Secondly, the death of Jesus arises out of his self-identification with sinners as expressed most profoundly in the 'cry of dereliction' from the cross.[18] Next, that it is a means of life for the world,[19] and a revelation, in fact *the* revelation, of God's love, for "love must be expressed in deeds".[20]

True forgiveness is not about punishment and penalty, but the restoration of relationship. Whilst the metaphor of ransom cannot be pressed too far, "a price had to be paid",[21] but this should not be seen in terms of propitiation, of which God is never the object in Scripture. Scripture is definite that what God requires is not sacrifice but obedience, and in the obedience unto death of Jesus true sacrifice has been made and therefore: "The death of Jesus thus provides in reality what the sacrifices of the Old Testament provide only in symbol".[22] For those who would question this whole scheme of salvation because of the so-called "scandal of particularity" (that is, how can a single event in time and space be of universal significance?), Newbigin neatly stands the argument on its head. Precisely *because* human beings are creatures of time and space, caught up in the stream of history, salvation must have historical form and expression. Thus:

> God, according to the Bible, is concerned with the redemption of the whole human race and of the whole created world ... the way of its working involves at every point the recreation of true human relationships and of true relationship between man and the rest of the created order. Its centre is necessarily a deed wrought at an actual point in history and at a particular place.[23]

That this is so depends upon the essential unity of humanity (and for that matter of the universe), for he argues always for the fundamental unity of the human race, there is only one story, one history. This means that the biblical story is not a separate story; rather it is part of the unbroken fabric of world history. Christians believe that it is in this place that the pattern has been disclosed, even though the weaving is not yet finished. "Christian faith is thus a way of understanding world

17 Newbigin, *Sin and Salvation*, p55.
18 Mark 15:34.
19 E.g. John 6 and 12:32
20 Newbigin, *Sin and Salvation*, p71; see also pp62-9 for Newbigin's more detailed commentary on the death of Christ.
21 Newbigin, *Sin and Salvation*, p82.
22 Newbigin *Sin and Salvation*, p87.
23 L. Newbigin, *The Household of God* (SCM, London, 1953) p99.

history which challenges and relativizes all other models by which the meaning of history is interpreted".[24]

Bound up with all of this is Newbigin's reassertion of the doctrine of election, which for George Hunsberger is the clue to Newbigin's whole theology.[25] Election involves the choosing of the one for the blessing of the many, beginning with the call of Abraham and the foundation of the 'Chosen People', through the notion of 'Remnant' (a *saving* remnant rather than one which is merely *saved*), until the final focus is upon the One, the Christ. Then the movement again becomes outward and expansive, from the first witnesses, through the Church to the whole world. The Bible thus compels the Church to say what it would not dare say for itself, "God leads the world to its consummation through the apostolate of the Church".[26] For Newbigin the doctrine of election is not only compatible with the nature of God and the nature of humanity, "it is the *only* principle congruous with the nature of God's redeeming purpose",[27] that is, redemption as relatedness and in relationships. A particular view of the nature of redemption or salvation is thus fundamental to Newbigin's thought, of which the doctrine of election is but a function. To sum up his whole argument let Newbigin again speak for himself:

There is an actual sphere of redemption, of which the historical centre is Jesus Christ incarnate, crucified, risen and ascended. From that centre the word of salvation goes out to all the earth, the nations are baptised, the Lord's table is spread, a real community is built up – all by the living sovereign working of the Holy Spirit. It is here in this visible community, that God is savingly at work reconciling the world to Himself, precisely because the salvation which He purposes is not merely private and spiritual but corporate and cosmic.[28]

It is clear from all of this that human life, both in sin and salvation, is corporate and, in the end, cosmic. Present experience of relationship is a pointer to the consummation of the divine purpose when all things will be caught up into that fully reciprocal relationship which is signified by the doctrine of the Trinity. Such discussion of the most fundamental points of Christian doctrine issues in the call to mission, the call to bear witness, and Newbigin emphasises that in all this the believer speaks "the language of testimony".[29] What is claimed is a relationship with 'Him who has spoken', and if the question is put 'Has He spoken?' the answer can only come in the realm of testimony and witness.

---

24 Newbigin, *Open Secret*, p99.
25 See his doctoral dissertation "The Missionary Significance of the Biblical Doctrine of Election as a Foundation for a Theology of Cultural Plurality in the Missiology of J.E. Lesslie Newbigin", Princeton Theological Seminary Ph.D. Thesis 1987. Subsequently published as *Bearing the Witness of the Spirit: Lesslie Newbigin's Theology of Cultural Plurality* (Eerdmans, Grand Rapids, 1998).
26 Newbigin, *Household of God*, p139.
27 Newbigin, *Household of God*, p101.
28 Newbigin, *Household of God*, p131.
29 Newbigin, *Foolishness to the Greeks*, p91.

The Christian Church is therefore the community of witness, living in the tension between what Newbigin has characterized as the "perfect and future tenses" based on the 'indicative' of the new reality experienced in Christ.[30] It expresses itself through the relationships of the new community which Christ forms, and in its words and actions. Newbigin is in no doubt about the validity of the Church, nor of its divine commission,[31] again arguing from his understanding of the nature of salvation as relational:

> God's way of salvation is not by enabling a few individuals to grasp the truth – either by mystical union, or by intellectual enquiry, or by being given one universal and inerrant revelation in code or book; it is by calling a people to Himself, that they may be with Him and that He may send them forth.[32]

The Church is thus chosen and called by God in order to be the bearer of blessing to the world. This pattern is congruous with the nature of God, the nature of the human race and the nature of salvation, as Newbigin has outlined it. Therefore the Church has a vital role in the process of salvation of which a "universalist" theology takes no account. For if God can and does bestow his grace indiscriminately, then the Church is no essential part of the whole scheme of salvation, indeed God himself ignores it.[33] Newbigin argues that such a position is intolerable, not only in that it fails to do justice either to the nature of the Church or the nature of salvation, but because it also violates the fundamental freedom which God has granted to humanity precisely to achieve that maturity and reciprocity of relationship which is his purpose in creation.

If salvation for the one depends on the salvation of the whole, does that not imply a form of universalism? Newbigin is naturally cautious at this point, recognizing that completion and consummation still lie in the future. He does not doubt God's purpose that all should be saved, but equally recognizes that his appeal to freedom of the will means that he cannot say that it is impossible that some will finally choose the idol rather than God, evil rather than good. Therefore, although salvation is by definition, universal and cosmic, this does not exclude the possibility that some may ultimately be 'castaways' – "To exclude this possibility would obviously be to depart completely from the gravely realistic teaching of the New Testament".[34] The claims of Jesus are absolute but not irresistible. However, despite what some of his critics may think, Newbigin argues strongly that one cannot assume from this position that those who have never been presented with the chance freely to decide for or against Christ must therefore be excluded from the possibility of salvation. He

---

30 L. Newbigin, *A Faith for this One World?* (SCM, London, 1961) pp84ff.

31 Newbigin is certain: "There can be no question that Jesus intended to be represented in all the plenitude of his power, by his own chosen and commissioned people." *Household of God*, p62.

32 Newbigin, *Household of God*, p63.

33 Newbigin, *Household of God*, p79.

34 Newbigin, *Household of God*, p140.

recalls Jesus' reluctance to speculate on the number of those who will be saved, and stresses that in the Gospels the severest warnings about judgement and exclusion from God's presence are reserved for those who presume their own inclusion in the company of the saved. Again the emphasis is on responsibility rather than privilege:

> The privileges to which conversion is the gateway are not exclusive claims upon God's grace; they are the privileges of those who have been chosen for special responsibility in the carrying out of God's blessed design. Their joy will be not that they are saved, but that God's name is hallowed, his will done and his reign perfected.[35]

He reiterates that to claim finality for Jesus Christ is not to assert either that the majority of men will some day become Christians, or to assert that all others will be damned. It is to claim that commitment to him is the way in which humanity can become truly aligned to the ultimate end for which all things were made.[36] Following John's Gospel, Newbigin argues that Jesus Christ is the light that enlightens *everyone* and the fundamental link between the Christian and other people is not any question of agreement or convergence between religion or ideology, but the plain fact of their common humanity.

This clear and simple theological framework to Newbigin's thought raises some important questions for our discussion. If salvation is a restoration of true relationship with God and with the rest of Creation, and if this is accomplished only through the saving activity of God in Christ to which the Church bears witness, and if it is appropriated by incorporation into the community of the people of God, how are those who do not encounter the witness of the Church to be brought into this relationship? Moreover, what of those whose experience of the reality of the Church is a denial of that true relationship for which they yearn and strive? Newbigin is clear that such folk are not necessarily consigned to perdition, but it does not seem at all obvious that he has answered his own question about how salvation becomes ours, in respect of such people.

Secondly, we must ask how adequate is Newbigin's account of human nature, especially in respect of freedom? Of course one would wish to endorse whole-heartedly his exposition of God-given freedom for true and reciprocal relationship, but does he really do justice to the bondage to which fallen human nature is subject? Are people who are presented with the testimony of the Church really free to respond positively or to reject it? How far are we bound by limitations of circumstance and culture? The balance between genuine freedom and determinism is a difficult one, but we must ask whether, for all his discussion of culture (to which we shall come in due course), he takes sufficient account of its strength.

Equally significant, and linking these first two points, is the question raised by his emphasis on the objectivity of the atoning work of Christ as accomplishing a new relationship between God and *the world*. If Christ has objectively achieved a

---

35 L. Newbigin, *The Finality of Christ* (SCM, London, 1969) pp112-3.
36 Newbigin, *Finality of Christ*, p115.

new relationship in this cosmic sense, how can individuals be free to align themselves with it, or indeed to reject it? Newbigin tries to avoid this difficulty by arguing for human freedom here, but in that case it would seem that the atonement is not really as objective, either in the personal or in the cosmic sense, as he has earlier suggested.

Thirdly, and of this Newbigin is well aware, there are those within the Christian tradition who would argue that the central planks of his argument, the doctrines of the Trinity and the Incarnation, are not only scandals to other faiths, but culturally conditioned expressions of the Christian faith which may well have outlived their usefulness, and this whole question of just what the essence of the Christian message is, would not be agreed by all. This is another important area to which we must return.

In this introductory section I have presented an outline of Bishop Newbigin's fundamental theological position. We have seen his clear conviction that the truth about human nature is to be discovered in relationship, a conviction that stems from his understanding of the nature and purpose of God as revealed in the divine action in Christ. This relational understanding is to be found in his view both of the nature of salvation and the mode by which it becomes ours through the witness of the Church. To hold this faith is to hold a clue, the vital clue, to the meaning and purpose of life itself, and to be drawn into that purpose in a responsible, free and creative manner. It is also to be commissioned to bear witness to that experience in order to widen the circle of relationship of which Christ himself is the centre and the goal. Finally it is a matter of personal commitment and confession:

> I speak of Jesus Christ as the one whom I know and confess as Lord of all that is, whom I know through the witness of the Christian tradition principally embodied in the canonical Scriptures, and whose coming to consummate all things I await.[37]

7.2 Religious Pluralism in Newbigin's Thought

As we noted in Part One of this volume recent discussion of the question of religious pluralism has tended to categorize the various Christian responses to this issue as "exclusivist", "inclusivist" or "pluralist".[38] Such discussions usually place the contributions of Lesslie Newbigin squarely in the 'exclusivist' camp (although Paul Knitter[39] recognizes a more complex situation and employs a more sophisticated analytical model which sees Newbigin representing the mainline Protestant tradition). Newbigin himself is reluctant to use this language at all for he believes that it stems from asking the wrong question in the first place and is anyway often inadequate to the task. In the fullest statement of his position on the

---

37 L. Newbigin, 'Christ and the Cultures', *SJT*, Vol. 31 (1978) pp9-10.
38 E.g. Alan Race, *Christians and Religious Pluralism*.
39 In his book, *No Other Name?* (SCM, London, 1985).

relationship of Christian faith to the religions,[40] he points out that his position cuts across these categories, combining elements which have been assigned to all three at various times. What he is always at pains to point out is that whilst he acknowledges the fact of plurality he does not accept the prevailing philosophy of pluralism. This section will trace the development of Newbigin's thought on this matter over a period of thirty years, before we assess the major criticisms of his thinking and evaluate the responses which he made.

Newbigin's first real venture into this area came in a small book called *A Faith for this One World?*;[41] the product of a lecture series given at Harvard in 1958. It deals with the apparent single world civilization which appeared to be emerging in the post war era, based on a western scientific world-view and a linear concept of history; neither of which could be totally separated from the Christendom in which they were formed. The issue at stake was which faith would provide the most adequate spiritual basis for the new world culture, because in a world where there is only one physics and one mathematics, "religion cannot do less than claim for its affirmations a like universal validity".[42]

This seems to suggest that out of the plurality of the human religious experience only one faith would emerge as commanding final and absolute allegiance for all people. The supremacy of the Christian faith is first worked out by Newbigin against this scenario of cultural unity. With hindsight it is clear that history in fact moved towards acceptance of plurality rather than uniformity, but nevertheless Newbigin maintains his position, adapting the arguments to suit the new situation. Many of the arguments which he applies to the plural society are to be found, in embryo at least, in his discussion of the proper faith for 'one world'. Of course there were other candidates for the position of "the world faith" and in the Harvard lectures Newbigin examined the suggestions of Radhakrishnan, Toynbee and Hocking.

Newbigin rejects Radhakrishnan's advocacy of a contemporary version of Hinduism because it offered tolerance rather than genuine unity. It was oriented towards the individual rather than the community or society at large. Radhakrishnan's analysis was based on a mystical approach to religion, which Newbigin consistently rejects for its inherent individualism. Such a view assumes the underlying unity of the human religious experience. Its apparent diversity is because the one truth has been refracted through a variety of cultural lenses and is received by individuals and communities at different stages of development. Newbigin argues that this denies the central assertion of the Christian faith that in a particular individual God has chosen to reveal himself in a decisive and ultimate way. Such an affirmation stretches the limits of Hindu toleration because it fundamentally contradicts the presuppositions of the traditional Indian world-view.[43]

---

40 L. Newbigin, *The Gospel in a Pluralist Society* (SPCK, London, 1989), especially chapters 13 and 14.

41 Published in the SCM Book Club (SCM, London, 1961).

42 Newbigin, *A Faith for this One World?*, p30.

43 Newbigin, *Faith for this One World?*, pp38-41.

Newbigin then goes on to analyse the suggestion of Arnold Toynbee that the "higher religions" ought to work together in the face of the common enemy, "the worship of collective man, of Leviathan".[44] This would mean for Christianity not only a shedding of its westernism, but also a rejection of any claim to uniqueness, which is an inevitable source of intolerance and pride. Toynbee argued that the central tenets of Christianity are present in other religions too. This of course is questionable as Newbigin recognizes, but he asks Toynbee the more fundamental question as to how we may verify the truth of the assertion of God's self-sacrificing love. Newbigin argues that, for the Christian, the truth of this is grounded in "the total fact of Christ" including the Resurrection.[45] It cannot be an induction from general human experience. But if Toynbee's rejection of Christianity's claims to uniqueness means a jettisoning of the uniqueness, finality and decisiveness of Jesus, then the whole basis for his common platform is destroyed. In fact this argument shows that Toynbee, mistakenly according to Newbigin, views Christianity as an idea, rather than as the announcement of an event. Moreover, for Newbigin, faith is that which commands one's ultimate allegiance, and is not to be used in the furtherance of some other purpose. When that happens religion becomes demonic.[46]

The third view which Newbigin discusses is that of W. E. Hocking as set out in his book *The Coming World Civilization*.[47] The first half of this analysis provided the basis for Newbigin's thesis of the single world civilization that lies behind *A Faith for this One World?* But, in the second half of the book, he rejects Hocking's notion that the spiritual basis for such a civilization will be provided by a confluence of the great religions resulting from a period of spiritual struggle. Hocking believed that Christianity would thus be universalised by this process, and specific names and places would no longer have any absolute significance. Newbigin again perceives that such a view is based on individual experience of timeless reality, rather than Newbigin's understanding of the biblical conception of God at work in and through human history. This inevitably means that Hocking is reluctant to be tied to particular people and events; there can be no absolute place for Jesus. But Newbigin argues that there can be no 'Christ concept' which is detached from the figure of Jesus of Nazareth: "If the word Christ is a plastic term whose meaning depends only upon the accumulated religious experience of a multitude of lone individuals in their search for reality, then we are left finally imprisoned in our own subjectivity."[48] In fact, as Newbigin acknowledges, Hocking does believe that the idea of love must be embodied in actual lives and deeds, but for Newbigin, and for traditional Christian faith, the crucial issue is the complete coincidence of the universal and the particular in "the Christ event". If the story of Jesus is but one of numerous examples of the embodiment of the love-ideal, then Newbigin believes that the truth of the assertion

44 A. J. Toynbee, *Christianity among the Religions of the World* (OUP, London, 1958) p85.
45 Newbigin, *Faith for this One World?*, p44.
46 Newbigin, *Faith for this One World?*, p45.
47 Published by Allen & Unwin, London, 1958.
48 Newbigin, *Faith for this One World?*, p50.

of the ultimacy of divine love remains an open question, and nor does it do justice to the gospel record.

Newbigin rejects these approaches for the same reasons as he rejects the later pluralism of Hick and others. He is not convinced of common human religious experience, especially when it is grounded in a form of mystical individualism. The question of epistemology is also raised by Toynbee's assumptions about the nature of God; how do we know what God is like? Newbigin is always concerned with the particulars of human existence and he suggests that Christian faith is a faith about history, not a form of idealism. He believes that all three attempts are doomed to failure and raises the question of whether twentieth century humanity might still believe in the possibility that Christian faith really could be a universal faith. Is this conviction merely the indication that we are prisoners of our tradition just as the mystic might be a prisoner of his experience? He answers by posing the question of what we might seek in looking for a universal faith, certainly nothing which is totally free of 'local colour', nor anything that is self-evidently universally acceptable – even the unity of the scientific culture does not provide that. A form of mystical unity would not do because it does not touch closely enough people's everyday existence. Rather, he suggests, that what is required is a harmony of wills redeemed from natural egotism, a reconciliation born of love, a righteous peace. Such love, peace and forgiveness is of God, not humanity, and God's love must be shown in action, and therefore of necessity in particular and local events.

It is this conviction which provides the rationale for the whole Christian mission. It cannot be justified by any appeal to results, which are in any case far too ambiguous, nor by dubious alliances with other causes, whether that of "civilization" or "democracy". The sole authority for the Christian mission is 'in the name of Jesus'. The world must be confronted with the 'total fact of Christ' and then allowed to respond as it will. This must be understood and interpreted within a biblical world-view, which includes the doctrines of creation, sin and redemption through election. This will include a proper respect for the spirituality of the non-Christian and a recognition of the place of the secular order, but will equally well find its focus in the cross of Christ, which profoundly disturbs all our finely balanced ethical judgements.

At this point Newbigin introduces what becomes a recurrent theme in his writing on the religions which we might sum up under the traditional heading of "the mystery of iniquity":[49] "it is often the higher religions, and those in them who are ethically farthest advanced, that offer the most bitter resistance to the preaching of the gospel".[50] This is of course enshrined in the gospel tradition where the religious authorities are the centre of opposition to Jesus and bring matters to the crisis of the cross. Newbigin believes that this pattern is repeated in the history of the mission of the Church and can be understood in the light of Paul's teaching in Romans on the law. Human efforts to obey the divine law, whether that of Torah or conscience, lead

---

49 Cf. Thomas Helwys, *The Mystery of Iniquity* (Amsterdam, 1612).
50 Newbigin, *Faith for this One World?*, p73.

only to estrangement from God because they stem from a self fundamentally alienated from God who is the source of love. Religion often becomes the focus of opposition to the gospel, which is frequently gladly received by the irreligious, just as in the ministry of Jesus.

This does not mean that such religion is mere illusion or falsehood; in fact Newbigin suggests that it is the response to the genuine witness of the divine Spirit ·in the heart of everyone. Nor does the Christian have any vantage point from which to stand in judgement upon such responses. However, he makes the Barthian point that the coming of the gospel means the end of all religion, in the sense that the true response to God which is the object of all religion can only be given by God, and has been given by him in Jesus Christ. Newbigin is quick to recognize that within Christianity itself there is plenty of evidence of legalism, rather than divine grace at work, and therefore what confronts all religions, including Christianity, is 'the Gospel'. Nor is divine grace restricted to operation only within the Church or the Christian traditions. Writing of the Hindu *bhakti* tradition he comments: "I cannot believe that God turns a deaf ear to these outpourings of devotion from men made in his image, or that they arise otherwise than through his witness in their hearts. I cannot believe that there is no contact between the soul and God in these prayers".[51] But for Newbigin such devotion has no grounding except in the human need of salvation, it does not lay hold of the reality of God's love seen in action, in events. It is this conviction which leads to an exposition by Newbigin of the doctrine of election that is so central in his thinking.

Newbigin argues that the particular can be the bearer of the universal, for him it is simply the logical consequence of belief in a personal God at all. He recognizes the moral dilemma posed by the "scandal of particularity", but suggests that it rests on a misunderstanding of the doctrine of election which focuses on privilege rather than responsibility. Humanity is related to God because we are his creatures and possessed by the "light which enlightens every one"[52] in virtue of that creation. People are related to God's saving activity by being related to the people called into being by God within a particular strand of history, which is nevertheless a part of the one universal history. It is the clue to world history, or better the mission of the Church is the clue to the meaning and end of history, existing only to fulfil the purpose of God in and for the world. Thus the particular, the Church, is the bearer of the universal, salvation. God's choice leaves no room for pride, nor for that disobedience so signally displayed by the disunity of the Church which is "a contradiction of its proper nature and a public abdication of its right to preach the gospel to all nations". Of course, the Church necessarily lives in the tension between that which has been accomplished in 'the event of Christ' and the consummation of God's universal purpose to which it points, it is the tension between the perfect and the future tenses, but it lives in the indicative of the new

---

51 Newbigin, *Faith for this One World?* p75.
52 John 1:9.

reality experienced in Christ and expresses that reality in its corporate life through its living together, its activity and its words of witness.[53]

All of this has profound implications for the pattern of the Christian mission to the nations. Whilst the Church cannot shed its exclusive claims in the sense in which Newbigin has expounded them, he is convinced that its "westerness" must be lost, for that which is so evidently provincial will never be recognized as universal. Historically it was the case that the great missionary activity of the Church was borne by the tide of expanding western culture, with both positive and negative consequences for all concerned. It must now be recognized that the pattern for mission must be that of the whole Church to the whole world, the Church is called upon not to support missions, but to be mission. This must be characterized by greater sensitivity, equality and mutuality than has usually been the case, and by "substantial progress· in the recovery of the Church's unity".[54] The denominationalism with which the Church's mission is scarred is a denial of that Gospel which the Church claims to proclaim and embody.

Although in many ways *A Faith for this One World?* is a slight book we have analysed the argument in some detail because it provides the basis of Newbigin's position, which is developed more thoroughly in later works. For example in another American lecture series in the following decade[55] published as *The Finality of Christ*,[56] Newbigin outlined possible approaches to the study of religion, both from outside and from within. He argued that, for the Christian, as for others with an "ultimate commitment", personal conviction cannot be ruled out of the discussion. Although in studying the religions Christians must strive for objectivity, in the final analysis criteria of judgement will always be shaped by ultimate commitments. Accurate description of religious phenomena may be achieved by some form of 'intellectual suspense', but true understanding depends on forming judgements about these phenomena that will inevitably be shaped by faith commitments of one sort or another.

The finality of Christ is not something for which the Christian can argue, it is the given from which one starts. Thus the pattern of the book is not an attempt to demonstrate Christ's ultimacy, but an exploration of what that faith commitment means and implies in relation to the religions, to the secular order and to history. We shall deal with Newbigin's approach to secular pluralism in the following chapter and therefore we shall continue to concentrate here on his understanding of the relation of Christian faith to the religions. But it should be noted that Newbigin affirms the distinction noted in Part One, between the Gospel or "the revelation of God in Jesus Christ",[57] and the phenomenon of Christianity as a religion, which is

---

53 Newbigin, *Faith for this One World?*, pp80-4. This reiterates what he has said about the nature of the Church in *The Household of God*, especially chapter 6.

54 Newbigin, *Faith for this One World?*, p124.

55 The Lyman Beecher Lectures at Yale, 1966, also delivered at Cambridge.

56 SCM, London, 1969.

57 Newbigin, *Finality of Christ*, p22.

judged by the Gospel as much, and perhaps more, than any other religion. The title of his book is *The Finality of Christ* and not *The Finality of Christianity*.

Newbigin builds his analysis by discussion of the on-going debate during the great World Missionary Conferences in the first half of this century. Edinburgh 1910 was characterized by the fulfilment theology of Farquhar and others. But Newbigin goes on to trace the decline of the notion of "fulfilment" as an appropriate model for the relationship of Christian faith and the religions during the ensuing conferences. In 1928 the Jerusalem conference tried to isolate the 'values' of the religions, but of course to assess such values some standard above them all must be assumed, and anyway claims for the finality of Christ relate to the whole of human life, not merely to those elements labelled religion. All this appeared in much sharper relief at the Tambaram conference in 1938 when the debate was focused by the work of Hendrik Kraemer, discussed at some length in the introductory chapter.

As we noted Kraemer draws a clear line between Christianity and God's self-revelation in Christ. Newbigin himself draws a similar distinction, but he suggests in his discussion of Kraemer that it is impossible to maintain complete separation between the Gospel and institutional Christianity. Equally Newbigin is unhappy with Kraemer's attempt to divorce human religious experience from divine revelation. He argues that if revelation has been understood and accepted then a religious experience has occurred. Moreover Kraemer was prepared to admit the sublime elements in non-Christian religious experience which implies the possibility at least of divine self-disclosure, and threatens his emphasis on the *sui generis* character of the Christian revelation.[58]

Newbigin highlights the debate between Kraemer and A.G. Hogg, which has been mentioned in the earlier discussion of Kraemer. Hogg asked whether a distinction might be made between non-Christian *religion* and non-Christian *faith*, in parallel to the separation between the revelation of God in Christ and organized Christianity. Kraemer agreed that this was valid and Newbigin too affirms the possibility of a genuine self-disclosure of God in non-Christian religious experience. Newbigin makes the practical point, which he reiterates in subsequent discussion, that total discontinuity is inconceivable and makes any communication of the Gospel impossible. Every translation of the Scriptures has to choose some word for "God", which will inevitably bear associations and connotations from the non-Christian tradition from which it is derived. Newbigin notes and affirms Kraemer's appeal to the mystery of iniquity at this point, but nevertheless suggests that Hogg's argument for real communion between God and the believer in non-Christian religious experience is not faced squarely by Kraemer and the truth of that experience must be affirmed. The debate cannot be conducted simply in terms of either continuity or discontinuity. For Newbigin the real questions are raised by the points at which continuity, or radical discontinuity, are identified and confronted.

Newbigin concludes this discussion by taking issue with Raimondo Pannikar, who provides an Indian Roman Catholic version of fulfilment theology in his book

---

58 Newbigin, *Finality of Christ*, pp33-5.

The Unknown Christ of Hinduism.[59] This is based on the Catholic doctrine of the universal salvific will of God, expounded clearly by Rahner amongst others. If God wills to save all of humanity he must provide the means to do so, and therefore the grace of God in Christ, who remains the universal redeemer, is made available through other channels than historic Christianity. Pannikar explains that in the context of India the traditional religion provided a channel for the divine grace to become operative in the life of the "good and bona fide Hindu". Newbigin argues that this fails to do sufficient justice to the terrible reality of sin which is focused in the cross; it merely provides another version of religion of law or morality, whereas the Gospel stresses that Christ came to save sinners rather than the righteous.

Pannikar's scheme also assumes that religion must be the channel of divine grace, whereas Newbigin again argues on the basis of John 1:9 that the light may shine in any area of human existence and not only, or even mainly, in the realm of religion. Newbigin argues that any version of fulfilment, whether Pannikar's or that outlined in the Papal encyclical *Suam Ecclesiam*, fails to do justice to the religions. They turn on different axes from Christianity and from each other, and cannot be judged on the basis of some supposed nearness to or remoteness from Christianity:

> ... what do concepts of 'near' and 'far' mean in relation to the crucified and risen Jesus? Is the devout Pharisee nearer or farther than the semi-pagan prostitute? Is the passionate Marxist nearer or farther than the Hindu mystic? Is a man nearer to Christ because he is religious? Is the Gospel the culmination of religion or is it the end of religion?[60]

In *The Finality of Christ* Newbigin again takes up the idea of Christ as the clue to universal history. He recognizes that Christians, as much as any other group, are obsessed with the notion of salvation, by which is meant the fate of the individual soul after death. But Newbigin argues passionately that the New Testament picture is of the cosmic fulfilment of God's work in Christ in which all things will be restored and united in him. Salvation means participation, both now and in the future, in this culmination of universal history. The 'event of Christ' is the decisive moment in this history, and its announcement provides the opportunity for all to commit themselves to it. It is of course possible to reject that opportunity and to lose the possibility of participation in the purposes of God, which is the true meaning of salvation. However, this does not mean that those who have not been confronted by the challenge of the Christian Gospel are necessarily excluded from participation in God's on-going work. Newbigin believes that we can do no more than repeat Jesus' urgent injunction "to repent and believe the gospel", and leave the rest in the hands of God.[61]

To speak of Christ as "the clue to history" means that a particular view of history is being affirmed. Newbigin draws on the distinction made between the cyclical

---

59 SCM, London, 1965.
60 Newbigin, *Finality of Christ*, p44.
61 Newbigin, *Finality of Christ*, pp60-2.

concept of history as a wheel, and the linear view of history as journey or road. Newbigin believes that such concepts of history form "a great divide" in human cultures, rather than slight variations on a theme. But he suggests that even those cultures which have traditionally held to a cyclical view of history, have been compelled to take the linear view more seriously since it underlies the secular world-view which is so widespread. Newbigin argues that this is a form of the biblical concept of the Kingdom of God, and can be understood from a Christian point of view as the drawing of people into a conscious form of historical existence as a consequence of the Incarnation.[62]

Christian faith must take history seriously for it is the sphere of God's self-revelation, the locus of his suffering interaction with estranged humanity. All this also means that history must be understood in some sense at least as a coherent whole, despite its apparent incoherence and meaninglessness. This is only possible because the Christian revelation is about the end of history. To speak of the finality of Christ is to express that conviction and to make the commitment which it implies, to live today and tomorrow in the light of it. In this way Christ is the clue to the meaning and end of universal history. Of course "the event of Christ" is only available to us through the Christian tradition, we have access to "the fact of Christ" only through the interpretation of the apostolic communities. Therefore no total distinction can be made between the self-revelation of God and the response of human faith. This is also true for all "facts" of history: they are only available because by accident or design they have been preserved for us and selected as significant. To claim finality for Christ is to endorse the initial judgement of those who responded to the events in faith. This is enshrined in a living, changing, but continuing tradition, and it is only meaningful when interpreted by that community which lives according to its truth. It is in this sense that Newbigin argues that there can be no total disjunction between "the Gospel" and the Church. Newbigin is convinced that "the original apostolic testimony" remains at the centre of the Church's life as the norm by which all development must be judged. Development is essential in order that the faith may be related to current situations, but the "original witness" acts as a check against aberrations and a constant source of renewal and reform.[63]

This process allows the Christian a constructive and creative engagement with history. From the clue, which is Christ, the beginning and the end may be known, but only in a parabolic way. It does not provide a blueprint or map for every by-way, as the extremists in every generation like to claim. This does not excuse the Christian from engagement with history and attempting to interpret what God is doing now; provided always that Christ remains the sole criterion of judgement, as crucified and risen Lord. The pattern of the Cross and Resurrection is the key to all such interpretation. In sum, "To claim finality for Christ is to claim that this is the true clue to history, the standpoint from which one truly interprets history and

---

62 Newbigin, *Finality of Christ*, p68.
63 Newbigin, *Finality of Christ*, pp75-8.

therefore has the possibility of being relevantly committed to the service of God in history now."[64]

From the discussion thus far certain key themes and questions in Newbigin's thinking on the issue of religious pluralism begin to emerge. One is what we might call the "soteriological question" in which he rejects individualistic concern for the fate of the soul in eternity. Instead he affirms what he believes is the biblical understanding of salvation as to do with the universal purpose of God in creation and redemption. This is related to the whole area of eschatology which he frequently discusses in conjunction with the meaning and purpose of history. As we have seen Newbigin is committed to the biblical, linear, understanding of history, as the sphere of the saving activity of God, the place for the unfolding and outworking of God's eternal purpose in relation to the whole of creation.

Another area might be labelled the "religious question", in which his fundamental beliefs about the nature and functions of religion have been shaped by the argument of Paul in Romans and confirmed by his long missionary experience. For Newbigin, religion symbolizes sin in the basic sense of man's independence of God, or better his alienation from God. This does not mean that all religion is therefore obviously evil, although there is plenty of evidence of the evil and harmful effects of the religions, including Christianity. The point is rather that, whatever sublime elements and indeed divine grace we may detect in certain religions or religious practices, beneath it there is always the attempt at self-justification which Paul discerned in the religion of the Torah. All such efforts are doomed to failure since they do not grasp that justification or salvation is the gift of God through his decisive self-revelation in Christ.

Behind all this there lies a third question, perhaps most fundamental of all, the "epistemological question" – how can we know any of this? Newbigin asserts that this is where the act of faith begins; this is where 'ultimate commitments' are revealed. For the Christian the starting point is always "the event of Christ" as God's self-revelation and therefore the most significant clue to the meaning and purpose of universal history. It is a commitment made in response to the witness of the Church, the embodiment of the Gospel, and the particular channel of the universal blessing of God made available through Jesus Christ. This is undoubtedly an act of faith, but every commitment to a framework for understanding the human situation is an act of faith. All of this is worked out in more detail and with greater rigour in his later writings, although his fundamental assumptions remain unchanged.

For example if we turn to *The Open Secret*,[65] we find that the question of the authority of the Christian mission has been expanded from the simple 'in the name of Jesus' to a fully Trinitarian exposition of the basis and purpose of the Church. But this continues to include specific personal commitment to the Lordship of Jesus Christ, a wagering of one's life on the ultimacy of Jesus, and therefore a faith

64 Newbigin, *Finality of Christ*, pp86-7.
65 Eerdmans, Grand Rapids, 1978; 2nd edition SPCK, 1995.

commitment which cannot be demonstrated or established from the basis of some other ultimate commitment. It is in the context of this discussion that Newbigin makes reference to the influence of Michael Polanyi on his thinking, particularly in his book *Personal Knowledge*,[66] with his plea for a post-critical philosophy. We shall consider the influence of Polanyi on Newbigin in more detail in the next chapter; for the moment suffice it to say that he provides the detailed philosophical platform on which Newbigin builds his epistemology. His essential argument is that which Newbigin has already independently articulated: knowledge is shaped by fundamental beliefs, which are "given" or assumed as an act of faith. There is a constant dialectical process between these assumptions and our ongoing exploration of the world, although always within the scope of our basic premises. It may be that this process might in the end lead us to abandon our original assumptions as inadequate, but any new starting point would include fresh assumptions also made as an act of faith. Thus Newbigin argues that the basic assumptions of Christian faith centre on Jesus but are more fully articulated in Trinitarian doctrine. This provides a model for understanding human life, "a model which cannot be verified according to the axioms of our culture, but which is offered on the authority of revelation and with the claim that it does provide the possibility of a practical wisdom to grasp and deal with human life as it really is".[67]

If we move from the epistemological questions to the issue of salvation and history we find that Newbigin is again expounding the scandal of particularity in terms of the doctrine of election. In the light of his greater emphasis on the doctrine of the Trinity in this later work it is no surprise to see his fundamental convictions expressed now with the emphasis on "interpersonal relatedness". Salvation must be that which not only binds the soul to God, but each to the other, and all to the world of nature. It cannot be received independently, privately, directly from God. It can only be passed from one to another, neighbour to neighbour, a process necessarily involving election, that is calling and response. God's blessing is indeed for all, but the very nature of that blessing means that it must be given and received in a manner that binds each to the other. Newbigin argues that such a view of the mission of the Church, based on this understanding of the doctrine of election, is essential if it is to touch the human situation as it really is, in relationships, in history and in the natural world.

He is again at pains to articulate the doctrine of election in a careful way in order to avoid the perversions which have accompanied it through its history: election is to responsible service not privileged status; it is a covenant not a contract; the faith in which God's promise must be received cannot be twisted into some ground for claims upon God over against the 'unbeliever' whose salvation is also part of the divine purpose.[68] Does this then imply a universalist soteriology? Certainly within the biblical material there is a strand of thought which has universalist overtones at

---

66 M. Polanyi, *Personal Knowledge* (Routledge & Kegan Paul, London, 1958, corrected edn, 1962).

67 Newbigin, *Open Secret*, p30.

68 Newbigin, *Open Secret*, pp79-86.

the very least. Newbigin highlights the unconditional Noachic covenant of blessing for the new humanity, and the promise to Abraham of the blessing for all the nations through his line. In the New Testament too, in those passages based on the parallel between Adam and Christ and in some of the Johannine literature, we may detect the influence of this line of thought.

This material must be held in tension with those many other passages which refer to judgement and the possibility of rejection. It is not possible to argue from the universal love of God to universal salvation. This fails to take seriously the freedom and responsibility that is entailed in personal being, granted to humanity by God in creation. Equally we must refrain from speculation about the ultimate destiny of others, for a characteristic element in Jesus' teaching on judgement is the element of surprise. In particular, much of Jesus' teaching on this topic was directed at those who claimed salvation as his right: it is by way of warning to the elect. Nevertheless, within the universal purpose which God is bringing to completion in Christ, there remains the awful possibility that the mark may be missed and we may find ourselves ultimately at odds with God and his purposes.[69]

How does all this relate to the question about "religion" outlined above? In *The Open Secret* Newbigin is careful to define the notoriously slippery concept of 'religion' with greater precision as "that which has final authority for a believer or a society, both in the sense that it determines his scale of values and in the sense that it provides the models, the basic patterns through which the believer grasps and organizes his· experience".[70] Of course, by this definition, that which a person confesses as his religion may not really be his true faith. Or he may so divide his life, for example between public and private spheres, that differing values operate in each. But the main issue is that point at which differing and discordant commitments meet and clash.

At this point Newbigin introduces (as he often does[71]) the well-known Indian parable of the blind men and the elephant. When presented with a different feature of the beast each man provides his individual comment as to what he has discovered. Each is partly correct, given the limited evidence available to him, but all are profoundly mistaken. The point is clear that each religious tradition is groping for that truth which is beyond its capacity fully to comprehend. As Newbigin points out, however, the story is told from a particular point of view – that of a king who *can* see, representing the Vedanta tradition, which implicitly corresponds to reality where all else is blindness. Again we are faced with an ultimate faith commitment beyond which it is impossible to go. Newbigin applies this point to the attempt of John Hick to bring about a "Copernican revolution" in the theology of religions, moving from a Christocentric model to a theocentric one.[72] Newbigin points out that any model we devise becomes our ultimate commitment – in this case it is

---

69 Newbigin, *Open Secret*, pp87-90.

70 Newbigin, *Open Secret*, p182.

71 E.g. *The Finality of Christ*, pp16-7.

72 See the discussion of Hick in Part One, where it is noted that he has since abandoned the theocentric model for a 'soteriocentric' version.

Hick's concern for "scientific truth" to which he is committed, as the fundamental ideology into which all else must fit.[73] Despite Hick's criticisms of the "confessional dialogue",[74] which Newbigin advocates, in favour of what he terms "truth-seeking dialogue", Hick himself assumes the truth of his own presuppositions.

Newbigin is clear that there is no dichotomy between "confession" and "truth-seeking" – confession is the starting-point of the search for truth, the standard by which all claims to truth will inevitably be assessed. For dialogue to be truly fruitful it is essential that the participants take seriously the full reality of their own faiths as the source for understanding the totality of experience. So Newbigin concludes:

> that no standpoint is available to any man except the point where he stands; that there is no platform from which one can claim to have an 'objective' view which supersedes all the 'subjective' faith- commitments of the world's faiths; that every man must take his stand on the floor of the arena, on the same level with every other, and there engage in the real encounter of ultimate commitment with those who, like him, have staked their lives on their vision of the truth.[75]

He recognizes that it is still possible for Christians who participate in this process of dialogue to come to it with various understandings of the nature of other faiths, and he proceeds to deal briefly with some of the common assumptions. It is worth noting here that Newbigin, so often classified as the champion of 'exclusivism', refuses to adopt some of the main planks of the exclusivist platform. For example, in response to the suggestion that other religions and ideologies are totally false, he suggests that any sensitive Christian mind cannot fail to recognize "abundant spiritual fruits" in the lives of non-Christian believers; he reiterates his point about the need for a common starting-point such as an understanding of the word "God"; again he refers to John 1:9 in commenting about the light made universally available. He does accept some truth in the suggestion of those who argue for a demonic element in the religions, but points out that this is a danger of *all* religion, including Christianity.[76]

In a discussion of other options, "fulfilment" theories, and Catholic teaching on the "concentric circles" model, he argues that none of this does proper justice to the nature of the religions, nor does it take account of the paradox of the mystery of iniquity. He is equally critical of Rahner's theory of "anonymous Christians", which also, in his view, fails to take the non-Christian faiths sufficiently seriously. Most

---

73 Newbigin, *Open Secret*, pp184-5.

74 That is, dialogue in which the partners meet recognizing that they begin from differing faith commitments of an ultimate nature and in which assessments of truth will be made according to their differing presuppositions and commitments. Newbigin articulated this in his article 'The Basis, Purpose and Manner of Inter-Faith Dialogue' (Division for World Mission and Evangelism, LCA 1975), modified as chapter 10 of *The Open Secret*.

75 Newbigin, *Open Secret*, p190.

76 Newbigin, *Open Secret*, pp191-3.

importantly, the whole theory is built on assumptions about the eternal destiny of the individual, which Newbigin believes that Christians are in no position to make. He will not accept the rebuke of Küng and others that unwillingness to pronounce on this issue is a failure of theological duty, and is "astonished" that any theologian would assume authority to do so. Our stance on this is vital for the manner of inter-faith dialogue, because "It is almost impossible for me to enter into simple, honest, open, and friendly communication with another person as long as I have at the back of my mind the feeling that I am one of the saved and he is one of the lost".[77] It is equally presumptuous to assume that the partner is "saved". All such assumptions and pronouncements go beyond human authority and undermine the possibility of genuine meeting. The Christian's position is simply that of witness within the context of a shared humanity, this is the sole basis of meeting.

All this is by way of clearing the ground and establishing what is not the case. More constructively Newbigin argues on the basis of his theology of creation, that the Christian is committed to the view that every human being is already in some relationship to Jesus, the Word through which all things are brought into being. This is an explicit recognition that the activity of Christ (Newbigin specifically refers to *Jesus*) is not confined to the area in which he is acknowledged. He is the light than shines within the darkness and no boundary can be drawn between these two areas. The Christian is a witness to this light. This light may be seen not only in the costly devotion of the followers of the various religions, but also in those committed to other ideologies such as humanism and Marxism even though they may have explicitly rejected the message of the Church. Christians will therefore meet all their fellow-humans as those who exist by the grace of the life-and-light-giving God, and rejoice in the evidence of response to him that they may discern.

It is just as important that the darkness be recognized as well as the light. The cross of Christ exposes the terrible fact of sin at the centre of human life. Sin is here defined as the capacity to pervert the grace of God, which is the basis of our lives, by twisting it into a claim over against God; the fundamental sin of independence is seen in man's characteristic state of alienation. The message of the Jesus crucified "by the powers of law, morals and piety", confronts every religion with a "radical negation". There is a sense in which Christ fulfils the "religion of law", but this is not apparent until his unconditional claim has been accepted and with hindsight one can look back to see, not the anticipated destruction, but true fulfilment. Newbigin sees the experience of Paul as articulated in Romans paralleled in that of modern day converts from other faiths. Through the process of human history, which finds its centre in the events which took place "under Pilate", God works towards his saving purpose. But this does not mean "the fulfilment of the personal spiritual history of each individual human being". Rather this process includes "the bringing into obedience to Christ" of the various treasures possessed by the whole of the human community, and this is what is meant by the Johannine saying of Jesus about the Spirit "guiding into all the truth" (John 16:13). The Church is commissioned to go

---

77 Newbigin, *Open Secret*, p196.

out into the world to receive as well as to give, and Newbigin highlights the enrichment of the Church through its encounter with the variety of human culture. Therefore the Church "must live always in dialogue with the world, bearing its witness to Christ but always in such a way that it is open to receive the riches of God which belong properly to Christ but have to be brought to him".[78] The Church is thus *in via*, open to the possibilities of change as it encounters new situations and ·cultures and lives in dialogue with them.

Newbigin concludes this discussion by suggesting that the purpose of "confessional dialogue" in obedient witness to Christ is *not* that Christianity should acquire another recruit. Rather with the partner we stand at the cross to receive judgement and correction, which changes the Church, the world and ourselves. Partners in dialogue meet as the common trustees of the one world, eager to listen and to receive, and to respond to the demands of the present context in which we meet. It necessarily involves vulnerability and risk; it means the putting aside of a considerable amount of "cultural baggage", although not the basic confession of the decisiveness of Jesus Christ; it is carried out in the expectation and hope that the Holy Spirit will use the encounter to convert *both* the partners to Jesus Christ, exemplified by the encounter of Peter and Cornelius in Acts 10. Only in this way will the Church fulfil the stewardship to which it is called.[79]

Much of this thought is helpfully summarised in Bishop Newbigin's contribution to the Lux Mundi centenary volume *Keeping the Faith*,[80] entitled *The Christian Faith and the World Religions*. Here he points to the "single global society", anticipated by *A Faith for this One World?*, but acknowledges that the result has been not a single culture but a plural one within a dominant secular materialism, at least in the Western world. Of course the world has always been plural in culture, but he points to the new factor of the widespread acceptance of "pluralism" as an ideology, reflecting a "privatisation" of religious belief with "tolerance" as the chief virtue.[81] Newbigin discusses his whole thinking in relation to the realities of contemporary society in his fullest volume *The Gospel in a Pluralist Society*.[82] In the ensuing chapter we will discuss both the basis for this thinking and its application to secular pluralism, but here we concentrate on his response to the most recent discussions of religious pluralism.

Newbigin recognizes that pluralism is now the "reigning orthodoxy", and any form of exclusivism is rejected as inappropriate to the urgent needs of the global society. What is required is a common commitment to shared "values" which, it is supposed, may be independent of any one tradition. This would provide the focus for unity in response to the nuclear threat and ecological disaster. All this assumes that truth is ultimately unknowable, and for Newbigin it is the final evidence of "cultural

---

78 Newbigin, *Open Secret*, p204.
79 Newbigin, *Open Secret*, pp206-14.
80 Edited by G. Wainwright (SPCK, London, 1989).
81 Wainwright (ed), *Keeping the Faith*, pp312-3.
82 SPCK, London, 1989. The Alexander Robertson Lectures given in Glasgow University 1988.

collapse". Total relativism provides no grounds for any talk of salvation at all; people and communities select their own absolutes, but absolutize merely their own wishful thinking or that of the most powerful factions. His own response underlines the way that this thinking depends on the unproven assumptions of modern western culture: the unknowability of truth; the elevation of the individual above the historic communities of which individuals are part; the appeal to abstract values such as "justice" and "love", without facing the difficult questions of "Whose justice?" and "What kind of love?"[83]

This type of thinking indicates a clear commitment to an ideology of pluralism by many Christian theologians, based on a "soteriocentric" view of "the universe of faiths".[84] Newbigin argues that this is in fact a reversal of the so-called Copernican revolution in theology. What now lies at the centre is the human self and its need for salvation, with no objective reality that can confront that self with the offer of salvation. It is the final step away from the "saving acts of God" to the "religious experience of the individual", and confirms Feuerbach's characterisation of theology as a form of anthropology: "It is the authentic product of a consumer society".[85]

Turning to a Christian response to other religions based on the confession of the Lordship of Christ, Newbigin makes his familiar distinctions: the sharp division between the religious and the secular cannot be maintained; in most societies religion is part of a wider culture or world-view and the whole of this must be seen in relation to Christ; Jesus regularly used the secular world as the basis for his parables and the Johannine prologue (again!) affirms that light shines on every human being whilst the world of religion is often in the deepest darkness. He once more rejects the "strictly exclusivist" view for the reasons which he has already given in his earlier writings. This approach also assumes that the Christian is in a position to know the ultimate fate of the non-Christian, and Newbigin constantly battles against that supposition from whichever quarter it comes. The discussion cannot be conducted around the question of who is to be saved; it is arrogant even to attempt to do so. It falsely removes the soul from the whole context of human history, and the individual from the historical realities of which he is a part.

Once more he notes the influence of Rahner's work, even amongst those who will not accept his main conclusions, and Newbigin comments that the notion that the non-Christian religions are to be understood as vehicles of salvation has become "a sort of orthodoxy and those who are not willing to accept it are dismissed as simply out-of-date".[86] For Newbigin proper discussion of this question must focus on "the amazing grace of God and the appalling sin of the world".[87] These two "poles" create a force field of creative tension at once both demanding and affirming.

---

83 Newbigin, *Gospel in a Pluralist Society*, pp152-66. Bishop Newbigin acknowledges his indebtedness to philosophers such as Michael Polanyi and Alasdair MacIntyre on these issues.

84 The work of John Hick is crucial to this whole discussion, see chapter 3.

85 Newbigin, *Gospel in a Pluralist Society*, p169.

86 Newbigin, *Gospel in a Pluralist Society*, pp173-9.

87 Newbigin, *Gospel in a Pluralist Society*, p175.

Attempts to reduce the tension by moving towards one or other pole lead inevitably to either strict exclusivism or easy universalism. Newbigin argues that the Christian must continue to live within the tension, confessing "the mighty work of grace in Jesus Christ" on which basis he makes this affirmation: "I believe that no person, of whatever kind or creed, is without some witness of God's grace in heart and conscience and reason, and none in whom that grace does not evoke some response – however feeble, fitful, and flawed".[88]

This has four implications. First, Christians must expect and welcome evidence of the grace of God from those outside the household of faith. It means, secondly, an eagerness to co-operate with people of all religions and none, in projects that reflect the saving purposes of God. Thirdly, within this context of mutual commitment, true encounter and dialogue will take place, in which, finally, the Christian will have the opportunity to "tell the story", that is the story of Jesus, the story of the Bible.

Ultimately, of course, the question of truth cannot be avoided:

> As a human race we are on a journey and we need to know the road. It is not true that all roads lead to the top of the same mountain. There are roads which lead over the precipice. In Christ we have been shown the road. We cannot treat that knowledge as a private matter for ourselves. It concerns the whole human family. We do not presume to limit the might and the mercy of God for the ultimate salvation of all people, but the same costly act of revelation and reconciliation which gives us that assurance also requires us to share with our fellow pilgrims the vision that God has given us the route we must follow and the goal to which we must press forward.[89]

7.3 Reaction and Response

Much of the discussion on these issues has been carried on using the categories of "pluralism", "inclusivism" and "exclusivism", and Newbigin's views are generally assigned to the latter category. It is recognized of course, that there are different nuances within these various broad groups, and the critics usually admit that Newbigin offers a more sensitive and developed approach than, for example, did Kraemer. Alan Race, for instance, recognizes that Newbigin genuinely believes in the manifestation of grace, characteristically "the light", in the lives of non-Christians, and indeed that Christians have much to learn in dialogue with people of other faiths and ideologies.[90] However, he detects a tension in this learning process, which for a Christian is one of "obedient witness" as we have seen. Race sees that this is resolved if the learning takes place after the conversion of the partner, but in fact Newbigin suggests that it is through the common experience of judgement before the cross, in which the non-Christian partner may be a channel of conviction of sin for the Christian, that the learning process begins. It is true that in the

---

88 Newbigin, *Gospel in a Pluralist Society*, p175.
89 Newbigin, *Gospel in a Pluralist Society*, p183.
90 Race, *Christians and Religious Pluralism*, p26.

example of Peter and Cornelius, which Newbigin uses on several occasions, Cornelius is converted to Christian faith, but Peter too is changed in the process and so is the entire self-understanding of the Church. Newbigin characterizes this experience as one in which *both* partners are converted more fully to *Christ*.

Gavin D'Costa agrees with Newbigin that the Church is not an invulnerable fortress of truth and cites approvingly his comment that the Holy Spirit may use the non-Christian partner in dialogue to convict the world of sin.[91] He also agrees that Christianity is enriched and fulfilled through its encounter with other faiths and new cultures and again quotes from Newbigin's writing on Christian witness in a multi-faith society.[92] Despite this measure of agreement, D'Costa suggests that "exclusivists", among whom he numbers Kraemer and Newbigin, do not fully consider the implications of their recognition of divine grace and revelation outside of Christianity and the Church. He comments that, "the exclusivists, when they do acknowledge revelation outside Christianity, either deny it any salvific efficacy or tend to minimize the implications of this admission".[93] He suggests, for example, that one implication which they ought to draw is that of the universal salvific will of God. Newbigin has responded to this sort of criticism with his argument that Christian theologians have no grounds to discuss the eternal destiny of other people. He believes that such an approach is patronizing and fails to do justice to the radical differences between the faiths. The centrality of the cross as the symbol of human alienation, means an inability to agree that a universal salvific will of God leads almost automatically to universal salvation, as so often seems to be the implication. If the response is made that not all are automatically saved, only the *bona fide* believers, then he argues that this is just another version of the religion of self-justification of which he is so severely critical.

Paul Knitter, in his important study *No Other Name?* uses a more complex analytical model in which Karl Barth is portrayed as the champion of conservative Evangelicalism, and missionary theologians such as Lesslie Newbigin and Stephen Neill are found in the "Mainline Protestant Model" which includes Brunner, Althaus, Tillich and Pannenberg. In fact, although Newbigin is often associated with Barth, like Kraemer he seems to have many affinities with Brunner who, as we have seen, viewed the Christian revelation as the crisis (or judgement) of religion, rather than simply its end. The main distinction which Knitter draws between the mainline Protestants and the Evangelicals, is the former's willingness to recognize genuine revelation outside the Christian tradition, even though, with the Evangelicals, they affirm salvation only through Christ.[94] From this it is obvious that although Knitter does not use the terminology of exclusivism-inclusivism-pluralism, in fact the soteriological question is a determining factor for his model. We know what Newbigin's response to this is!

---

91 D'Costa, *Theology and Religious Pluralism*, p136.
92 D'Costa, *Theology and Religious Pluralism*, p124.
93 D'Costa, *Theology and Religious Pluralism*, p75.
94 Knitter, *No Other Name?*, pp104-6.

Knitter does recognize the importance of the "happenedness" of the Christ event for the theologians in this category, a point which much of the discussion overlooks, and he helpfully underlines the traditional protestant requirement to be associated with this event by "the word".[95] Knitter himself is unwilling to tie salvation to the Christ event in this way. This discussion raises an important point for Newbigin in the area of soteriology and revelation.

Quite properly Newbigin understands all revelation not simply as propositional, but as the self-communication of God in his grace and sovereign freedom. Given that he believes no human being is without this grace, nor beyond some form of response, however flawed this may be, it implies that, in his terms, all are involved, at least to a minimal extent, in the saving purposes of God. Is it then necessary to have this historical connection with the Christ event? He clearly believes that while salvation is not automatic, it is quite possible for those outside of Christ, to be caught up in God's final purpose of uniting all things in him. It may be that this recognition of the extent of revelation undermines Newbigin's assertion of the centrality of the Christ-event. He argues that the Christ-event provides the objective basis for the receiving of grace and the response of faith, but given that he is prepared to acknowledge both grace and revelation outside the Christian tradition, might this not imply some objective basis, even if not of the unique and decisive nature of Christ, in other strands of the one human story?

A second question raised by this discussion is whether Newbigin's interpretation of the biblical record is not somewhat forced and over-schematic. For example, is the doctrine of election quite as central for the self-understanding of Israel and the Church as he maintains? Certainly it is a key feature, but there are also other voices, such as that of Wisdom, which offer alternative approaches to the tradition. Again, is it fair to interpret all religion by using Paul's interpretation of first century Judaism and his reaction to his own experience of law and grace? It may be that this is not such an all-embracing interpretative key as Newbigin believes.

There is a dialectic in his method, seen for example in his discussion of the tension between the two poles of divine grace and human sin. This has its parallel in the radical discontinuity between the Gospel and the religions, which is yet not a total disjunction. Similarly, it is the Christ-event which is ultimate and decisive rather than Christianity, but that event is only accessible to us through the Church in all its limitations and cultural conditioning. To argue that the Gospel stands in judgement on the Church is true, but then the Gospel itself is necessarily clothed in the cultural assumptions of its time, a condition of its being actual 'event'. Newbigin says that he does not wish to reject the findings of two centuries of biblical scholarship, (although much of its assumptions are based on the post-enlightenment philosophy of which he is so critical). But his appeal to Scripture (most frequently to Paul and the Fourth Gospel) seems to take little account of critical scholarship. He is right to emphasize the decisiveness of Christ as the Christian starting point, but a more fully articulated Christology would help us to

---

95 Knitter, *No Other Name?*, p105

see the implications of Newbigin's confession of Christ's Lordship more clearly. Moreover, while his appeal to history and objectivity is a welcome corrective to over-abstract arguments in recent years, does his understanding of the relationship between the human and the divine pay enough attention to the point that these are two subjects, albeit communicating through objective realities? Is not the element of subjectivity an inescapable aspect of personal being? His recognition of the centrality of subjectivity in human knowing stands in tension with his appeal to the objective "happenedness" of history.

Newbigin's contributions to the debate are always set in the context of culture and society and this contextualization is most welcome and a real strength. But, as we have already noted, the development of his argument has taken place within the shift from *A Faith for this One World* to *The Gospel in a Pluralist Society.*[96] Has this shift been sufficiently noted in the development of the argument? It may well be that his most significant and lasting contributions are the questions that he raises about method and assumptions. His analysis of the basis of the ideology of pluralism is penetrating and fundamental, and his exposition of the questions of epistemology, although technical, is clear and relevant (and this from one who claims to be a pastor not a theologian!). This aspect of his work has not always received the attention nor the response which it deserves. Fuller discussion of this will be reserved to the following chapter on his approach to secular ideologies and his basic methods and procedures, but it seems fair to note at this point that it is his grasp of this range of underlying assumptions that prevents his being classified as neatly as much of the discussion tries to do. Thus he concludes his fullest discussion of religious pluralism in this way:

> The position which I have outlined is exclusivist in the sense that it affirms the unique truth of the revelation in Jesus Christ, but it is not exclusivist in the sense of denying the possibility of the salvation of the non-Christian. It is inclusivist in the sense that it refuses to limit the saving grace of God to the members of the Christian Church, but it rejects the inclusivism which regards the non-Christian religions as vehicles of salvation. It is pluralist in the sense of acknowledging the gracious work of God in the lives of all human beings, but it rejects a pluralism which denies the uniqueness and decisiveness of what God has done in Jesus Christ.[97]

---

96 Cf. Wainwright, *Theological Life* p205
97 Newbigin, *Pluralist Society*, pp182-3.

CHAPTER 8

Newbigin and Secular Approaches to Pluralism

8.1 The Discussion in Outline

In the previous chapter we discussed Bishop Newbigin's response to the issue of religious pluralism, and noted the development of his thinking over a period of some thirty years. The question presented itself to him in two forms: initially in his personal encounter with the Indian world-view during his missionary experience in India; later in his opposition to the pluralist theology of religions which had developed in Western culture over the post-war period. The aim of this chapter is to discuss his analysis of Western culture, which is found, in the main, in his later writings. We may regard this as a new exercise in contextualization for Newbigin the missionary. His return to the European world in 1974 after twenty-seven years as a bishop in the Church of South India, proved to be a considerable culture-shock,[1] and much of his writing after his return to Britain was concerned with a Christian critique of contemporary Western society and its culture.[2] All this was produced over a relatively short period of time, in the context of his relocation into the plural society of Birmingham and the pluralist theology of (especially) John Hick, then H. G. Wood Professor of Theology in the University of Birmingham. After a brief description of the development of his position, we will look more fully at two key aspects of his analysis: the question of history as the sphere of God's activity, and the problem of culture as the medium of human experience of that activity.

It is typical of Newbigin's thinking that although the bulk of his writing in this area was among his most recent, the roots of this work can be traced in some of his very earliest material. For example in his influential book on the nature of the Church, *The Household of God*, he stresses the missionary and eschatological character of the Christian community. This underlines the cosmic nature of the divine purpose, which is concerned with the redemption of the whole human race and the whole created world. It is not about the salvation of individuals abstracted from that context of community which is the very essence of their humanity.[3] Already, in Newbigin's view, questions of history and culture are necessarily at the heart of a Christian concept of salvation. Newbigin was of course well aware of the secularization of Western society before his return to the multi-cultural Britain of the

---

1 See Newbigin's account of this experience in *Unfinished Agenda*, chapter 18, pp239-50, and *The Other Side of 1984* (WCC, Geneva, 1983) pp1-4.

2 The key works are: *The Other Side of 1984* (1983); *Foolishness to the Greeks* (1986); *The Gospel in a Pluralist Society* (1989); *Truth to Tell* (1991).

3 Newbigin, *The Household of Faith*, p99.

nineteen seventies. He tackled the issue directly in his 1964 Firth Lectures given at Nottingham University,[4] in which he distinguished between 'secularization' as a process and 'secularism' as an ideology. He suggested that 'secularization' is a unifying experience for the human race, based on "a shared secular terror and a shared secular hope". The terror referred to the nuclear threat, the hope to common expectations about the future dominated by the concept of 'development', a vogue word the content of which was filled out by goals determined largely by Western economic and industrial needs and values.[5] Newbigin argued that this process of secularization could be understood biblically, for the Bible itself is largely concerned with secular events, interpreting them in line with its view of history as the sphere of the divine activity as well as the human.

In fact, suggested Newbigin, secularization, based as it is on the modern scientific world-view, has its roots in the biblical belief that the world is comprehensible to human beings and susceptible to human reason. The notion of development can likewise be interpreted as a secular version of the biblical hope for a new age and a new order of existence, a secularised form of the Kingdom of God. He follows up the suggestion of A.T. van Leeuwen,[6] that secularization is the process in which the non-western world meets biblical history: the dissolution of the "ontocratic" pattern of society in the non-western world could be viewed as a new phase in the fight of prophetic religion against a totalitarian "sacral" society. Newbigin warns that the new order emerging from the secularization process may be as enslaving as previous patterns of society unless a rediscovery of human responsibility before God is made:

> I suggest that if the mastery which is given to man through the process of secularization is not held within the context of man's responsibility to God, the result will be a new slavery; that if the dynamism of 'development', the drive to a new kind of society, is not informed by the biblical faith concerning the nature of the Kingdom of God it will end in totalitarianism; and that if the secular critique of all established orders is not informed and directed by the knowledge of God it will end in self-destructive nihilism.[7]

Perhaps his later writing can be interpreted as a response to a contemporary situation in which some, at least, of these prophetic words have been fulfilled.

Although secularization could be interpreted and related to a biblical view in this way, Newbigin was critical of contemporary attempts to relate the Gospel and western culture. The influence of existentialism had led to an individualism foreign to the scriptures, and to a flight from history as the place of God's action, reminiscent of the old paganism in its search for a "timeless philosophy" untouched

---

4 L. Newbigin, *Honest Religion for Secular Man* (SCM, London, 1966).

5 See Newbigin's interesting description of this process in modern India, *Honest Religion*, pp14-9.

6 Arendt van Leeuwen, *Christianity in World History* (Edinburgh House Press, London, 1964).

7 Newbigin, *Honest Religion*, pp38-9.

by contingency. He raised the question of the resurrection of Christ as a key issue here, and to this he returns in other presentations of his argument.[8] Newbigin is also critical of those who deny the reality of God over against man, and who regard "God-talk" as expressive of attitude rather than any form of affirmation about 'how things are'. Clearly we are not able to make statements about God in the way that we do with objects open to empirical observation; rather Christian talk of God has the nature of testimony, "confessing that one has been known, loved, called, redeemed by Another whom one only knows because he has so acted".[9] This understanding of the nature of the Christian witness as the personal testimony of the Christian community is one of Newbigin's key insights. Such language is understood by the speaker as an account of reality, not just as an expression of ethical attitudes. Love for God and love for neighbour cannot be equated simply in order that the former may be dispensed with; in the biblical view, the obligation of neighbourliness stems from the existence and nature of God.[10]

Although belief in God has been a fundamental element in the human story, it is no longer part of the 'mental furniture' of secular humanity. But this question, of whether and how we may know God, cannot be tackled apart from an understanding of how we know or believe anything – even at this early point in his thinking the issue of epistemology is crucial for Newbigin.[11] He begins here the development of an epistemology based on the work of Michael Polanyi in *Personal Knowledge*, stressing knowledge as subjective human experience formed within a framework of community. Knowing is an activity of *persons* in *community* involving both *risk* and *commitment*. However important the role of scepticism and doubt, the active principle in the expansion of knowledge is faith, and this is nowhere more true than in our knowledge of persons. To know another person is to recognize another centre of decision beyond our control; to ignore the difference between our knowledge of persons and our knowledge of things, to "use" someone or be "used" by them, is legitimately described as impersonal or even inhuman behaviour. This develops a similar point made in Newbigin's first book, where he writes:

> When I turn from dealing with natural objects to dealing with another person, I am in a quite new world. I am no longer in the position of a subject dealing with objects; I am no longer the single centre of decision and action. I am now in the presence of another subject, another such centre of decision and will, and a centre which is inaccessible to my will in a way that nothing in the natural world can ever be.[12]

---

8 See *Honest Religion*, pp53ff; *Finality of Christ*, pp85-6; *Foolishness to the Greeks*, pp62-3; see below for a fuller discussion.

9 Newbigin, *Honest Religion*, p58.

10 See Newbigin's more detailed presentation of this argument in *Honest Religion*, pp65-76.

11 Newbigin, *Honest Religion*, p79.

12 L. Newbigin, *Christian Freedom in the Modern World* (SCM, London, 1938) p45.

Knowledge of God not only falls within this area of personal knowing – the knowledge of encounter – but points to the profoundly personal character of all our knowing.[13] To this extent all knowledge is subjective and grounded in faith. But faith in God is faith in someone "other than myself", and such knowledge as it brings is partial and depends on the willingness of the other to disclose himself to me, and my willingness to attend and to respond: "The man of faith knows that he does not know, but knows that he is known".[14]

Newbigin reiterated his position in *The Finality of Christ* in two central chapters entitled, "The Gospel as a Secular Announcement" and "The Clue to History". Similar material appeared in *The Open Secret*. His arguments here will be discussed in the following sections, together with his current concerns which have been expressed more recently in books following rapidly one upon the other. The issues were briefly outlined in *The Other Side of 1984*, and followed up more fully in *Foolishness to the Greeks*. Bishop Newbigin's mature thinking is found in its most developed and fully articulated form in his major book *The Gospel in a Pluralist Society*. The particular nature of the truth of the Christian message is examined in *Truth to Tell*. In all this the questions of faith and history, and culture and epistemology are central and to these major areas we now turn in more detail.

8.2 Faith and History

It is virtually impossible to read anything ever written by Lesslie Newbigin without gaining a sense of his feel for history, his awareness of being part of a story, indeed of being caught up in *the* story of the unfolding drama of the purposes of God. One of his major criticisms of post-Enlightenment culture is the elimination of teleology, both in the natural sciences and in the human. He argues that purpose continues to play a vital role in human life; it is in fact "an inescapable element".[15] Such a sense of purpose is central to the thought of the Bible which he defines in terms of access to God's purposes: "I would want to speak of the Bible as that body of literature which – primarily but not only in narrative form – renders accessible to us the character, actions and purposes of God".[16] Such a sense of purpose, human and divine, cannot be privatised to some separate world of values; if it is to retain any meaning at all it must relate to the public world of facts, to nature and to history. His whole argument centres on the conviction that the "scriptural explanation" is the true one; that is, that 'the way things are' has to do with the divine purpose. This Gospel perspective may stand in judgement on post-enlightenment culture just as validly as the assumptions of that culture have

---

13 Newbigin, *Honest Religion*, pp88-9. He goes on (pp88-92) to take issue with John A.T. Robinson's interpretation of knowing God in his well-known book *Honest to God* (SCM, London, 1963) pp43-9, which has clearly influenced Newbigin's own title.
14 Newbigin, *Honest Religion*, p99.
15 Newbigin, *Foolishness to the Greeks*, pp34-5.
16 Newbigin, *Foolishness to the Greeks*, p59.

endeavoured to judge the Gospel over the last two hundred years.[17] This sense of purpose is closely related to an understanding of history as the *locus* of the divine activity in Newbigin's thinking.

He approaches the question on a more personal level in thinking about "revelation in history".[18] He contrasts his own stress on the "happenedness" of the Christ-event, (he has summed up the Gospel as "news about things which have happened"[19]) with the pietist emphasis (from whatever tradition) on a living relationship with God now. If the latter is separate from the nexus of relationship in which human beings exist, it is a false abstraction. On the other hand, involvement means relationship to, and even dependency upon, the contingencies of real life, including that history of which we are a part.

Life for most people in contemporary Western society is lived in terms of cause and effect; God is either a redundant hypothesis, or is relegated to the privatised sphere of religion and morals. Is it still possible to talk meaningfully of divine activity in a world so full of alternative explanations for the way things are? Different scientific disciplines will analyse and explain in varying ways: chemical, physical, sociological and psychological explanations may be equally valid ways of interpreting the same event. But they do not seem to contradict each other in the way that talk of human and divine agency seems to do. Newbigin suggests that we may understand this dichotomy as the difference between external viewpoint and participant observation. The scientific view of cause and effect depends upon an event being closed, completed, past. It may then be analysed and conclusions drawn. But for the participants within an event, the future remains open and real choices must be made: human intention can make a difference in the world of action and event. Newbigin argues that a parallel can be drawn between this and the activity of God in the world. The Christian tradition does not believe that every aspect of the world is an expression of the divine intention, but this may be explained by God's choice to limit his freedom and grant a measure of independence to his creation.

The question then arises as to how we are to discern what reveals the character and purpose of God, and what is its contradiction. Such judgements about meaning must always be made when writing history or telling a story, for material is always selected on the basis of relevance to our understanding of the story. This means that some judgement, however provisional, has already been made as to the significance of what is told. Newbigin argues that the Christian tradition holds that God has made his purpose known through some, and not all, events in human history, and therefore to some, and not all, people of the world – a strong reaffirmation of what is usually known as the scandal of particularity.[20]

As we noted in the previous chapter, it is through the doctrine of election that Newbigin deals with the issue of particularity. This aspect of his thinking has been

---

17 This is the argument of the whole of *Foolishness to the Greeks* and much of *The Gospel in a Pluralist Society*.

18 Newbigin, *Pluralist Society*, chapter 6, pp66-79.

19 Newbigin, *Truth to Tell*, p5.

20 Newbigin, *Pluralist Society*, pp69-72.

the subject of a major study by Dr George R. Hunsberger,[21] where he argues that Newbigin's understanding of the doctrine of election is fundamental to his thought. Important though election undoubtedly is, I want to suggest that it is his concept of *history* that is more basic to Newbigin's position. The doctrine of election is the interpretative key to the resolution of the tension between the Bible as universal history and the problem of particularity. History reveals the purposes of God: election explains how those purposes are brought to completion. As he argued briefly in a short paper contributed to the *festschrift* for Dr E. A. Payne,[22] it is a doctrine of *history* which is "indispensable" for the mission of the Church: there must be some kind of faith about God's intention for the world.[23] But this is precisely what modern thought will not allow. Human origins are a matter of "public truth", taught and discussed in the classroom. Human destiny, however, is perceived to be a matter of private opinion, despite its significance for our understanding of what it means to be human.[24]

The chapter on election in *The Gospel in a Pluralist Society* is the second of four that deal with the overall question of revelation in history and its relation to Scripture and to Christ.[25] The objections which are often raised to the doctrine of election are frequently based on an individualism which is foreign to the biblical world-view, and Newbigin suggests that the doctrine cannot be treated in isolation from the Bible's characteristic understanding of the human situation as relational rather than solitary. Mutual relatedness "is not merely part of the journey towards the goal of salvation, but is intrinsic to the goal itself". He reiterates the argument of *The Open Secret*[26] that revelation is always mediated, coming not directly, 'from above' as we might put it, but indirectly through our neighbour, who is not an interim guide but a partner with whom we enter into salvation. Again he refers to his key text on this issue, Romans 9-11, citing especially 11:32: "For God has consigned all men to disobedience, that he may have mercy upon all" (RSV). Even the elect, in the end, receive salvation through the non-elect according to this divine 'logic of election'. Newbigin believes that, correctly interpreted in this way, election

---

21 "The Missionary Significance of the Biblical Doctrine of Election as a Foundation for a Theology of Cultural Plurality in the Missiology of J.E. Lesslie Newbigin", Princeton Theological Seminary Ph.D. Thesis 1987. I am indebted not only to Dr Hunsberger's study, but especially to his splendid bibliography. Now published as: *Bearing the Witness of the Spirit: Lesslie Newbigin's Theology of Cultural Plurality* (Eerdmans, Grand Rapids, 1998).

22 Newbigin, 'The Church in its World Mission', in L.G. Champion (ed.), *Outlook for Christianity* (Lutterworth Press, London, 1967), pp109ff – the one essay which seems to have escaped Dr Hunsberger's notice, it is unlisted in his bibliography.

23 *Outlook for Christianity*, p118. Note again the close link between history and purpose.

24 Newbigin, *Truth to Tell*, pp24-5.

25 Newbigin, *Pluralist Society*, pp66-115.

26 Newbigin, *Open Secret* pp78-9, and elsewhere.

can be defended against charges of privilege and exclusivism: the grace of God is always sovereign and free.

The cross of Christ exposes the twin realities of human sin and divine grace, but these universal verities are revealed through the particularity of this historical event. Just as the logic of the gospel works from the particular to the universal, so too with the logic of election, which means that:

> [T]his particular body of people who bear the name of Jesus through history, this strange and often absurd company of people so feeble, so foolish, so often fatally compromised with the world, this body with all its contingency and particularity, is the body which has the responsibility of bearing the secret of God's reign through world history.[27]

Newbigin has made the point that what he terms "the logic of election" is parallel to his understanding of the Gospel, 'the logic of salvation' and to this issue we now turn. He has for many years been convinced that Christ is "the clue to history" and his recent chapter of that name[28] is anticipated in his earlier writing, especially in *The Finality of Christ* where he comments that the question of the finality or absoluteness of Jesus Christ must be posed with respect to his meaning for the secular history of humankind.[29] He firmly believes that Christianity is dependent on the history of the Gospel events. *This* history points to the meaning of *all* history. He had already argued that if some form of "Christ concept" could be detached from the figure of Jesus of Nazareth, it would be tantamount to unbelief from the perspective of the Bible: "On the question of whether the word Christ is or is not indissolubly and finally riveted to the name of Jesus hangs the whole issue of life and death for man".[30] It is only through the Christ *event* that the Christ *principle* is decisively revealed, for the Gospel is not merely a narrative vehicle for the presentation of ideas but the activity of God himself within human history.[31] "The Christian faith is a particular way of understanding history as a whole which finds in the story about Jesus its decisive clue".[32] Newbigin is not so naive as to suppose that such an event could be isolated from its interpretation; he is clear that we do not know exactly what Jesus said or did.[33] The point is that the "secret" of the Gospel was communicated to a community which lives its current story in the light of the story about Jesus and in constant dialogue with it, reinterpreting it as situations change. Thus the understanding of God's action in history is always an insight of faith, never one of an unchanging or unquestionable certainty.

---

27 Newbigin, *Pluralist Society*, p87.

28 Newbigin, *Pluralist Society*, chapter 9, pp103ff.

29 Newbigin, *Finality of Christ*, p45.

30 Newbigin, *Faith for this One World?*, p50.

31 Newbigin, 'The Christian Faith and the World Religions', in Wainwright (ed), *Keeping the Faith*, p328.

32 Newbigin, 'The Centrality of Jesus for History', in M. Goulder (ed), *Incarnation and Myth: The Debate Continued* (SCM, London, 1979) p200.

33 Newbigin, *Pluralist Society*, pp94-5.

Nevertheless, Newbigin is convinced of the basic trustworthiness of the gospel record in relation to the "happenedness" of the central events, including the resurrection. For Newbigin the resurrection of Jesus is the crucial issue for Christian faith because it is *the* act of God, *par excellence*. The resurrection is "a fact of history" in the same sense as any other, that is, it calls out from us a judgement of the evidence. To interpret the resurrection as an event only in the inner spiritual journey of the disciples is to privatise it in a way which would make it impossible to affirm the universal Lordship of Christ.[34] The Kingdom of God, present in Christ, is the recognition of the reign of God in the realm of human history, and of that claim upon our lives. In the crucifixion we see man's rejection of that claim, but in the resurrection we see God's pledge that the claim stands and demands a response.[35] A positive response will be conversion experience, not only for the heart and will but also for the mind,[36] for "it has never been possible to fit the resurrection of Jesus into any world-view except a world-view of which it is the basis."[37] To illustrate this point, Newbigin uses the well-known story of Bukharin's address in Kiev during the early years of the Communist revolution in Russia. The battery of rationalist argument against religion, deployed for a whole hour in Bukharin's address, is shattered by the ancient affirmation of the Church spoken by an Orthodox priest, "Christ is risen". The whole assembly rose and proclaimed the response "He is risen indeed!" Such a confession sums up for Newbigin "the total fact of Christ" which requires from humanity a response. To those who respond in faith, "in the name of Jesus" is their only authority.[38] It is the warrant for the Church's mission, the basis of its eschatological hope, and the ground of its understanding of history. The meaning of the story can only be understood from the end, and in "the total fact of Christ", his life and ministry, his death, resurrection and exaltation, the "end" of all things has been decisively disclosed:[39]

> The resurrection of Jesus from the dead is the beginning of a new creation, the work of that same power by which creation itself exists. We can decline to believe it and take it for granted that we have only the old creation to deal with. Or we can believe it and take it as the starting point for a new way of understanding and dealing with the world. Here two mutually incompatible ways of understanding history meet each other.[40]

For the Christian Church, the resurrection of Jesus Christ shapes its entire world-view or "plausibility structure",[41] and calls into question the world-view and

---

34 Newbigin, *Finality of Christ*, p85.
35 Newbigin, *The Other Side of 1984*, pp36-7.
36 Newbigin, *Truth to Tell*, p2.
37 Newbigin, *Honest Religion*, p53.
38 Newbigin, *Faith for This One World?*, pp59-60.
39 A central theme, e.g., *Faith for this One World?*, p98; *Honest Religion*, p49; *Finality of Christ*, pp62-3.
40 Newbigin, *Truth to Tell*, pp11-2.
41 A phrase that Newbigin adopts from Peter Berger – see next section.

plausibility structures of all other societies including contemporary Western culture. According to Newbigin it is precisely the business of the Christian Church to challenge existing plausibility structures in the light of God's revelation of the real meaning of history. In order to do this the Christian community needs to step outside of contemporary culture, indwelling or inhabiting the story which the Bible tells, understanding the world through the text of scripture, just as we understand the world through the body and the senses.[42] This notion of 'in-dwelling' as a mode of knowledge was developed by Polanyi in relation to any systematic interpretation of life, including not only religious but also mathematical and artistic apprehensions of the universe.[43] We do not merely regard the fragments of experience, but look through these clues in order to determine the whole and its significance; we indwell them. The Christian way to do this is as part of that community shaped by the biblical understanding of life, namely the Church.

Any form of rationality or plausibility structure is embodied in a community, and the Christian Church is that community which lives in continuity with the apostolic community which first responded in faith to the story of Jesus. This story is but part of the entire human story which is one – the biblical story and the story of Jesus cannot be 'fenced off' from the rest of life. The Church witnesses that in this particular part of the story it finds the centre and meaning of the whole. This is what Newbigin means by his repeated reference to the Bible as universal history.[44] It is significant that the story is history: it is not just a matter of "this is how things are" (myth), but "this is what happened" (history).

> The Bible does not tell stories which illustrate something true apart from the story. The Bible tells a story which is *the* story, the story of which our human life is a part. It is not that stories are part of human life, but that human life is part of a story. It is not that there are stories which illustrate 'how things are'; it is that we do not begin to understand how things are unless we understand how they were and how they will be.[45]

Newbigin develops with a particular eschatology E.H. Carr's definition of history as a continuing conversation between past and present *about the future*.[46] The shape of the future has been disclosed in Jesus, which is why he is the clue to history. Critical questions are vital because it matters "what really happened", but the believer comes to the critical questions with a fundamental faith-commitment to the Lordship of Christ which radically challenges the critical orthodoxy of contemporary scholarship.

In the end it is not really a question of faith and history but of two faiths, two views of history. In one what finally matters is the individual and the ideal:

---

42 Newbigin, *Pluralist Society*, pp97-8.
43 Polanyi, *Personal Knowledge*, e.g., pp280-3.
44 E.g. *Open Secret*, chapter 7, pp73ff; *Pluralist Society*, chapter 8, pp89ff.
45 Newbigin, *Open Secret*, p92.
146 E.H Carr, *What is History?* (Penguin, London, 1960).

humankind is to be understood in terms of our inner life, our spirituality alone. For Newbigin this is never what the biblical tradition is about. Throughout his work he constantly argues for an understanding of humanity in relation to the world and to history. To reject the significance of history is to reject "the full humanity of man";[47] this is ultimately what is at stake.

Running through this discussion of questions about faith and history have been related questions about culture and epistemology, which are even more fundamental, and it is to these that we must now turn.

8.3 Epistemology and Culture

As we noted briefly in the outline of his position given at the beginning of this chapter, Newbigin is committed to a theory of knowledge based on the influential work of the Hungarian-British scientist and philosopher Michael Polanyi (1891-1976). Polanyi began his scientific career (after initial training in medicine) as a physical chemist and held the chair in that subject at the University of Manchester from 1933-48. He became increasingly disillusioned with the philosophy of science and turned his attention to this area when Manchester University created a special non-teaching post for him as professor of Social Studies, which he held from 1948-58. He gave the Gifford Lectures at Aberdeen in 1951-2 and the result of some nine years work was given in *Personal Knowledge*. In this book he develops an epistemology in reaction to the prevailing positivism and logical formalism of the day which stressed the process of scientific *justification* of ideas rather than the processes of *discovery* which, though possibly of interest, were regarded as mere matters of psychology.[48] By contrast Polanyi believed that intuition and the creative intelligence play a significant part in scientific breakthrough, which theory and justification catch up with at a later stage. (He himself caricatured his position as "shooting first and asking questions afterwards" and apparently voiced this opinion during the *viva voce* examination of his doctoral thesis when some minor discrepancy was pointed out to him![49])

Polanyi's concept of personal knowledge recognizes the involvement of the knower in all acts of understanding. It is not, however, mere subjectivism, since comprehension brings genuine contact with the reality of what is known. This human dimension is not an unfortunate flaw, to be eliminated, since this is logically impossible. Rather it is to be accepted as a vital component of true knowledge. Polanyi believed that modern Western culture is at a turning point in the development of what he termed "post-critical philosophy" similar to that of the Hellenism of the fourth century. Augustine brought the history of Greek philosophy to a close with his recognition of all knowledge as a gift of grace. In our post-

---

47. See his essay 'The Centrality of Jesus for History', p203.

48. See the lengthy article by Stephen E. Toulmin, 'Philosophy of Science' in *Encyclopaedia Britannica* Vol. 16 (1973) pp375-93, esp. pp386-7.

49 Reported by Drusilla Scott, *Everyman Revived: The Common Sense of Michael Polanyi* (Book Guild, Lewes, 1985) pp2 and 4.

Enlightenment culture we must recognize that the Christian heritage has been exhausted in the oxygen of a rediscovered Greek rationalism, and accept once more the role of faith in knowing. Faith or dogma and doubt must be brought back into balance for only in the creative tension of these twin poles is true knowledge possible.[50]

This approach has been described as "romantic anti-rationalism",[51] but this fails to do justice to Polanyi's penetrating discussion of the nature of rationality and his critique of the positivist empiricism which dominated thinking at the time. This aspect of Polanyi's thought, together with the Augustinian analogy have certainly influenced Newbigin's presentation of the argument which he reiterates at some length in both *The Gospel in a Pluralist Society*[52] and in *Truth to Tell*.[53] It was against this same "scientific" secularism that Newbigin also reacted and it is not surprising that Polanyi's thought immediately struck a chord and is mentioned in the first book Newbigin wrote after the publication of *Personal Knowledge*, where he refers to the "creative and imaginative leaps" by which the great scientific advances have been made and argues that reality "is almost by definition that which does not submit to our rules but requires us to submit to its". It is in this context that he talks of faith as the active principle in knowing, for it is by the "leap of faith" that all advances in human understanding are achieved.[54]

Although this area is not a major feature of *The Finality of Christ*, Newbigin does highlight the issue at the outset when, commenting on the question of inter-religious relationships, he remarks that "the real decisions are made at the beginning of the argument not at the end. The decisive question is the question of starting-point".[55] In other words *all* knowledge is based on an ultimate commitment of some sort, which is inevitably a *faith* commitment. It is to this question of the ultimate commitment reflected by Western culture that Newbigin turned his attention most frequently in his later studies.

Post-Enlightenment culture is characterized by a thoroughgoing individualism, focused on the autonomous human person with all his or her attendant rights including, according to the constitution of the United States of America, "the pursuit of happiness". The Enlightenment was the exchange of one set of explanations of "how things are" for another; the promise of heaven was swapped for the pursuit of happiness, to be secured by the emerging nation-states in which the unforgivable sin was now treason.[56]

Despite his radical questioning of the Enlightenment heritage and culture which we share, Newbigin is no mere reactionary; he recognizes that there can be no going back to some form of pre-enlightened innocence. We can only raise the sort of

---

50 Polanyi, *Personal Knowledge*, pp264-8.
51 Toulmin 'Philosophy of Science'.
52 See chapters 1-3.
53 See pp19-33.
54 Newbigin, *Honest Religion*, pp84-6.
55 Newbigin, *Finality of Christ*, p15.
56 Newbigin, *Other Side of 1984*, pp5-15.

fundamental questions which he is wanting to raise, because of battles won during the Enlightenment, against the stifling constrictions of the Church as much as anything else. Not only must we acknowledge our debt but complete the unfinished agenda set for us in the eighteenth century in areas such as true human rights and real freedom for all. Nevertheless, the expectations of the Enlightenment remain largely unfulfilled, and many struggle to find meaning in their existence: the accepted explanations now seem neither acceptable nor explanatory.

Just as the Enlightenment itself emerged out of the disintegration of the old order, at this point in Western culture and history we stand in need of a new framework for the integration of human experience. Newbigin (following Polanyi) argues that what is required is a recognition of the role of dogma in such an enterprise. In the eighteenth century dogmatism was the enemy of reason, the agent of superstition and ignorance. A radical scepticism was needed in order to achieve liberation from the bonds of ignorance and to awaken European culture from its "dogmatic slumbers". Newbigin persuasively develops the Polanyian point that, in the end, doubt is necessarily a secondary feature of the cognitive process; critical questioning can only be done on the basis of at least some unquestioned assumptions. There must first be the act of attending or "receiving" something within our total environment. For Newbigin: "This primal act is an act of faith".[57]

When we try to relate this to our experience the role of doubt becomes vital, or else we are at the mercy of superstition and fancy, but the initial action is one of attention or faith. The Enlightenment saw a fundamental change in the balance between faith and doubt. In fact Polanyi says that one of these two cognitive faculties (faith) was totally repudiated so that the critical mind relied only on the other (doubt), but, he continues, "We must now recognize belief once more as the source of all knowledge".[58] Newbigin affirms this in his most recent discussions of epistemology where he comments, "There is no knowing without believing, and believing is the way to knowing".[59] At this stage Newbigin helpfully develops a point which Polanyi had noted but not expanded, that the exception to this general rule of doubt, was the realm of religion in which faith was recognized as a form of personal conviction, which, however, still fell short of knowledge.[60] Christianity, in accommodating itself to the post-Enlightenment situation, has allowed itself to become privatised, withdrawing from the public realm of "fact" to a world of individual piety and personal morality. Thus the Western Church has fallen into one of the two classic pitfalls of the missionary by accepting post-Enlightenment culture so uncritically that its message can be absorbed without a radical challenge:

> ... contemporary British [and most of western] Christianity is an advanced case of syncretism. The Church has lived so long as a permitted and even privileged

---

57 Newbigin, *Other Side of 1984*, p20
58 Polanyi, *Personal Knowledge*, p266
59 Newbigin, *Pluralist Society*, Chapter 3.
60 Polanyi refers to Locke's *Third Letter on Toleration* where he talks of faith as "persuasion, short of knowledge", *Personal Knowledge*, p266.

minority, accepting relegation to the private sphere in a culture whose public life is controlled by a totally different vision of reality, that it has almost lost the power to address a radical challenge to that vision and therefore to 'modern western civilization' as a whole.[61]

Newbigin has already made the point that the Church exists precisely to confront and question the reigning 'plausibility structures' through the affirmation of the Gospel which provides the Church with a radical alternative vision of "how things are".[62]

Newbigin links Polanyi's notion of fiduciary framework with Peter Berger's concept of plausibility structure,[63] to demonstrate that for all cultures a widely accepted social structure of belief and practice provides the boundaries within which plausibility may be assessed. Berger suggests that for modern Western culture such a framework has broken down and all that is left is private judgement, but Newbigin highlights here the contrast between the public world of so-called facts and the private world of belief. In the world of fact truth is assessed by reference to objective criteria based on the tenets of empirical science; by contrast in the realm of belief only subjective criteria can apply for the truth of beliefs can never ultimately be judged. Here all is opinion, each as valid as the other, and all that can be assessed is the sincerity of the believer.[64]

The root of our secular pluralism is thus revealed, but it is a pluralism only in the world of values and beliefs; in the public world of facts the reigning plausibility structure is an unquestioned acceptance of post-Enlightenment scientific culture. Culture provides the "lenses" through which we view the world; contemporary Western culture provides different sets of lenses with which to view different aspects of our existence. Newbigin is arguing for a new "fiduciary framework", which will overcome this dichotomy between the public and private worlds and restore the teleological element which has been eliminated from so much of secular thinking. Such a move will require a conscious "act of faith", a willingness to accept something as given even when unproven by the tenets of current notions of proof. In other words this would be a return to dogma.

However, Newbigin argues that there would be two safeguards against a return to dogmatism. As Polanyi has shown, and Berger concurs, all such frameworks are held in community. The history of the Church demonstrates there is a constant internal dialogue about the nature of the faith which is held and shared by the community. That dialogue includes regular reference back to the sources of the faith, Scripture and tradition, by which the Christ-event was originally expressed. This internal dialogue provides the first safeguard against dogmatism. The second is found through external dialogue, that is, dialogue with other faith communities, those who hold other

---

61 Newbigin, *Other Side of 1984*, p23.

62 Newbigin, *Pluralist Society*, p8.

63 Berger, *The Heretical Imperative: Contemporary Possibilities of Religious Affirmation* (Collins, London, 1980): "human beliefs and values depend upon specific plausibility structures", p19.

64 Newbigin, *Pluralist Society*, pp14-5.

fiduciary frameworks. Pluralism holds that there will always be a variety of such frameworks and structures that are virtually water-tight and self-contained; they must co-exist in mutual toleration. Newbigin believes that through dialogue between such communities of belief and practice, we may actually reach the point at which all such frameworks are radically challenged. Genuine dialogue entails risk, the risk that may lead to that rejection of one framework and the acceptance of another which in mission is called conversion.[65]

Although the Church with its fiduciary framework is a social and political fact, and a potential challenge to all other frameworks and structures by which society understands and orders itself, Newbigin is clear that he is not pleading for a return to a Constantinian form of society. The name of Church, the *ecclesia Theou*, indicates a self-understanding of this community as the public assembly to which all humanity is summoned by God. But all genuine response must be voluntary. The difficult task for the contemporary Church is to embody Christ's claim to Lordship over all life, without falling into the "Constantinian trap".[66] The regular injunction to the Church to keep out of politics reflects the fundamental dichotomy between public and private worlds which Newbigin has outlined. But to bow to such pressure is to recognize a limit on Christ's Lordship, which is a denial of the Christian gospel. Of course many people are content to regard science and religion as alternative and perhaps complementary ways of understanding the world, but for Newbigin this is never enough, for he is concerned about *reality*. Only if a mystical view of religion is adopted can these two plausibility structures easily co-exist, and this he regards as just another version of privatised religion. The Church "can never accept an ultimate pluralism as a creed even if it must – as of course it must, acknowledge plurality as a fact".[67]

This brings us back to Newbigin's concern for purpose. For in order to understand the true nature of reality, of 'how things are', we must have some view of purpose. Of course it is quite possible to explain the constituent parts of the universe, including human beings, by reference to their function within the whole scheme, but this does not then provide any explanation of the whole. Newbigin develops an analogy first in relation to machines, then with reference to animals, in which lower level explanations, condition the higher level but do not replace them. Description of what is happening is no substitute for understanding, which requires a wider vision of the place of this component within the whole. When it comes to human beings the new element of the possibility of full reciprocity of understanding is introduced. Although partial reciprocity is possible in the relationships between humanity and some animals, full reciprocity is a feature of mature human relationships in which "each tries to communicate to the other his perception of what is the true objective of purposeful action, in other words, of what is good" meaning absolutely good, or good for all.[68] For human beings to enjoy this fully reciprocal relationship, it

---

65 Newbigin, *Other Side of 1984*, p31.
66 Newbigin, *The Other Side of 1984*, pp33-4.
67 Newbigin, *Foolishness to the Greeks*, p115.
68 Newbigin, *Foolishness to the Greeks*, p86.

requires a mutual acknowledgement of 'the good' or something similar by which conflicting purposes are assessed.

In this recognition of "that which is beyond" we reach the limits of the natural theology which Newbigin has been articulating, for no analysis of nature can bring any knowledge of a purpose beyond ourselves, we have come to the limit of inductive reason. That does not mean we can have no further knowledge however, for it may be that we have been addressed from "the beyond", and here we move into the realm of testimony and confession. It is the witness of the Church that in its foundation events, that which Newbigin sums up as 'the total fact of Christ', God has both spoken and acted for and with humanity, his purpose and character have been revealed, and the true nature of reality has been disclosed. God's purpose is thus revealed as fundamental to all that is, and therefore it is impossible for the Christian plausibility structure to co-exist with another from which any sense of teleology has been excluded.

This raises the familiar issue of the relationship between revelation and reason and this Newbigin has discussed in *The Gospel in a Pluralist Society.*[69] It is inappropriate to speak of reason as though it is a source of knowledge to be equated with Scripture and Tradition as the Anglican Communion has often done and which was re-examined for example in the *Festschrift* for R. P. C. Hanson.[70] As Vatican II affirmed, tradition is not a separate source of revelation, but the on-going application of Christian truth to fresh circumstances. Similarly reason is not a source of truth but the faculty by which the various elements of human experience are apprehended and integrated into a coherent whole which makes sense. Reason forms a part of the plausibility structures which Berger has identified, and is therefore culturally conditioned, expressed in the language and thought-forms of particular communities, determined by a heritage of discussion and debate, related to the economic, social and political development of the society of which it is a part. Despite these limitations, Newbigin follows Alasdair MacIntyre,[71] in objecting to the complete relativism which might seem to be the corollary of this view of reason.

MacIntyre attempts to rescue 'virtue' from these nihilistic tendencies through co-operative 'practice', expressing the human capacity for excellence. Although the goals of such activity change, they are carried on within a coherent social tradition, another of MacIntyre's key notions. Through the practice, the tradition itself is constantly renewed and transformed, whilst continuing to belong within the same story. This understanding of a narrative structure to life has clear links with Newbigin's sense of being part of a story, indeed the story, as we have already seen. Modern life stresses the isolation of the individual; MacIntyre looks to traditional communities where co-operative patterns of life persist. As Ross Poole has

---

69 In Chapter 5, 'Reason, Revelation, and Experience', pp52-65.

70 Richard Bauckham and Benjamin Drewery (eds), *Scripture, Tradition and Reason: A Study in the Criteria of Christian Doctrine. Essays in honour of Richard P. C. Hanson* (T & T Clark, Edinburgh, 1988).

71 A. MacIntyre, *Whose Justice? Which Rationality?* (Duckworth, London, 1988) chapters 18 and 19.

suggested,[72] there is an inherent nostalgia to MacIntyre's reasoning at this point which seems to look backwards rather than forwards. The communities which MacIntyre identifies, for example in Irish Catholicism and Orthodox Judaism, have not only resisted external pressure but also internal renewal. Newbigin too has been accused of a nostalgia for the days of Christendom and a return to a Constantinian pattern of society. Clearly there are parallels here and Newbigin is overtly sympathetic to MacIntyre's analysis and solution. For both the essential requirement is to be active within the stream of living tradition, finding meaning and identity and purpose as part of the whole.

Newbigin points out that plausibility structures do change in response to developments in human experience and understanding. Traditions of reason are subject to "the test of adequacy to the realities which it seeks to grasp". Where they are outdated and unconvincing they must change or die. Sometimes the change is slow and keeps pace with the new experience, at other times systems of thought are caught up in a paradigm shift (a favourite Newbigin expression borrowed from the scientific analysis of Thomas Kuhn[73]). Rival systems of rational discourse are subject to the same test: "Which is more adequate for grasping and coping with reality with which all human beings are faced?" All plausibility structures, all forms of rationality, are limited and judged by the reality which they seek to express and make coherent. If the relativist claims that reality is finally unknowable, that is in itself a claim about the nature of reality stemming from a particular cultural context. The context in question is that of western cosmopolitan society where, according to MacIntyre, rootless individuals exist without a firm or stable social tradition.[74] Another root of contemporary pluralism is thus exposed.

Scientific reason relativizes other plausibility structures in the same way that Christianity must relativize scientific reason in the light of the Gospel. But this reason is not a neutral faculty which can arbitrate between these two alternative apprehensions of reality. Lessing's famous ditch disappears because there are no such things as "universal truths of reason", only those apprehensions of reality worked out within a particular historical tradition. All forms of reason, in this wider sense of plausibility structure, including Christianity, are necessarily particular and contingent.

> The true opposition is not between reason and revelation as sources of and criteria for truth. It is between two uses to which reason is put. It may be put to the service of an autonomy which refuses to recognize any other personal reality except its own; which treats all reality as open to the kind of masterful exploration that is appropriate to the world of things, where the appropriate phrase is: 'I discovered'. But it may equally well be put to the service of an openness which is ready to listen to, be challenged and questioned by another personal reality. In neither kind of

---

72 R. Poole, *Morality and Modernity* (Routledge, London, 1991) pp149-50.

173 T. Kuhn, *The Structure of Scientific Revolutions* (University of Chicago Press, Chicago, 1962).

74 MacIntyre, *Whose Justice? Which Rationality?* pp366-9 and 388.

activity can we engage except as rational beings. When reason is set against revelation, the terms of the debate have been radically confused. What is happening is not that reason is set against something that is unreasonable, but that another tradition of rational argument is being set against a tradition of rational argument which takes as its starting point a moment or moments of divine self-revelation and which will therefore naturally continue to say, not 'We discovered,' but 'God spoke and acted.'[75]

8.4 Assessment and Response

We conclude this chapter by attempting some assessment of the strengths and weaknesses of Newbigin's approach to the pluralism of the modern world together with the response of his critics. On the understanding of history his most substantial debate was with the late Professor Maurice Wiles and some indication of the issues at stake is given in the follow-up discussion to *The Myth of God Incarnate*,[76] published as *Incarnation and Myth*[77] to which we have already briefly referred. In an article to which Newbigin drew attention,[78] Wiles asks the question, *In what sense in Christianity a "Historical" Religion?* and argues that the phrase "historical religion" means different things to different people. In any case the verdict of historical research on many of the so-called foundation events of the faith must be "not-proven", and even where we believe that we may be on firm ground there can never be absolute *certainty*. Scriptural accounts are capable of a number of historical reconstructions. Therefore Wiles concludes that there is no reason to isolate certain historical events from the more general historical experience of humanity.[79]

Newbigin suggested that Wiles' approach is typical of post-Enlightenment understanding, which views history as a process of development in which it is impossible to isolate certain events from the broad context in which they occurred. This means that the story is understood from a new centre, as the unfolding of imminent forces within an unbroken chain of cause and effect, from which the possibility of divine intervention is excluded in principle.[80] While Newbigin did not dispute the first of these points, the second, related, point is crucial in that by definition, it excludes the possibility of attributing finality to Jesus in relation to the history of the world. Wiles took a contemporary philosophy of history as his starting point, whereas Newbigin began from the notion of the centrality of Jesus for the understanding of all history.

---

75 Newbigin, *Pluralist Society*, p62.
76 John Hick (ed.) (SCM, London, 1977).
77 Michael Goulder (ed.) (SCM, London, 1979).
78 M. Wiles, 'Christianity a "Historical" Religion?', *Theology* Vol. LXXXI No. 679 (January 1978), pp4-14.
79 Wiles, 'Christianity a "Historical" Religion?', p12.
80 Newbigin, *Incarnation and Myth*, pp199-200.

In direct response to Wiles' conclusion, Newbigin argued that "general historical experience" can only be grasped through specific and particular historical experiences which provide insight or clues to the meaning of the whole. Some events are significant in that they change the course of the story, not just the way human beings think about the story. Newbigin characteristically stressed the importance of events as part of the public life and history of the world, and constantly fought any attempt to 'privatise' significance and importance to the 'inner' world of the soul. What we are is to be seen in what we do, and the community of which we are a part. Thus "In the end it is the question whether the shared public life of mankind has a place in the ultimate purpose of God, whether 'salvation' refers to the destiny of a soul conceived as an entity apart from the total human person, or to the destiny of the human person considered realistically as part of history and nature."[81] The key word here is *realistically* for it underlines Newbigin's antipathy to any form of idealism and highlights his own understanding of anthropology which is expressed in his relational soteriology.

Wiles challenged Newbigin on two main areas: first he wants to know why there must be *one* event of a different order of decisiveness, when frequently we come to an understanding through a *series* of clues. Following from this he challenged Newbigin's "extreme and exclusive insistence on Jesus as the source of any true knowledge of God as a narrowing and distorting perspective" which destroys any possibility of continuity between Jesus and the faith of Israel, let alone between Jesus and other faiths.[82] In the last chapter, however, we argued that Newbigin believes in a radical but not a *total* discontinuity between Christ and religion. We should also note that positions similar to that of Newbigin have their defenders amongst the leading theologians, and although he does not himself make the link, much of what Newbigin says can be paralleled in the work of Pannenberg, for example. The whole notion of revelation *as* history is close to what Newbigin was trying to argue.[83]

Pannenberg's argument at least partly answers the first criticism of Wiles, as to why there must be only one event of real decisiveness: "A multiplicity of revelations implies a discrediting of any particular revelation, for then the form of the divine manifestation is no longer the singularly adequate expression of the revealer".[84] It was in response to the difficulty of this area that Pannenberg formulated his theory of "indirect self-revelation" as a reflex of the divine activity in history. The self-revelation of God to which the Scriptures bear witness, is indirect, brought about through God's action in history, but this revelation will be comprehended only at the

---

81 Newbigin, *Incarnation and Myth*, p205.
82 Wiles, 'Christianity a "Historical" Religion?', pp211-2.
83 The allusion is of course to the seminal work of the Pannenberg 'group' *Offenbarung Als Geschichte*, W. Pannenberg (ed.) (Vandenhoek & Ruprecht, Göttingen, 1961, rev. edn, 1965), E.T. *Revelation as History* (Sheed and Ward, London, 1965). All references to this English edition.
84 Pannenberg, *Revelation as History*, p6.

end of history, and history receives its unity only from this goal.[85] There are clear parallels here with Newbigin's focus on "universal history", with its indirect revelation and cosmic purpose, and it is interesting to note that for Pannenberg as well as Newbigin, this is closely tied up with Jesus' death and resurrection: "it is only in view of the end [of history] that we can say that God has proved himself in the fate of Jesus as the one true God ... in the fate of Jesus as the anticipation of the end of all history, God is revealed as the one God of all mankind ..."[86] It is only in the light of the resurrection that we are in a position to judge the truth of Jesus' claim to be the agent of God's purpose: it is a claim made directly only for his message, his proclamation of the Kingdom, but indirectly the claim is for himself as proclaimer of the message, the personal embodiment of the Kingdom. This claim "is supported by the realisation of eschatological salvation in his own resurrection from the dead".[87]

Like Newbigin, Pannenberg is not satisfied with a merely subjective account of the resurrection such as that offered by Bultmann for example. He too traces the roots of this line of argument to a Kantian division between facts and significance, but what is required is a reinstatement of the unity between fact and meaning. In relation to Jesus and the resurrection this means that:

> Jesus of Nazareth is the final revelation of God because the End of history has appeared in him. It did so both in his eschatological message and in his resurrection from the dead. However, he can be understood to be God's final revelation only in connection with the whole of history as mediated by the whole history of Israel. He is God's revelation in the fact that all history receives its due light from him.[88]

Again we see support for a Newbigin-like linking of the particular with the universal, based on what Braaten has called "a radically realistic doctrine of the resurrection".[89]

Such realism is characteristic of Newbigin, especially in his discussion of the resurrection as an event in public history. Like Pannenberg, Newbigin leaves himself open to the criticism of William Hamilton that all that is required is correct historical technique to discover God in history, and any technique which fails to find God is, by definition, inadequate. Hamilton labelled such a view "justification by method".[90] Clearly there is a real danger here that just as contemporary historiography must exclude God, the Newbigin-Pannenberg approach will

85 Pannenberg, *Revelation as History*, p133.

86 Pannenberg, *Revelation as History*, p134.

87 Pannenberg, 'The Revelation of God in Jesus of Nazareth', in James M. Robinson and John B. Cobb Jr. (eds), *New Frontiers in Christian Theology. Vol. III: Theology as History* (Harper & Row, New York, 1967) p116. See also Pannenberg, *Jesus God and Man* (SCM, London, 1963) chapter 3.

88 Pannenberg, 'The Revelation of God in Jesus of Nazareth', p125.

89 Carl. E. Braaten (ed.), *New Directions in Theology Today. Vol. 2: History and Hermeneutics* (Lutterworth Press, London, 1968) p31.

90 Hamilton in Braaten (ed.), *History and Hermeneutics,* pp180-7.

inevitably discover him. But both Pannenberg and Newbigin recognize that they are speaking "from faith to faith", and what Newbigin in particular is trying to establish is that critical scholarship does precisely the same within the plausibility structure of modern Western culture.

Wiles' second criticism of Newbigin on the question of continuity can also be paralleled in Pannenberg, who argues that the decisive message of Jesus was anticipated in the faith of Israel, albeit inadequately. God "was not known aright"; otherwise the message of Jesus would not have been rejected. Nevertheless, through the Christian mission the Gentile world was enabled to recognize the God of Israel as the one true God. Although Pannenberg does not use the language of election it is clear that this is essentially what is argued by Newbigin through his use of the doctrine of election, and the key passage of Romans 9-11 is also reflected in Pannenberg's discussion.[91] Likewise Pannenberg makes a similar point to Newbigin when emphasizing that humans as contingent, finite beings, can only approach God through the world of finitude. Particularity is inevitable, with its inherent danger of distortion and misunderstanding, but that is all there is:

> Through the veil of the finite, men become aware of the infinite God. Therefore their perspective is always one-sided and distorted. But at the end of the veiled way revelation from God can occur, the self-unveiling of the God already provisionally known through all the obscurities of the veiling.[92]

Human beings, mortals as they are, constantly attempt to "finitize" God, and this process is frequently reflected in the religions. But for Pannenberg, God is essentially "the future God" who makes himself known proleptically in Jesus: "who or what God is becomes defined only by the Christ event".[93]

Both Pannenberg and Newbigin affirm this particularity and radical discontinuity, despite Wiles' misgivings. But both recognize that total discontinuity would be impossible and itself undermine the central doctrine of the incarnation. The hermeneutical and missionary task remains to unfold the meaning inherent in the revelatory events in the language and culture of the hearer; that is within the framework provided by the context of history and tradition. Such a process is always open to new insights, because the God who has revealed himself, unveils himself as that kind of God, finally to be known only in that future to which he is working.[94]

This leads from questions of faith and history to those of faith and culture, especially epistemology, which Newbigin posed most sharply for Western society. In his moving personal tribute to Bishop Newbigin in the *International Review of*

---

91 Pannenberg, 'The Revelation of God in Jesus of Nazareth', pp104-9.

92 Pannenberg, 'The Revelation of God in Jesus of Nazareth', p118.

93 Pannenberg, *Jesus: God and Man*, pp130-1; see also the discussion by Knitter, *No Other Name?* pp97-108.

94 Pannenberg, 'The Revelation of God in Jesus of Nazareth', pp128-31; cf. Newbigin, *Open Secret*, p95; *Foolishness to the Greeks,* pp62-3; *Pluralist Society*, p78, pp114-5.

Mission published following Newbigin's eightieth birthday in December 1989, Bernard Thoroughgood gently makes a significant point about the shock of returning to the "family home" only to discover that the "body-building foods" of Newbigin's youth (for example Farmer, Barth, Kraemer and others), are dismissed and undervalued. But, warns Thoroughgood:

> There is a risk of over-reaction. In seeking to discover the missionary approach and the language in which to commend Jesus Christ, we may see all the negative aspects of western culture and therefore the over-against-ness of the biblical revelation rather than those positive elements which carry forward the healing and reconciling work of Christ.[95]

David Stowe also made this point in a dialogue with Newbigin in the *International Bulletin of Missionary Research.* Stowe argued that: "Newbigin appears to ignore major positive elements of Western modernity that are intrinsic to its sensibility and spirit".[96] He suggests as examples of such oversight, the modern emphasis on democratic consensus, and the humanist consensus that governments and social systems are for persons rather than *vice versa.* Certainly Newbigin's critique of post-Enlightenment culture is as pointed as his rejection of religions as potential means of salvation, but there he does at least leave open the possibility that *other* aspects of non-Christian society may prove to be channels for "the light which lightens everyone"; a possibility which, as Thoroughgood and Stowe suggest, he seemed to overlook in contemporary Western culture.

In response to such criticism Newbigin affirmed that he was indeed grateful to God for the good things in modern culture, but was equally convinced that Western society is based on the fallacy that there can be human self-fulfilment apart from the creator God who made us. He rejected Stowe's process approach, which begins from the concept of creativity, rather than from the self-revelation of the Creator in his "costly act of reconciliation through the cross".[97] Newbigin conceded that this will not now be widely accepted as public truth, in the sense that it will gradually prevail in the course of reasoned dialogue to win the assent of all reasonable people. But the Church still has the responsibility to proclaim it publicly as that which is true for all, the vital clue to that universal history of which every human life is a part.

It is this understanding of public truth which Newbigin identified as the crucial difference between himself and Stowe, and which played such a central role in the "Gospel and Culture" movement, initiated by Newbigin's energy and vision. We may see a development of such ideas in *Truth to Tell: The Gospel as Public Truth,* where he argued for a distinction between agnostic and committed pluralism. The former believes that truth is unknowable; there are no criteria available by which to discriminate between the varied and conflicting truth claims of our modern plural society. What is required is toleration and freedom for all. Committed pluralism, on

---

95 *IRM*, Vol. LXXVIX (No. 313 (January 1990) p78.
96 *IBMR* Vol. 12 No.4 (October 1988) p148.
97 *IBMR* Vol. 12 No.4 (October 1988) pp152-3.

the other hand, whilst recognizing that "full apprehension is always beyond us" does not abdicate the human responsibility of the search for greater and deeper truth. Building on Polanyi's notion of the republic of science (a living community of interpretation in the MacIntyre mould), Newbigin argued that fundamental truth ought to be held and debated in common. Differing opinions should not be left to co-exist in some pluralist suspension, but brought together, tested and debated and resolved as in the scientific community.

Newbigin was convinced that there is a reality to be grasped, if always partially and provisionally.[98] This would lead to the development of a truly free society, for freedom requires a grasp of truth; freedom does not necessarily mean truth, but truth always brings freedom.

Freedom through truth is true freedom, not mere anarchy or randomness. Such a grasp of truth is the only alternative to the inevitable decay expressed in the Second Law of Thermodynamics, in which nature's ultimate word is death. The Christian faith "is that the cosmos is created by the word of God, and that word is continually active in the whole of the cosmos to renew and to create out of decay new patterns of order, to raise the body of Jesus from death to a new creation in glory, to renew the face of the earth and to renew the whole life of humanity".[99] For Newbigin, truth is inevitably and ultimately Christological.

Charles C. West identified this point in his summation of the Newbigin-Stowe discussion.[100] He suggests that what Stowe advocates is a logos-Christology based on Whiteheadian idealism, which stands in contrast to the *Christus Victor* figure of Newbigin's crisis theology. West comments, "It is wrong to set Christ the logos in opposition to Christ the crucified or to exalt one without the other, but I would have to confess that faith begins with the event in history, the word made flesh, where God took hold and redeemed the whole rebellious structure of God's sinful creation".[101] He thus endorses the basic point that Newbigin is making and argues that only this approach is adequate to undergird the mission of the Church. But he goes on to say that it would be helpful to see more clearly how biblical reference and the person of Christ inform his analysis. Newbigin's biblical reference, through his understanding of history and election seem clear enough, but as I suggested earlier, a more developed, or perhaps a more fully articulated Christology, would provide a firmer grounding for his approach.

A related question is whether Newbigin pays sufficient attention to a theology of the Holy Spirit, at least in any explicit way. This may seem a strange point to make of the one who first introduced a Pentecostal model of the Church to stand alongside the categories of Catholic and Protestant.[102] But the question centres not upon the role of the Spirit within the Christian community, but upon the divine activity in

---

98 Newbigin, *Truth to Tell*, pp56-8.

99 Newbigin, *Truth to Tell*, p63.

100 *IBMR* Vol. 12 No.4 (October 1988) pp153-6.

101 C. C. West, 'Mission to the West: A Dialogue with Stowe and Newbigin', *IBMR* Vol. 12 No.4 (October 1988) p154.

102 In *The Household of God*.

the world as a whole. He began to tackle both of these issues in *The Open Secret* with his Trinitarian model for mission, but paid less attention to them subsequently.[103] However, as we have seen both in this chapter and the last, Newbigin was sure that human history is the sphere of divine action, and that this activity cannot be restricted to the realm of some biblical or "sacred history". Rather the unfolding of the biblical drama reveals the divine involvement in *all* history. The question which he avoids is how the biblical material enables us to identify the divine action beyond the Judaeo-Christian tradition.

Lamin Sanneh, in a thorough discussion of the issues raised by *The Gospel in a Pluralist Society*, also wonders whether the analogy with rationality is not pressed too far and assumes too large a role in Newbigin's apologetic. He feels a similar unease to that which we expressed over Newbigin's use of the concept of election at the conclusion of the previous chapter: it might almost become "the rule by which faith acquits itself"[104] – a recurrence of justification by method? Although conceding Newbigin's Polanyian understanding of epistemology as fundamentally an act of faith, Sanneh points out that this leaves us with a dilemma over Newbigin's main plank of the resurrection of Christ. If there is no knowing without believing, "the disciples could not have known the empty tomb existed without a predisposition to belief".[105] Sanneh is keen to argue that the analytical reasoning which Newbigin uses so competently himself, and which figured so largely in his later analogies, in fact has a subordinate role in matters of faith and religion which often operate on different, but no less important levels. As should be apparent from our discussion above, the main point of Newbigin's analogies is not to suggest that faith operates like scientific knowledge, rather he argues that such so-called factual knowledge is also built on assumptions or acts of faith and personal commitment in exactly the same way as religious belief is grounded; nevertheless, the dilemma about the resurrection identified by Sanneh remains.

Stowe, in the article already cited, accused Newbigin of a "shallow scientism" that is "a distortion of true science", which, for Stowe, is "an imaginative *search*, a quest that is spiritual",[106] but this seems far too idealistic a portrayal of the reality of science encountered by most people. Newbigin denied that he was attacking science; rather he wanted to argue the case for the Gospel on the same basis as the scientist defends his theories "with universal intent" – a phrase borrowed from Polanyi.[107] This is what underlies Newbigin's appeal to public truth. Furthermore, if some truth be granted to Stowe's allegation, the point is that it is such a view of science that

---

103 Newbigin, *Open Secret*, chapter 5 'Sharing the Life of the Son: Mission as Love in Action', and chapter 6, 'Bearing the Witness of the Spirit: Mission as Hope in Action'. How significant is it that the latter is one of the shortest chapters in the book?

104 'Particularity, Pluralism and Commitment', review article by Lamin Sanneh in *The Christian CENTURY* (January 31 1990) p103.

105 Sanneh, 'Particularity, Pluralism and Commitment', p104.

106 West, 'Mission to the West: A Dialogue with Stowe and Newbigin', p149.

107 West, 'Mission to the West: A Dialogue with Stowe and Newbigin', p151.

lies beneath much of popular culture in the West,[108] and it is this prevailing culture of which Newbigin provides so searching a critique.

Is it, however, a critique that is fully justified? In his book *Revelation and Reconciliation*,[109] Stephen Williams argues that Newbigin's approach is too narrowly based on the issue of epistemology and revelation, and ignores broader moral questions raised during the eighteenth century, even though he acknowledges his debt to Charles Cochrane's *Christianity and Classical Culture*,[110] in which the moral realm of the will is more important than the intellectual realm of knowledge.[111] Williams argues that neither Newbigin nor Polanyi give an adequate account of Locke who in fact recognises broader approaches to the relation of faith and knowledge.[112] What we have is a falsely weighted presentation of the Enlightenment.

Finally, given that many of these questions began to be formed for Newbigin as a result of living in two cultures, the Indian and the Western, expressed in different languages and thought-forms, it is a pity that he does not address in more detail the questions raised by George Lindbeck in his influential book *The Nature of Doctrine*.[113] Lindbeck articulates an alternative approach to doctrine as neither propositional in the classical sense, nor experiential-expressivist on the other, but cultural-linguistic, a grammar learned within a particular historical, cultural and linguistic context. Although Lindbeck's recognition of the cultural-linguistic context of all human reasoning and discussion has clear affinities with Newbigin's approach, it also implies a relativism with which, one suspects, Newbigin would have been uncomfortable, even though Lindbeck specifically rejects assumptions about a common core of human religious experience which the various faiths articulate differently. Instead he views them as "cultural-linguistic systems within which potentialities can be actualised and realities explored that are not within the direct purview of the peoples of Messianic witness, but that are nevertheless God-willed and God-approved anticipations of aspects of the coming kingdom".[114]

Newbigin's concern for cultural context stems always from his missionary motivation: "True contextualization happens when there is a community which lives faithfully by the gospel and in that same costly identification with people in their real situations as we see in the earthly ministry of Jesus".[115] When he is criticized for conducting the discussion at too theoretical a level[116], this context should be borne in

---

108 This was certainly the author's own experience in ten years of teaching religion to teenagers whose common assumption was that 'science has "disproved" religion'.
109 Cambridge University Press, Cambridge, 1995.
110 Clarendon Press, Oxford, 1940.
111 Williams, *Revelation and Reconciliation*, p5.
112 Williams, *Revelation and Reconciliation*, p27.
113 SPCK, London, 1984.
114 Lindbeck, *The Nature of Doctrine*, pp54-5.
115 Newbigin, *Pluralist Society*, p154.
116 E.g. in a discussion of *Foolishness to the Greeks*, *Expository Times* Vol. 98 No.3 (December 1986) pp65-6, 'Talking Points from Books'; a similar point was made in

mind. Perhaps a more telling question is whether his whole approach assumes "a highly idealized Church",[117] but from his earliest days he has retained and devoted his life to a high view of that community which reflects his high estimate of her Lord. This raises an important question. Given the decisiveness of Christology for this whole discussion, ultimately it is true of Newbigin, as it was of Kraemer, that he never articulates fully the detailed Christology which is required. The emphasis is always on event, especially the Cross and Resurrection, but the content of the Person revealed in times the events, and the implications for the mission of the Church, are not adequately addressed. What sort of a Christ do we see in all this? We miss the sort of wrestling with the issue of "Jesus and the Hindu" or "Jesus and the secularised westerner" that we discovered in Cragg's discussion of "Jesus and the Muslim" and "Muhammad and the Christian". As Wainwright points out this engagement is more fully reflected in Newbigin's biographical material but scarcely features in his analytical work.[118]

Newbigin is forced to admit the activity of grace and the self-revelation of God beyond the sphere of the "household of faith", but one feels with D'Costa that he never came to terms with the implications of this admission. Strangely, despite his affection for John 1:9 and the "light which enlightens all people", he never developed either a Logos Christology or a doctrine of the Spirit which might connect the Christ event with the recognition of God's universal self-revelation in so many channels of human life. Rather Newbigin seems always to be looking for a single key to unlock the questions that he faces; the doctrine of election, the negative view of religion, epistemology and the enlightenment, all serve similar functions in providing a single interpretive approach to complex multi-faceted phenomena. They make for clarity and consistency, yet in the end leave one both grateful for the insights given, but dissatisfied with the conclusions reached. Christology and Ecclesiology cannot be separated as radically as the Kraemer-Newbigin missiological tradition might suggest. Perhaps what is important is that the priority lies with a Christology determined by the crucified and risen Christ. In Part Four, therefore, we turn therefore to some key Christological discussions.

---

conversation to the present author by a local minister, also about *Foolishness to the Greek*.

117 *Expository Times* Vol. 98 No.3 (December 1986) p66.

118 Wainwright, *Theological Life*, pp205ff.

Part 4

Developing a Missiology for a Plural Society

Having examined in some detail the perspectives of Bishops Cragg and Newbigin in relation to pluralism and mission, we must now consider what their approaches might contribute to the current debate, and whether in drawing together the two main strands of missiological reflection on inter-faith relationships, the notion of fulfilment might provide a model which is both adequate to contemporary needs and true to Christian tradition in holding together the elements of continuity and discontinuity. The first section of this conclusion will ask what Christological affirmations are appropriate to this discussion. The second will focus more specifically on the biblical concepts of "fullness" and "fulfilment", and the third will outline a dialogical approach to mission in the light of the contributions that Cragg and Newbigin have made.

CHAPTER 9

Christology and Inter-Faith Relations

Central to much of the discussion thus far is a recognition that Christology is of vital importance in this debate. As John Robinson put it, "The fundamental affirmation of Christianity is that in Jesus is to be seen the clue to the mystery of the Christ – of what the divine process is about and what the meaning of human existence is."[1] In the encounter with Jesus, Christians claim that we are meeting the holy, God is present and active confronting us and challenging us to make an existential choice; Christ calls us to respond, making an affirmation about what we believe the universe to be about and how human life fits in to the pattern. Christians claim to have seen in Jesus not only the meaning of true human existence, but also the key to the way the world is. Such affirmations lie close to the heart of Christian relationships with people of other faiths. Christology is not in the end only about the person and work of Jesus Christ, but is actually an expression of fundamental Christian insights into the nature of God and the world. These insights have usually been expressed in the language of incarnation in an attempt to convey both the human and cosmic dimensions in the life and work of Jesus. The classical Christologies, in responding to this encounter with the divine in Christ have worked "from above", that is they began with what was known, or rather believed, about God and tried to relate that to the human situation as then understood. Most modern writers now reject the possibility of starting "from above" in order to decide how the divine became human; rather it is a question of starting "from below" to see how this human being may be spoken of as divine.

Contemporary people regard this world as real in a sense which Hellenistic thought did not allow. For this reason traditional Christologies always have a docetic feel about them for the modern age. Certain doctrines, originally intended to affirm the genuine humanity of Christ whilst at the same time preserving his divine attributes, tend to reinforce this "latent docetism". Clear examples would be the virginal conception of Jesus and the perpetual virginity of Mary. Leaving aside historical considerations (for there is little historical evidence here), the theological points made by such doctrines tend to militate against the reality of Jesus' humanity. For the early Fathers, Christ was human if he had what they believed to be the constituents of other human beings. For modern thought it is not enough to "possess" the correct components, one must also be the product of the processes of

---

1 J.A.T Robinson, *The Human Face of God* (SCM, London, 1973) p10.

the world and its nexus of relationships. Without this Christ may be *like* us, but not one *of* us: "a genuine man can only come out of the process and not into it."[2]

For the same reason the doctrine of the pre-existence of Christ is also seen as a threat to the humanity of Jesus, no longer credible to modernity if it implies a break in the continuity of existence. The traditional doctrine of the sinlessness of Christ, a function of soteriology, has also reinforced the "latent docetism" of traditional views, together with the notion of Jesus as representative Man, true humanity *par excellence*. As Baillie put it: "it is nonsense to say that he is 'Man' unless we mean that he is a man."[3] Such discussion brings us to the heart of the Christological issue, recognizing the tension that Christianity both affirms the identity and continuity of Jesus with the rest of humanity, but at the same time affirms difference and discontinuity. Stephen Sykes remarks that "Christology cannot function at all unless some statements are made which indicate a *special* activity of God in Christ;"[4] but such activity cannot remove Christ from the human realm, for if it did the human condition would remain unchanged. Therefore, "The humanity of Christ, however conceived, contains elements of continuity with all other human beings. But I can see no a priori reason for supposing that the humanity of Christ may not itself contain genuine elements of novelty; and it these novel elements which provide us with the factual reasons for embarking upon Christology at all."[5] In other words, whatever we may say about the common humanity of Jesus, it is his distinctiveness, which leads us to talk of his divinity. The danger of such a position is that it may lead to some form of Antiochene division in which the various sayings and events of Jesus' life are attributed to his humanity, where we identify with them, or his divinity where we see them as novel, leading to a "triple-decker" model of God, Christ and Jesus, descending from divinity to humanity. Robinson verges on this when he says of Jesus, "he is the clue to the mystery of Christ in the same way that the Christ is the clue to the mystery of God."[6] This would seem to lead, not to the "human face of God", but to the "human face of Christ" who is in turn the "superhuman face of God". Robinson seems here to fall into the trap, of which he warns others, of thinking of the Word (or the Christ) as "a being" rather than as an expression of Divine Being.

Among others, Maurice Wiles and John Hick suggest that the problem lies in a confusion of language when we attempt to speak of incarnation of the divine in human life. Language about "pre-existence", for example, does not give expression to a hypothesis about the ontological relationship of the divine and human in Jesus

2 Robinson, *Human Face*, p37.

3 D. Baillie, *God was in Christ* (Faber, London, 1956) p87.

4 S.W. Sykes, "The theology of the humanity of Christ", in S. Sykes and J. Clayton (ed), *Christ, Faith and History* (CUP, Cambridge, 1972) pp59-60.

5 Sykes, "The theology of the humanity of Christ", p65.

6 Robinson, *Human Face*, p11.

Christ, but is rather a poetic image designed to evoke the response of faith. In other words we are dealing with the language of "myth".[7] Wiles' argues:

> There are many things to be said which give grounds for seeing the life and death of Jesus as part of the human story which is of unique significance in relation to seeing the human story as a whole, as a true story of divine redemption at work. To ask for some further ontological justification of that vision would be to succumb to the category mistake of confusing the human historical story with the divine mythological story.[8]

But there must be *some* connection between the human history and the divine myth for the story of Jesus to possess this "unique significance". As Robinson notes, "that of which the interpretation is the interpretation must have sufficient validity in the man-language series if the God-talk is to be credible."[9] This connection between "human-language" and "God-talk" is linked to the experience of redemption. In John Knox's words: "The uniqueness of Jesus was the absoluteness of what God did in him."[10] It is not, as some theories of atonement would have it, that God is so moved by the death of Jesus that he is persuaded to avert his wrath, but that God is personally involved in this death as an expression of his limitless love for his creation. John Hick affirms this, not in the traditional language of "substance", but in terms of Jesus' and God's common agapé. Jesus was conscious that "in this agapé he was at one with God himself, so that in his actions God's agapé was enacting itself".[11] Thus, for Hick, Christological language is essentially functional, and as such more truly reflects the Hebraic thought forms of the first Christian communities. Similarly Robinson suggests that Christ *does* what God *does* and therefore he *was* "God for us".[12] In such views Jesus shares with the rest of humanity a continuity of being; ontologically he is human. But he shares with God a continuity of event; functionally he is divine.

Such a scheme commends itself for a number of reasons. It takes seriously contemporary understandings of what it means to be human, yet at the same time takes seriously the biblical witness that in the events of the life, death and resurrection of Jesus, people were confronted with the activity of God. If the concept of divine immanence is given its due weight, then we can say that through the processes of the world the life of Jesus emerges as the fulfilment of the divine purpose and initiative: less incarnation from without, more irruption from within, which is arguably equally compatible with the notion that the "Word became flesh".

---

7 "Myth" here is used in a technical sense to mean a way of communicating a theological, metaphysical or mystical reality in language which is ahistorical rather than nonhistorical.

8 Wiles, "Does Christology rest on a mistake?" in Sykes and Clayton (eds), *Christ, Faith and History*, p11.

9 Robinson, *Human Face*, p119.

10 J. Knox, *The Death of Christ* (Collins, London, 1959) p125.

11 Hick, *God and the Universe of Faiths*, p163.

12 Robinson, *Human Face*, p179.

This is particularly reflected in the Johannine tradition with its emphasis on unity of will and purpose between the Father and the Son, which C.F.D. Moule characterizes, in somewhat Rahnerian language, as "perfection of response". He suggests that here lies the resolution of the paradox of Jesus' continuity and discontinuity. In him we see "a perfection such that the result is seen and experienced as a new and creative event, rather than merely a better example than anything that had gone before".[13]

But does such a functional view take sufficiently seriously the link between person and work, being and function? Is it not the case that what a person *does* reveals what they *are*, in their very being? John Macquarrie makes the point well: "The question is really whether a human being can be reduced to a collection of roles or functions, or whether there is not also a person who is the centre and subject of these roles or functions".[14] Moreover is a merely functional view adequate to the Christian understanding that what happens in "the Christ event" is not simply something new in human experience, but also in the experience of God? As H.D. Lewis expresses it, God "had the experiences of Jesus, in fully human form, had them and yet without ceasing to be God, infinite in wisdom and majesty".[15] In the end the manner of Jesus' living (and his dying and rising) forces us to ask questions about his being, "because Jesus is constrained by the coming rule of God and talks about it in his parables, while at the same time his life is itself a striking parable of it, we cannot avoid the question: 'who is he?'"[16]

Wolfhart Pannenberg and Karl Rahner both recognize that Christology must start "from below", but this does not for them restrict the theological enterprise to functional statements only. Pannenberg argues for the "revelational presence" of God in Christ, recognising that revelation, properly understood, is never simply propositional, but is indeed self-disclosure. The Revealer and what is revealed are identical, the medium is not alien to God and therefore: "Jesus belongs to the definition of God, thus to his divinity, to his essence",[17] Rahner comments: "the 'function' of Jesus reveals his 'essence'".[18] Likewise Edward Schillebeeckx argues that "if there is a unique universality in Jesus, it must lie in Jesus' actual being-as-man, not behind or above it. The form of God's revelation is the man Jesus. Thus God's-being-God will be disclosed in Jesus being-as-man".[19] For both Pannenberg and Rahner this is made explicit in the events of the crucifixion and resurrection of Jesus (Schillebeeckx finds all this rather more ambiguous[20]). In the cross Jesus

---

13 C.F.D. Moule, "The manhood of Jesus in the New Testament", in Sykes and Clayton (eds), *Christ, Faith and History*, p110.

14 J. Macquarrie, *Jesus Christ in Modern Thought* (SCM, London, 1990) p7.

15 H.D. Lewis, *Jesus in the Faith of Christians* (Macmillan, London, 1981) p73.

16 E. Schillebeeckx, *A Schillebeeckx Reader* (T&T Clark, Edinburgh, 1986) p143.

17 Pannenberg, *Jesus – God and Man*, p130.

18 Rahner, *Foundations of Christian Faith*, p251.

19 E. Schillebeeckx, *Jesus: An Experiment in Christology*, (Collins, London, 1979) p597.

20 For Macquarrie this is his weak point, cf. *Jesus Christ in Modern Thought*, pp310-11.

declares his ultimate allegiance to his mission and to the God who calls him to it, and in the resurrection God declares the divine allegiance to the mission and work of Jesus. The resurrection is the vindication of the whole of Jesus' work and activity and "the light which falls back on the pre-Easter Jesus from the resurrection involves his person as a whole".[21]

Rahner points out a further aspect of the Easter tradition in that, "according to the New Testament the experience of resurrection contributed to the *content* of the interpretation of the essence of the person and work of Jesus, and was not merely the divine confirmation of a knowledge already clearly expressed by Jesus before the resurrection".[22] Pannenberg puts it similarly when he comments that Jesus "was not only unrecognisable before Easter, but he would not have been who he was without the Easter event".[23] He does acknowledge that the Christian tradition also links the revelation of Jesus' identity with God to other key events such as the transfiguration, the baptism and his birth, but all of these Pannenberg attributes to what he terms the "retroactive significance" of the resurrection, a perspective which reveals that Jesus was previously one with God, and indeed if he reveals the divine essence, must carry some notion of "pre-existence".[24]

John Macquarrie agrees that the so-called Christology of descent is but the corollary of a Christology of ascent, based on the Easter experience. Rahner argues that it implies both a Son and a Logos Christology. Jesus feels in relationship, not to the Logos, but to the Father. He is in the relationship of a son and therefore is the Logos in historical form. In this way the notion of pre-existence may be retained by a Christology from below, but only so long as the resurrection of Jesus takes precedence over the doctrine of incarnation to which it gives rise. Such an approach has important implications for our understanding of the whole notion of revelation, and for Christian relationships with people of other faiths. Schillebeeckx comments that "In one way or another God's transcendent, creative activity will come to expression in our world; otherwise there would be no ground, no occasion even, for justifying our talk of God's action in our history".[25] Such a Christology therefore shapes our understanding, not simply of the person and work of Jesus but of human nature and the nature of the world as a whole, for "Only if there is *in all human beings* a possibility for transcendence and a capacity for God, can there be such a possibility and capacity in the man Jesus; and only if God makes himself present and known in and through creation generally can there be a particular point at which he is present and known in a signal way".[26]

---

21 Pannenberg, *Jesus – God and Man*, p141.

22 Rahner, *Foundations*, p279.

23 Pannenberg, *Jesus – God and Man*, p137; cf. Schillebeeckx, *Jesus*, p510: "He is not appointed, not *constituted*, 'Son of God' at the resurrection, but not until then did it appear."

24 Pannenberg, *Jesus – God and Man*, p150,

25 Schillebeeckx, *Jesus*, p627.

26 Macquarrie, *Jesus Christ in Modern Thought*, p381.

This echoes the sort of Christology we have seen advocated by Kenneth Cragg[27] where he talks of the process of prophecy, and indeed all revelation, as "incarnational" in character. If God's self-disclosure were not "relatively present everywhere",[28] then it would not be the sort of world in which God's absolute revelation in Christ could take place. The significance of this ultimate self-disclosure is that it reveals "new and glorious criteria" by which we may understand the true nature of God. Such a Christology seems much more helpful for inter-faith understanding than Newbigin's more traditional position, although we have noted that Newbigin regularly argues that the light of the Logos which became incarnate in Jesus, is the same light which enlightens all people.[29] As we have seen, Newbigin never fully develops or works out the implications of this admission.

This sort of Christology argues that two things are revealed in the incarnation, the true nature of God and the true nature of humanity: God is a God who can express the divine reality in the humanity of Jesus of Nazareth, and humanity is so constituted as to allow such self-expression. The *imago dei* is thus given a new lease of life through such a Christological approach. If we then ask the question what makes *this* revelation absolute and others relative, Pannenberg, Rahner, Newbigin and Cragg all point us to the resurrection. This means that in Christian theology the question of truth has only one measure and that is Jesus Christ. It is not possible to remove the figure of Christ from the centre of our theological universe, whether we attempt to replace him with the "Christian Father God" or whether we select the more neutral "soteriocentric" approach. Although it is commonly assumed that Christology is a problem for positive inter-faith relations, I want to suggest to the contrary that the problem in this whole debate is that we simply have not been Christological enough.

The Christian starting-point, the *a priori* if you like, is a Christlike God. In Michael Ramsey's fine words (expounded in John V. Taylor's equally notable book), "God is Christlike and in him is nothing unChristlike at all".[30] But Christians throughout their history have struggled to come to terms with the redefinition of our human concepts of God which the Christ-event brings. We continue to attempt explanations of how this man Jesus can also conform to our preconceptions of God. To start "from below" means that God has demonstrated in Jesus Christ who and how God is, destroying many of those preconceptions in the process. To have seen Jesus is, as the fourth evangelist correctly perceived, to have seen the Father; it is to have encountered God as the divine reality, albeit within the confines of the incarnation. The man Jesus in his life, death, resurrection and exaltation, is the fundamental Christian definition of God. But the Christ event does not reveal a God who is otherwise absent from his world, rather it identifies the God who is ever-present.

27 See above Part 2
28 Cragg, "Islam and Incarnation", in Hick (ed), *Truth and Dialogue*, p134.
29 See above Part Three.
30 J.V. Taylor, *The Christlike God* (SPCK, London, 1992).

As John Robinson pointed out in one of his lesser-known books,[31] to give up the centrality of Christ is to give up the only thing that Christianity has to offer. Christianity is Christ or it is nothing. But, as he goes on, to say that God is best *defined* by Christ is not to say that God is *confined* to Christ; indeed the whole point of the doctrine of the Trinity is to attempt to explain how the God who is revealed definitively in Christ is also the eternal Creator and the ever-present Spirit. Thus we suggest that a way forward for Christian theology in the realm of inter-faith relations is to retain its Christological criterion within a Trinitarian context.

This re-affirmation of the so-called "scandal of particularity" need not imply an "exclusivist" soteriology. One of the confusions in the debate has been that "exclusivism" has been used in two related but quite distinct ways. First, in making "exclusive" claims for Christ, which we are arguing an adequately *Christian* theology must do. Secondly, in drawing conclusions about the "exclusion" of certain groups from salvation, which I want to suggest we need not do, and if we take Christology sufficiently seriously we should not do. A properly Christological account is of the One who, in Barth's splendid extension of the parable of the loving father, "journeys into the far country" in search of a lost humanity.[32] This brings us to the heart of a missiological approach, the *Missio Dei*, the mission of the Christlike God. The measure of this divine love and commitment is nothing less than Calvary itself. The Cross not only reveals that there are no lengths to which God will not go in order to redeem a lost creation, but actualises that salvation in time and history.

Here is sufficient ground for the affirmation of the universal salvific will of God. One route from this axiom may lead to universalism, that is, ultimate salvation for every creature, which begs the important question which needs more discussion than space here allows of what we really understand salvation to be. We must, however, take seriously the scriptural witness to God's redemptive purpose as cosmic in scope.[33] How cosmic is a salvation from which the majority of the humanity God created to be a partner in creation is to be excluded? But we need not go this far if we remain convinced, like Newbigin for example, of the terrible possibility that some will choose to remain apart from God. That is, however, their free choice, not a reflection of the divine will and purpose.

Christians have traditionally affirmed that in Jesus we see the ultimate and absolute expression of God's mission to the world, that Christ is the fulfilment of the divine hope and that through his life, death and resurrection, is accomplished the divine purpose in creation and redemption. Cragg and Newbigin both have roots in the Evangelical tradition, which understands such affirmations to have biblical warrant and authority. The Christological discussion of this chapter drives us back to the biblical sources of Christian tradition in which the roots of such Christological thought are to be found. Gerald Anderson has noted a diversity in biblical tradition here, or even a divergence of tradition, where one stream emphasizes the broadly

31 J.A.T. Robinson, *Truth is Two-Eyed* (SCM, London, 1979).

32 K. Barth, *Church Dogmatics* (T&T Clark, Edinburgh, 2004) Volume 4.1, pp157ff.

33 Most obviously in Romans 8:19-22, also found, e.g., in Ephesians 1:10; Colossians 1:20, etc.

inclusive continuity of God's action in Christ, whilst the other is more narrowly exclusivist and discontinuous. He comments:

> In faithfulness to biblical revelation, both of these traditions must be affirmed and maintained, but this is difficult to do when some persons affirm continuity with doubtful uniqueness and others affirm uniqueness without continuity. What is needed in our theology of religions is uniqueness *with* continuity.[34]

This is precisely what I am concerned to achieve.

---

34 G.H. Anderson, "Theology of Religions and Missiology", in C. Van Engen, D. Gilliland and P. Pierson (eds), *The Good News of the Kingdom* (Orbis, Maryknoll, NY, 1993) p201 and pp205-6.

CHAPTER 10

Biblical Ideas of Fullness and Fulfilment

Since the earliest times Christian believers have wrestled with the particularity of their experience and the absoluteness of their faith commitment and attempted to relate this understanding to their wider experience of religious faith and the world in which they lived. Extremists from either wing have sought and found proof texts from Scripture to justify their own assumptions. Rather than follow this ultimately fruitless procedure, we must trespass briefly into the world of New Testament studies in order to examine a key theme in New Testament thought which is essential for our discussion, namely the whole area of fullness and fulfilment. We shall argue that through their use of this language the first Christians articulated their experience of both continuity *and* discontinuity with the past, and also tried to express the cosmic and eschatological dimensions of God's revelation in Christ. Perhaps here we may locate that "uniqueness *with* continuity" for which Gerald Anderson hopes.

Fulfilment language evolved in the specific context of the relationship of Christian faith to its Judaic roots and we must always be sensitive to the uniqueness of that relationship. However, first century Judaism was already a faith in dialogue with Hellenism, and as Christianity expanded into the Roman world beyond Palestine, its engagement with Greco-Roman culture became increasingly significant. So we shall examine in detail not only the first gospel with its special concern for the relationship with the parent faith, but also the Colossians-Ephesians literature with its alertness to the wider cultural picture. In any case, one might argue that for a convert or where Christianity takes root in a new cultural context, there may be parallels to be drawn between the relationship of Christianity and the indigenous culture and that of Christianity and Judaism. We must also note that fulfilment language has a cosmic dimension in relation to the divine purpose for the universe, and an eschatological reference to the future as the consummation of this purpose as well as to the past as the arena of fulfilment for previous promises.

A key issue for the first Christians was the question of the relationship between their new-found faith in Jesus and the Jewish heritage in which it was so clearly rooted. The question may have taken different forms for different communities, especially for predominantly Jewish-Christian or Gentile-Christian groups, but it is such a central question that it runs like a thread throughout the New Testament material, sometimes addressed directly, as in Romans 9-11, but often appearing in indirect form, especially in the shaping of the Gospel narratives which describe the relationship of Jesus and Judaism. There is no scope here for a detailed account of the process of separation between the Jewish and Christian communities.[1] Recent studies have, however, emphasized the significance of the group of *plerow* words for this discussion, and these have played a vital role in the development of missiological thinking in the late nineteenth and early twentieth centuries. A brief examination of recent biblical scholarship raises the question as to how far this earlier application of the term "fulfilment" was true to its New Testament range of ·meaning.

Walther Zimmerli, in a seminal contribution to the understanding of the fulfilment theme, has suggested that it is the core of the New Testament preaching[2] and R.T. France agrees that it is in some sense the theme of the whole New Testament and the bone of contention between the early church and Judaism.[3] It is necessary to examine the word-group with some care however, because it is "the epitome of Biblical eschatology" and therefore "an unexamined cliché" as C.F.D. Moule noted in his significant discussion[4] of this issue. Part of the difficulty is that the words are used inexactly by the biblical writers themselves, but Moule identified three areas in which they are commonly to be found. First, argues Moule, they underlie the concept of prediction and verification, secondly that of undertaking and achievement, and finally they express the notion of covenant-promise and fulfilment. Only in this latter sense do they really reflect the sense of finality and insurpassibility in which is fulfilled "all the promise and hope attaching to all that is epitomized in the Bible by God's covenant with his people".[5] To this end the *plerow* words are appropriate with their root sense of "filling to capacity" or, as the Theological Dictionary of the New Testament suggests, "rich fullness". Indeed it can be said that the words of this group are virtually a technical term in relation both to the fulfilment of scripture and the fulfilment of time in an eschatological sense.[6]

C.F.D. Moule suggests that even in the basic and perhaps crude application of *plerow* to the verification of prediction, as seen for example in the formula-quotations of Matthew's Gospel, an important principle is highlighted: "Those who are sensitive can recognize God's pattern of relationship as it shapes itself out of the different materials of successive generations ..."[7] Later generations look back to discern the pattern of God's dealings with his people and to discover the promises given within the covenant relationship. In their own time they look to the affairs of the nation and the wider world in anticipation of the pattern being repeated and the

---

1 See on this J.D.G. Dunn, *The Partings of the Ways* (SCM, London, 1992).

2 In his essay "Promise and Fulfilment" in C. Westermann (ed) *Essays in Old Testament Interpretation* (ET SCM, London, 1963) p113.

3 R.T. France *Matthew: Evangelist and Teacher* (Paternoster Press, Exeter, 1989) p166.

4 C.F.D. Moule, *Fulfilment-Words in the New Testament: Use and Abuse* (New Testament Studies 14, SCM, London, 1967-68), pp293-320.

5 Moule, *Use and Abuse*, p294.

6 C. Brown (ed.), *New International Dictionary of New Testament Thought* (Paternoster Press, Exeter, 1976) Vol. 1, p735.

7 Moule, *Use and Abuse*, p298.

divine pledges being redeemed. This detection of pattern assumes that God is at work to fulfil his purposes and achieve his goals and therefore even within the basic prediction or verification level of thought, "teleological development" is implied. From a Christian perspective Bultmann underlined that Christ must be regarded as the goal of history *first* before such an undertaking can be begun.[8] This is the assumption which governs the process.

The finality attributed by Christians to the story of Jesus is not in the end related to a unique number of verifications of prediction, rather it stems from the quality of Jesus' filial relationship to God which was understood to be the realization of the goal of the covenant-promise. Clearly what the New Testament offers is an interpretation of the purpose of God based on the Hebrew Scriptures, which are used as an *interpreted* authority, interpreted within the Church as the Spirit-filled community. Such interpretation is necessarily determined by the present experience rather than the past, and so different writers offer variations on the theme depending upon the exact nature of their present situation. This can mean the apparent abandonment of the Old Covenant altogether and James Dunn highlights as examples of this process the antitheses of Matthew 5:21-49, the critique of ritual law in Mark 7:1-23, and Stephen's attack on the Temple in Acts 7. In the end, he argues that, "The experience of Christ, the freedom brought by Christ, called for such a radical interpretation of the Old Testament that some of its revelatory functions had to be consigned to an era dead and gone".[9]

The significant point is that the *plerow* words seem able to embrace this discontinuous element within the notion of fulfilment. It need not, indeed it must not, be assumed that fulfilment implies only continuity, an unbroken line of development from promise to completion. In the essay already referred to, Zimmerli adduces Jeremiah 31 as evidence that there is a divine prerogative of sovereign freedom in the fulfilment of the covenant promises which involves a shattering of expectations precisely as part of their fulfilment.[10] Matthew chapter five has already been mentioned, and Moule identifies Matthew 5:17 as the single most significant passage on the fulfilment theme. Since this also provided the basis for the most important missiological interpretation of fulfilment in Farquhar's *The Crown of Hinduism*, it will be helpful to examine the usage of the *plerow* words and the significance of fulfilment theology within the first gospel.

10.1 Fulfilment in the First Gospel

There would probably be broad agreement with Graham Stanton's conclusion that "for much of early Christianity, and for Matthew in particular, the relationship

---

8 R. Bultmann, 'Prophecy and Fulfilment', in Westermann (ed) *Essays in Old Testament Interpretation*, pp50-75.

9 J.D.G. Dunn, *Unity and Diversity in the New Testament* (SCM, London, 1977) pp94-9.

10 Zimmerli, "Promise and Fulfilment" in C. Westermann (ed), *Essays in Old Testament Interpretation*, p118.

between Christianity and Judaism was the central problem for Christian theology".[11] The gospel emerges from a period of long dispute between church and synagogue and is written for a new community of both Jews and Gentiles who now define themselves over against the local synagogue. Stanton thus comes down for a date after the final break with Judaism rather than immediately before it, but whether or not we accept this particular conclusion it does not materially affect our view either of Matthew's problem or his proffered solution. R.T. France agrees that the relationship with Judaism is the central problem in the study of Matthew, the setting being late enough for clear distinctions and even hostility to emerge, but sufficiently early for the relation still to be a live issue. Whether the argument is *intra or extra-muros* is impossible to decide on the available evidence, but it certainly reflects the tension which resulted in the *birkath ha-minim*. As Stanton puts it:

> There is now general agreement that in the decades after 70 far-reaching reconstruction and consolidation of Judaism took place which included a more careful drawing of the boundaries of acceptable diversity within Judaism. The separation of Matthean Christianity from Judaism was almost certainly part of this process.[12]

France notes that in any case the implementation of the excommunication decree varied in time from place to place. He goes on to argue forcefully that "fulfilment" is the central focus of Matthew's theology. He endorses H. Frankmolle's opinion that it is Matthew's fundamental theological idea,[13] although he would not share Goulder's controversial view that the fulfilment theme so dominates the evangelist's picture that the non-Markan material is created in order to expand this theme.[14] The strength of the "fulfilment" interpretation of Matthew is based on a cumulative case which draws not simply on the use of *plerow* and allied words, but also includes the so-called "formula-citations", and the sense of movement through the gospel from the prologue which traces the "genesis" of Jesus through David to Abraham and the covenant-promise of the blessing of all nations, to the climax of the gospel where the Great Commission sends the disciples out to the nations. The infancy narratives, the Moses typology, chapter 12 where the authority of Jesus is shown to be greater than that of David, Solomon and Jonah in turn, all reinforce this fulfilment theology.

It is perhaps the formula-quotations with their clearly distinctive form that have attracted the most discussion. France argues for a complex dialectic between text and tradition in which: "the narrative tradition is the motive for the selection and shaping of the texts, but the texts have become the organising principle for the narrative".[15] Stanton believes that Matthew's use of the ten formula-citations is his most

---

11 G. Stanton, *A Gospel for a New People* (T&T Clark, Edinburgh, 1992) p168.

12 Stanton, *Gospel for a New People*, p145.

13 France, *Matthew*, pp166-7 and ch 5 *passim*.

14 M.D. Goulder, *Midrash and Lection in Matthew's Gospel* (SPCK, London, 1974).

15 France, *Matthew*, p181.

distinctive Christological contribution and suggests that while drawing on existing tradition, the evangelist has carefully selected and adapted the material to reflect his fulfilment theology.[16] Robert Banks seems to shift the emphasis away from innovation in favour of existing tradition that Matthew extends in application.[17] Whatever the emphasis the fundamental point is clear that they are part of a total theological outlook that runs like a connecting thread throughout the first gospel:

> The Formula-Quotations are simply one expression of the total fulfilment theology which undergirds Matthew's presentation of Jesus thought, surfacing sometimes in formula-quotations, sometimes in verbal echo, sometimes in the way a story is told...[18]

As Zimmerli has already hinted, it is important to recognize that "fulfilment" is not an unbroken or steady development. We have noted that the particular theme of the typological chapter twelve is "greater than". In Jesus is present that which is greater than David or Solomon or Jonah. Fulfilment for Matthew evidently includes a strong element of transcendence or excess which in fact is also present in the apparently conservative pericope 5:17-21, which concludes:

> Unless you can show yourselves *far better than* the scribes and Pharisees, you can never enter the kingdom of Heaven. (Matthew 5:21 REB)

The antitheses which follow, as Davies and Allison have pointed out,[19] underline the attitude and behaviour appropriate to the disciple of Jesus whose standards surpass, *without contradicting*, the Torah itself. The whole section concludes with the call to perfection (5:48). Similarly Robert Banks has noted that the teaching of Jesus neither simply confirms the Law, nor does it abrogate it; rather, "it is a surpassing or transcending of the Law that is the keynote thought".[20] France agrees that "this element of transcendence is found throughout Matthew's emphasis on fulfilment in Jesus".[21]

As used in the first gospel the fulfilment language embraces both continuity and discontinuity and it is difficult to establish where the emphasis lies. This may be because it varies from place to place, and perhaps between the struggles of Jesus' own day and those of the Matthean communities. An illustration of this tension surrounds the issue of the relationship of the new community to the old Israel. France comments:

---

16 Stanton, *Gospel for a New People*, p363.

17 R. Banks, *Jesus and the Law in the Synoptic Tradition* (SNTS Monograph 28, CUP, Cambridge, 1975) p175.

18 France, *Matthew*, pp184-5.

19 W.D. Davies and D.C. Allison, *Matthew 1-8* (International Critical Commentary, T&T Clark, Edinburgh, 1990).

20 Banks, *Jesus and the Law*, p203.

21 France, *Matthew*, p190.

Fulfilment implies both continuity and discontinuity. There remains a people of God, in which the hopes and destiny of Old Testament Israel find their culmination. But the very existence of a newly constituted community of the people of God, and one which is not purely Jewish, calls in question the status of the existing Israel, the 'sons of the Kingdom'.[22]

He goes on to recognize that Matthew is referring to the creation of a new nation (21:43), not simply a new leadership, but then cites approvingly C.H. Dodd's description of this process as "not a matter of replacement but of resurrection".[23] This seems to underline the element of continuity through the discontinuity. In this sense the church is not Israel's rival but its fulfilment.[24] Stanton, on the other hand, argues that the new people are not a new Israel, for this would imply a greater continuity than Matthew 21:43 admits.[25] Certainly the experience of the Matthean community and the strong anti-Jewish polemic of the Gospel point to a very real rivalry and a genuine disruption within the processes of fulfilment. Banks' comments on 5:17 seem pertinent here:

> Precisely the same meaning should be given to the term *pleroun* when it is used of the law as that which it has when it is used of the prophets. The prophets teachings point forward (principally) to the actions of Christ and have been realized in them in an incomparably greater way. The Mosaic Law points forward (principally) to the teachings of Christ and have been realized in them in a more powerful manner. The word fulfil in 5:17, then, includes not only an element of discontinuity (that which is more than the Law has now been realized) but an element of continuity as well (that which transcends the Law is nevertheless something to which the Law itself points forward).[26]

Ben Meyer characterises this process as a realization of the "inner dynamism" of the Torah, in which it is indeed transcended, "but only in its own direction", an obsolescence of external form and limit. This apparent discontinuity does not contradict or nullify the Law.[27]

Perhaps we just have to accept that Matthew does not expound the relationship between new and old with the sort of clarity and consistency which modern interpreters would like.[28] What *is* clear is that his fulfilment theology is stretching

---

22 France, *Matthew*, p213.

23 C.H. Dodd, *The Founder of Christianity* (Collins, London, 1971) p90.

24 France, *Matthew*, p241.

25 Stanton, *Gospel for a New People*, p11.

26 R. Banks, 'Matthew's Understanding of the Law: Authenticity and Interpretation in Matthew 5:17-20', *Journal of Biblical Literature* 93 (1974) p233. See also G. Strecker *The Sermon on the Mount* (T&T Clark, Edinburgh, 1988) p54: "The Old Testament Torah in itself does not carry its own validity but needs realizing fulfilment and authorizing confirmation through Jesus Christ. Here [5:17] the verb *pleroun* also contains a critical element."

27 Ben F. Meyer, *The Aims of Jesus* (SCM, London, 1979) pp143-8.

28 Stanton thinks so, *Gospel for a New People*, p383.

language in order to contain both the continuous and discontinuous elements of the Christ-event. God is faithful in bringing his pattern to completion and fruition, but he is also free to innovate and surprise his people by the manner of the fulfilment which he offers. The reality of the redemption exceeds the promise of the pledge, and that which is found in Christ transcends the imagination, even of Moses and the prophets. Zimmerli argues that it is the cross which intersects and interrupts any comfortable notions of progress and fulfilment, and as we have seen both Cragg and Newbigin recognize its centrality for such a discussion. The factors which led to the cross were of course inexorably at work throughout the ministry of Jesus. Although it is a matter of some controversy as to how far and in what detail he perceived its inevitability, there can be little doubt that Jesus anticipated suffering and death as a real possibility, and in due course, probability.

Matthew, writing in the light of the cross and resurrection, now sees the issue more clearly and with a new perspective. He is not so much concerned with the attitude of Jesus towards the Law, what matters is: "how the Law stands with regard to him, as the one who brings it to fulfilment and to whom all attention must now be directed".[29] In Jesus the last hour has arrived, the last Adam is come, but, argues Moule, this is "a collective and corporate fulfilment, as well as an individual one".[30] What is the meaning of all this for the Church?

10.2 Fullness in Colossians-Ephesians

In relation to this aspect of the discussion we must also note the usage of the cognate noun *pleroma* or "fullness", which is especially significant in the late Pauline (or deutero-Pauline?) epistles, Colossians and Ephesians. Here the Christological and (especially in Ephesians) the ecclesiological content of the term is at its most developed point within the New Testament. C.F.D. Moule has also been influential in the discussion of this noun form of the word-group, and has argued that context is more important than purely linguistic considerations in determining its meaning.[31] Elsewhere he suggests that in the plethora of complex theories about the background and usage of the term, "the most commonsense non-technical interpretations may be nearest to the truth . . . the word-group spans both 'realized' and 'futurist' eschatology, and in both Christ is Himself the central point".[32]

The Colossian "heresy" is now regarded as fundamentally Jewish, albeit a Judaism strongly influenced by Hellenism, and especially Stoicism. The use of *pleroma* in this context draws as much on the Old Testament of the Septuagint as anywhere and the lines of interpretation converge[33] at Colossians 1:19:

---

29 Banks, *Jesus and the Law*, p226.

30 Moule, *Use and Abuse*, p320.

31 See for example his note in International Dictionary of the Bible (Abingdon Press, New York, 1962) Vol. II, p826.

32 *Scottish Journal of Theology* Vol. 4 (1951) p86.

33 P.T. O'Brien *Colossians and Philemon* (Word Biblical Commentary, Waco, TX, 1987) p53.

For in him (Jesus) all the fullness [*pleroma*] (of God) was pleased to dwell. (NRSV)

This verse of the famous (pre-Pauline or even pre-Christian?) wisdom hymn is applied to the presumed incipient gnosticism of the Colossian situation in 2:9-10:

For in him the whole fullness [*pan to pleroma*] of deity dwells bodily, and you have come to fullness [*pepleromenoi*] in him. (NRSV)

F.F. Bruce paraphrases thus: "Christ ... incorporates the plenitude of the divine essence ... those who are members of Christ realize their plenitude in him".[34] And Moule comments: "It appears that Christ is thought of as containing, representing, all that God is; and that the destiny of Christians, as the Body of Christ, is to enter in him into that wealth and completeness".[35] Such sentiments are not unique in the New Testament for they are similar to those found in the Christ-hymn at the beginning of the fourth gospel (John 1:14-16) and the opening verses of Hebrews.[36] This suggests that whatever the development reflected in the Colossian-Ephesian material, it is not without foundation in the wider stock of Christian tradition.

The opening chapter of Ephesians contains significant echoes of the Colossian hymn, but scholars generally suggest that the writer, whether Paul or another, further extends the application of the pleroma-language in ecclesiological terms. The whole movement of thought reaches its climax in the notoriously obscure verses 22-23: "he (God) has put all things under his (Christ's) feet and has made him the head over all things for the church, which is his body, *the fullness of him who fills all things*" (RSV). The Greek is capable of a number of constructions, but the piling up of such all-comprehending terms is clearly highly significant: "*to pleroma tou ta panta en pasin pleromenou*".

H.M. Barth[37] provides a detailed review of the *pleroma* terminology, and he concurs that a cosmic interpretation is required in this context. Christ is not only God's fullness for the church but for the world. Although Ephesians places the emphasis on the filling of the church and indeed all things by Christ, whereas Colossians concentrates on the fullness of God in Christ, "neither excludes what is specifically explained by the other".[38] Barth concludes:

In Ephesians and Colossians fullness and filling denote a dynamic unilateral relationship: the revelation of God's glory to the world through Jesus Christ; the power extended by God in Christ and in the church for the subjection of the powers and the salvation of all mankind; the life, greatness and salvation given by Christ

---

34 F.F. Bruce, 'St Paul in Rome 3. The Epistle to the Colossians', *Bulletin of the John Rylands Library* Vol. 48.2 (1966) p279.

35 C.F.D. Moule *Colossians & Philemon* (CUP, Cambridge, 1957) p169.

36 In John 1:16 we find *pleromatos* whilst Hebrews 1:3 uses the characteristic *hypostaseos*.

37 In the Anchor Bible (Doubleday, New York, 1974).

38 H.M. Barth, *Fulfilment* (SCM, London, 1980) p200.

to his body; or, in brief, the presence of the living God and his Messiah among his chosen people for the benefit of all mankind.[39]

Clearly this was hardly written with a modern multi-faith world in mind, but Ephesians does have a particular interest in the relationship of Jew and Gentile within the Christian community, which is symbolic and representative of the new humanity God is creating in Christ. This process will eventually embrace the entire universe and God's purposes in creation and redemption will be complete. In George Caird's words: "In Christ is already seen the full character of God, and that fullness is now being imparted to the Church as the first decisive step in the process by which it is to be imparted to the universe at large".[40]

10.3 Implications for the Contemporary Debate

In the light of this discussion we may endorse C.F.D. Moule's conclusion that proper Christian discussion of this promise and fulfilment theme "must be along the lines of an achievement, by God himself in Jesus Christ, of the covenant promise in terms of a fully personal relationship - which, through its long history has been struggling towards such a fulfilment".[41] However, with Zimmerli, we should also affirm that this personal fulfilment also takes on the character of promise, and, as the Colossians-Ephesians material suggests, a promise which looks in turn to its consummation in the same Christ in whom the original promise is fulfilled. Such promise has an openness about it: open to misunderstanding and abuse certainly, as so often in church history, but also open to new insights and correction in the sovereign freedom of God.[42] Fulfilment is about promise and openness to all that God may yet do in and through the cosmic Christ.

Even at this early biblical stage we can see emerging some of the later characteristics of fulfilment theology. It is highly Christological in character, and experientially rooted in the life of the Christian community as it wrestles with the question of religious faith outside of Christ. The theme of fulfilment relates both to the purposes of God in creation and redemption, and to the spiritual aspirations of humanity for salvation and liberation. In Christ meet both dimensions of fulfilment. What perhaps was not sufficiently emphasized in the late nineteenth and early twentieth century interpretations of this doctrine, is that fulfilment is as much about discontinuity and radical transcendence as it is about continuity and completion. The cross of Christ contradicted many expectations of how God would fulfil the ancient promises, and a doctrine of fulfilment that is true to the New Testament will include this less comfortable aspect.

It is just such a creative tension of which this whole area stands in greatest need according to David Bosch, who criticizes all the current approaches for simply being

---

39 Barth, *Fulfilment*, p209.
40 G.B. Caird, *Paul's Letters from Prison* (OUP, Oxford, 1976) p43.
41 Moule, *Use and Abuse*, p320.
42 Zimmerli, *Promise and Fulfilment* p110.

too neat, with no loose ends, "The various models seem to leave no room for embracing the abiding paradox of asserting both ultimate commitment to one's own religion and genuine openness to another's, of constantly vacillating between certainty and doubt".[43]

Like Kenneth Cragg, he sees the need for poetry more than theory, for a meeting of hearts as much as of minds.[44]

---

43 D. Bosch, *Transforming Mission* (Orbis, Maryknoll, NY, 1991) p483.

44 It is perhaps worth noting that in his short study *The Gospels in World Context* (BRF, London, 1979) Cecil Hargreaves chose the work of Cragg by which to interpret the Gospel of Matthew.

CHAPTER 11

A Dialogical Approach to Mission

To return to our opening question, how may people of faith remain faithful to their confession in a world of many faiths? How is it possible for the contemporary Christian to confess the Lordship of Jesus Christ in our religiously plural world? In the light of our discussion we have seen that this is a question that attracts a variety of responses, but we are attempting to rediscover what might be entailed in a missiological approach. Many have suggested, like Stanley Samartha, that the whole notion of mission is inappropriate in a post-colonial world; that mission, with all its imperialist overtones, is no longer an option. The best that can be expected is mutual understanding and tolerance brought about through creative reflection and sensitive dialogue. The veteran missiologist Gerald H. Anderson noted that, "while there may be more consciousness of religious pluralism today, the churches in the West are not prepared to deal with it missiologically".[1] While sensitivity and dialogue are essential to the process of inter-faith encounter, to abandon the whole notion of mission is for Christianity, as indeed for some other faith communities, to deny the essential character of the faith. Might dialogue in some sense fulfil the Christian calling to mission through its commitment to faithful witness?

11.1 Mission and Dialogue

From the beginning the Church has existed in multi-cultural and multi-religious situations, but the nineteenth and especially the late twentieth century brought a new sense of what Kenneth Cragg has called "conscious pluralism".[2] I have suggested that it might better be characterised as "conscious *plurality*",[3] that is a genuine awareness of different faiths, cultures and ethnicities, which has contributed to an assumed but perhaps unconscious *pluralism*. According to Lesslie Newbigin it is important to distinguish between the fact of *plurality* and a philosophy of *pluralism*:

---

1 G.H. Anderson, "Theology of Religions and Missiology", in C. Van Engen, D. Gilliland and P. Pierson (eds), *The Good News of the Kingdom* (Orbis, Maryknoll N.Y., 1993) p201.

2 K. Cragg, *The Christian and Other Religion* (Mowbray, London, 1977) p7.

3 N. Wood, *Confessing Christ in a Plural World* (Whitley, Oxford, 2002) p13.

The church can never accept an ultimate pluralism as a creed, even if it must acknowledge plurality as a fact.[4]

The Inter-Faith Movement is now over a century old,[5] but this more recent and widespread consciousness of plurality, even if not necessarily acceptance of pluralism, has meant that, over the last forty or so years especially, the Church has developed a form of critical engagement with the other world religions in the form of *dialogue*.[6] Its apparent novelty is the cause of suspicion for some, although scholars as theologically diverse as Kenneth Cracknell and John Stott recognise its presence in the New Testament itself.[7]

Stott's definition of dialogue is taken from that which was framed at the National Evangelical Anglican Congress held in Keele in 1967:

Dialogue is a conversation in which each party is serious in his approach both to the subject and to the other person, and desires to listen and learn as well as to speak and instruct. (Paragraph 83)[8]

Following initial discussion on dialogue at the World Council's New Delhi Assembly in 1961 and further discussion at Uppsala in 1968, at the World Council of Churches Fifth Assembly in Nairobi in 1975, five people of other faiths were invited to take part in discussions about seeking community where inter-faith dialogue was to be debated. Fears were aired that any concession would lead to syncretism against which the 1928 Jerusalem meeting first warned. It was also noted that dialogue could mean compromise of the faith and the uniqueness of Christ and that it may rock the heart of the church's mission. It was not surprising to find that it was Asian voices in particular that promoted dialogue, as they had done in Tambaram in 1938, arguing that this was the only way forward in the pluralistic world which the church inhabits. The 1975 Assembly set a clear agenda of the need for clarification regarding the nature, purpose and limits of interfaith dialogue with special reference being made to the issues of syncretism, indigenisation, culture and mission.

In 1977 a meeting entitled "Dialogue in Community" was held in Chiang Mai, Thailand, to clarify the Christian basis for seeking community: "The Chiang Mai consultation affirmed that dialogue is neither a betrayal of mission nor a 'secret weapon' of proselytism, but a way 'in which Jesus Christ can be confessed in the

---

4 Newbigin, *Foolishness to the Greeks*, p115.

5 See M. Braybrooke, *Pilgrimage of Hope* (SCM, London, 1993).

6 The process is helpfully outlined in C. Hallencreutz, *Dialogue and Community* (WCC, Geneva, 1977).

7 K. Cracknell, *Towards a New Relationship* (Epworth Press, London, 1986) ch. 2; and J. Stott, *Christian Mission in the Modern World* (Kingsway, Eastbourne, 1986) ch. 3.

8 Stott, *Mission in the Modern* World, p60.

world today'".[9] It was the Chiang Mai meeting which led to the formulation of the *Guidelines on Dialogue* adopted by the WCC Central Committee in 1979, and subsequently condensed by the British Council of Churches into the "four principles of dialogue"[10] discussed below.

11.2 The Context of Mission

Christianity, like Buddhism and Islam, has always been a missionary faith and so the meeting of faiths takes place within a history and context of missionary encounter. Over recent centuries this missionary encounter has been predominantly, but not exclusively, in the context of western colonialism and imperialism.[11] This has complicated relationships and often clouded the issues at stake between faith communities. It is this which has led some Christians, and others˙ like Rabbi Jonathan Romain,[12] to suggest a moratorium on mission, especially evangelism. In this context some faith communities are suspicious that the recent Christian interest in dialogue is a subterfuge for evangelism, a "deceitful dialogue" as Romain has characterised it. Equally, some Christians see the interest in dialogue as symptomatic of a post-colonial crisis of confidence and as a betrayal of the missionary commission of the Church.

Christians from both Asia[13] and Africa[14] have defended the language of mission even in a post-colonial world, but some would still argue that nevertheless Christians must make a choice as to whether they are committed to dialogue on the one hand or evangelism on the other; or at the very least to make it clear which activity they are about in any given moment.[15] The implication is clear that even if mission and evangelism remain part of the contemporary agenda of the church they must be clearly distinguished from the altogether different activity of dialogue. But is this really the case or is it rather a false dichotomy?

---

9 http://www.oikoumene.org/en/resources/documents/wcc-rogrammes/interreligious -dialogue-and-cooperation/interreligious-trust-and-respect/guidelines-on-dialogue-with-people-of-living-faiths-and-ideologies.html.

10 *Guidelines on Dialogue with People of Living Faiths* (WCC, Geneva, 1979); *In Good Faith: The Four Principles of Inter-Faith Dialogue* (CTBI, London, 1992, earlier versions in 1981 and 1983).

11 As Brian Stanley has demonstrated it should not be too readily assumed that mission was always at the service of the colonising powers; in not a few examples Christian mission was a restraining and even a subversive element in the process. See Stanley, *The Bible and the Flag*.

12 J. Romain, *Your God shall be my God* (SCM, London, 2003).

13 E.g., Thomas Thangaraj, *The Common Task: A Theology of Christian Mission* (Abingdon Press, New York, 1999).

14 E.g. Lamin Sanneh, *Whose Religion is Christianity?* (Eerdmans, Grand Rapids, MI, 2003).

15 See K. Cracknell, *In Good and Generous Faith* (Epworth Press, London, 2005) p144.

Kenneth Cracknell, drawing on the approach of the Indian theologian Thomas Thangaraj, outlines a missiology for the twenty-first century, which suggests that dialogue and witness are not incompatible but rather illustrate David Bosch's wish for a 'mission in bold humility'.[16] There is no scope here for a full exploration of the parameters of contemporary mission and evangelism, but for our purposes today we need to explore further what we think dialogue might be.

11.3 What is Dialogue?

Problematically, dialogue means different things to different people as the World Council of Churches acknowledged:

> Some see dialogue primarily as a new and creative relationship within which one can learn about the respect others but also can give authentic witness to one's own faith. Others see it as an important historical moment in the development of religious traditions, in which each of the faith traditions in dialogue is challenged and transformed by the encounter with others. Still others view dialogue as a common pilgrimage towards the truth, within which each tradition shares with the others the way it has come to perceive and respond to that truth.[17]

All these understandings at the very least imply a recognition that God is the God of the whole world and all its peoples. Bishop Michael Nazir-Ali reminds us that in the Bible, God is spoken of as a universal God:

> The God of the whole world ... the God of every nation, of every people ... God, if he is the God of the whole world, of every people, must be working in the histories of those people.[18]

The implication might be that through encounter, engagement and dialogue it would be possible to discern the ways of God in the histories of all people.

There have been various attempts to delineate the scope of such dialogue, many of them variations on the influential typology of Eric Sharpe. As a religious studies scholar Sharpe[19] identifies four distinct types of dialogue, each with its own goals:

1. Discursive dialogue – deliberate meeting for intellectual enquiry. This recognises that faith traditions often have distinctive worldviews, which are frequently underpinned by sophisticated philosophical systems. This sort of dialogue then requires a certain technical expertise in at least one's own

---

16 Bosch, *Transforming Mission*, p489
17http://www.oikoumene.org/en/resources/documents/wcc-programmes/interreligious-dialogue-and-cooperation/interreligious-trust-and-respect/guidelines-on-dialogue-with-people-of-living-faiths-and-ideologies.html
18 M. Nazir-Ali, *Mission and Dialogue* (SPCK, London, 1989) p78.
19 E. Sharpe, "The Goals of Inter-Religious Dialogue", in J. Hick (ed.), *Truth and Dialogue* (Sheldon Press, London, 1974) pp77-95.

tradition and is likely to be mainly the sphere of the expert or the religious professional. It will also mean deliberate or 'set-piece' meetings, which are likely to have agreed agendas and procedures. Through intellectual discussion of beliefs a clearer picture can emerge both of distinctives and of those things which might be held in common between traditions.

2. Human dialogue – which arises from encounter in ordinary relationships. This recognises that religion is frequently not so much about belief but about practice and this is as much the concern of the ordinary believer as it is of the expert. Such dialogue is about the ordinary and everyday and occurs not in deliberate meetings of experts but in the accidental encounters of people in the meetings of everyday life. It may be that 'encounter' is really a better word than 'dialogue' here, since the latter does seem to suggest a degree of planning and purpose. But out of such encounter there should be no doubt that genuine relationships can be formed and searching dialogue can take place.

3. Secular dialogue – in which people of different traditions co-operate in matters of common concern. It is widely agreed that because of the territorial problems that the meeting of faiths can produce, the neutral realm of the secular world can often provide the forum for constructive meeting of different faith communities. There are often matters of concern within a community, which may involve people of all faiths and none. Such things might be co-operation over events or facilities, sharing in the life of a school or community association, local politics and so forth. Sharing a common purpose is a strong base for building good relationships and offers the possibility of building trust which enables the discussion of faith questions at the appropriate time.

4. Interior dialogue – this focuses on the spiritual elements within various traditions. This approach to dialogue recognises the centrality of the spiritual quest in many traditions, and offers the possibility of a depth of encounter to the devout practitioner of faith, whether expert or professional in the formal sense, or simply a devout believer. Inevitably this may also impinge on the vexed question of worship which for many traditions is the obvious expression of their spirituality. Experiencing a religious tradition in its worship is often a way to understand the heart of a tradition in a very immediate way, but there are important questions about integrity and authenticity which need to be considered by all parties involved.

This might all suggest, as others like Hick seem also to imply, that dialogue is fundamentally about moving towards *agreement*, whereas in the experience of some it is equally as significant for its recognition of *difference*. Thus Bishop John V. Taylor in an essay on "The Theological Basis of Inter-Faith Dialogue" suggests that:

Dialogue is a sustained conversation between parties who are not saying the same thing and who recognise and respect the differences, the contradictions and the mutual exclusions between their various ways of thinking. The object of this dialogue is understanding and appreciation, leading to further reflection about the implications for one's own position on the convictions and sensitivities of other faith traditions.[20]

Alan Race expresses the tension between agreement and distinctiveness helpfully when he writes:

> Dialogue assumes neither harmony between religions nor isolationist self-sufficiency, but mutual accountability. In this sense, the space between the assumption that "we're all the same" and the insistence that "we're all different" is where dialogue flourishes.[21]

This "space between" is perhaps what Michael Barnes calls "living in the middle".[22]

However, John Stott, while accepting the importance of dialogue with other faith traditions, also suggests that there is need for encounter with them, and even for confrontation:

> In which we seek both to disclose the inadequacies and falsities of non-Christian religion and to demonstrate the adequacy and truth, absoluteness and finality of the Lord Jesus Christ.[23]

Nazir-Ali agrees, but recognises that this is a mutual process of witness:

> I cannot see dialogue in its fullness without the opportunity for both sides to witness to their faith in trust that the partners recognise each other's integrity … we must be committed to let the light of Christ shine through our conversation and reflection, without that dialogue remains unfulfilled for the Christian.[24]

Such dialogue is clearly not in Nazir-Ali's or in Stott's minds incompatible with their commitment to evangelism, but is this an adequate understanding of the nature of dialogue?

---

20 J.V. Taylor, 'The Theological Basis of Inter-Faith Dialogue', in J. Hick and B. Hebblethwaite (eds), *Christianity and Other Religions* (Fount/Collins, London, 1980) p212.

21 A. Race, "Interfaith Dialogue: Religious accountability between Strangeness and Resonance", in A. Race and P. Hedges (eds), *Christian Approaches to Other Faiths* (SCM, London, 2008) p156.

22 M. Barnes, *Theology and the Dialogue of Religions* (CUP, Cambridge, 2002) p232.

23 Stott, *Mission in the Modern World*, p69.

24 Nazir-Ali, *Mission and Dialogue*, p83.

11.4 The Four Principles of Dialogue

In response to the WCC Guidelines on Dialogue noted above in 1981 the then British Council of Churches' Committee on Relations with People of Other Faiths published four "Principles of Dialogue", which were reissued with a commentary in 1991 as *In Good Faith*. In brief the four principles are:

1. Dialogue begins when people meet each other. Although apparently self-evident, this first principle is an important reminder that for too many people dialogue can seem a remote and academic exercise rather than an encounter between "people who live in houses not books".[25] Too much of the discussion has been without genuine encounter and real meeting with actual people of faith. In genuine encounter stereotypes are undermined, common humanity is discovered, and actual particularities are exposed.

2. Dialogue depends upon mutual understanding and trust. This of course requires a willingness to listen and hear what others are really saying. "Partners in dialogue should be free to define themselves. Dialogue should allow participants to describe and witness to their faith in their own terms".[26] It is interesting that "witness" occurs at this point in relation to all participants in the dialogue. It is a recognition that dialogue, if it is to be meaningful, is about the sharing of convictions not the suspension of belief.

3. Dialogue makes it possible to share in service to the community. Actually, as the Baptist response to this principle points out, often the dynamic works the other way: "Our discussion ... leads us to reflect on whether dialogue leads to service, or rather in reality, common action in the community leads to dialogue".[27] This confirms the point made above in relation to Sharpe's typology as "secular dialogue", but recognises that even where the secular world provides the space or opportunity for mutual co-operation, religious communities will be motivated by the ideals and demands of their own particular faith commitments in relation to "justice, compassion and peace".[28]

4. Dialogue becomes the medium of authentic witness. Where encounter has led to trust, whether through common action or simply by neighbourly involvement there may come a point where, according to *In Good Faith*, we cannot "honestly avoid witnessing to our faith. The complaint of some critics that dialogue replaces evangelism is unfounded".[29] This will clearly avoid any sense of coercion, and a recognition of the mutuality of dialogue which

---

25 *In Good Faith*, para 1.1 p1.
26 *In Good Faith*, para 2.3 p3.
27. N.J. Wood (ed.), *A Baptist Perspective on Inter-Faith Dialogue* (Joppa Publications, Alcester, 1992) pp12-3.
28 *In Good Faith*, para 3.3, p5.
29 *In Good Faith*, para 4.1, p6.

involves receiving as well as giving. But in the end: "Dialogue assumes the freedom of a person of any faith including the Christian to be convinced by the faith of another ... Christians will wish both to be sensitive to their partners' religious integrity and also to witness to Christ as Lord of all".[30]

In the context of this discussion on the relationship of dialogue and witness it is this final principle which requires some further consideration.

11.5 Dialogue and Witness

The British churches' fourth Principle of Inter-faith Dialogue is that dialogue becomes the medium of "authentic witness". What might this mean? First there must be a clear repudiation of power relationships and any use of force or coercion. Sadly this has been the experience of too many in the recent mission history of the church in the colonial era:

> Interreligious dialogue cannot shy away from recognising the effects of uneven power relations and the impact of mutual perceptions, no matter how distorted they are.[31]

This is a complex process in the present British context since members of minority religions often believe the Christian community to be more powerful and influential than it feels itself to be. Equally Christians often attribute to other faith communities, especially Muslims, an influence they do not themselves feel. Such dialogue will mean jettisoning the baggage of this recent past and the repudiation of colonial stereotypes, which still influences the mutual perceptions of both western Christians and members of other faith communities.

Further, authentic witness will not stop at mere recognition but also involve repentance for past and present racial, ethnic and religious prejudice and discrimination. As a recent writer in a denominational newspaper put it:

> We indigenous Christians have a poor record when it comes to religious hospitality towards the stranger. Witness the Black Majority Churches, whose original members could find no room among white Christians in the 'Mother Country'. If this is how we treat those who are different, but of our own faith, little wonder we are not interested in, and consider ourselves superior to, those who are different and of another faith.[32]

---

30 *In Good Faith*, para 4.6, p7

31 http://www.oikoumene.org/en/resources/documents/wcc-programmes/interreligious-trust-and-respect/guidelines-on-dialogue-with-people-of-living-faiths-and-ideologies.html.

32 S. Nolan, 'The Logic of Hospitality', *Baptist Times* 27 June 2002, p5.

This approach also recognises the need for a genuine appreciation of cultural diversity, which extends beyond the widespread but superficial taste for curry,[33] and might include for example acceptance of diverse patterns of social and family life and unfamiliar religious observance. This suggests an openness and humility, a readiness for vulnerability and risk, which is entailed in genuine encounter.

As the WCC guidelines on interreligious dialogue outline, it will also necessitate taking the position that Christians do not have the only experience of God's revelation but that others, of other faith traditions and none, might also be recipients of God's wisdom and truth. This need not threaten the Christian commitment to the ultimacy of God's self-revelation in Christ, although the authors cited in this paper take a variety of positions on this question. In the Christological discussion above I have argued that given the sort of God whom Christians claim to encounter in the life, death and resurrection of Jesus Christ, we should positively expect such a God to be experienced and encountered by people in all cultures and throughout human history. To appreciate this will mean Christian people making themselves vulnerable to the possibility that God speaks in many and various ways to his people in many times and places,[34] and the words contained in the scriptures are to be interpreted by the whole community of God's people, as they listen to each other.

This does of course require that people are willing to share the convictions that lie at the heart of their respective traditions, confident that they will be heard with respect, even where there may still be disagreement. Therefore "authentic witness", like all other aspects of dialogue, will be characterised not only by deep conviction but also by humility, integrity and sensitivity. Michael Nazir-Ali comments:

> There can be no authentic witness without prior dialogue. Unless we understand people's beliefs, their culture, the idiom of that culture, their thought forms, the intellectual tradition, the artistic tradition, the faith tradition, unless we understand these we will not be able to witness to people authentically as Christians.[35]

Does this approach exemplify Jonathan Romain's so-called deceitful dialogue? I don't believe so, provided that all parties share this expectation to give and to receive the witness of others. This is not the same as using dialogue as a mere subterfuge for an evangelism which simply instrumentalises dialogue. Rather it is to recognise mutual witness as an inherent element in the dialogical process. In other words there must be mutuality, or what Alan Race calls "mutual accountability". In my experience people of other faiths often feel cheated by Christians who are too inhibited to share the heart of their faith tradition or discuss their spiritual practice. There must be a willingness by all sides to be faithful to the tradition which has nurtured and formed them.

---

33 A recent poll named Chicken Tikka Masala as Britain's favourite dish, interestingly a hybrid of eastern and western tastes!

34 So Hebrews 1:1-2.

35 Nazir-Ali, *Mission and Dialogue*, pp82-3.

I suggest that in Christian thought such faithfulness is represented not so much by attempts to impose a particular worldview through argumentation, as by testimony to a powerful and transformative encounter with the divine in the person of Jesus Christ. This nevertheless needs to retain the openness and vulnerability which I believe is characteristic of the Christ of the New Testament. Witness in the Hellenistic Greek of the New Testament is of course *martyria*, from which the word martyr is derived and which encapsulates the commitment to gracious and sacrificial service to others so distinctive of Christ himself; but perhaps this is all too rarely discerned in some of his more strident disciples. Authentic witness for the Christian must be Christ-like in character as well as Christological in substance. Dialogue at its best is characterised by the faithful, gracious and open testimony of all parties. Such mutual witness, far from being inimical to dialogue, is I believe its most crucial component.

11.6 A Theology of Mission for a Plural Context

Christian mission is rooted in the mission of the Triune God. David Bosch, in his magisterial analysis of the history and theology of Christian mission, has drawn attention to the emerging consensus from Catholic, Conciliar, Evangelical and Orthodox circles alike, that the Church is missionary in its very nature.[36] Tim Gorringe is right: God engages! Not just in history but in the present moment, not just with those who manage to find their way into the sheepfold of the Church, but with the whole earth and all her people. The Spirit continues to move over the face of the earth. As the Church goes out in mission she does not move into a God-forsaken void but follows the call of the God who goes before us and who beckons us on; as we go in mission we seek to identify the gracious presence of the Christ-like God and with all peoples celebrate the reality of saving grace.

Bosch argues that the Church does not therefore possess mission: mission does not originate with the Church for mission begins with God; and the Church is not the purpose of mission for its goal is his Kingdom. Rather the Church is the "sacrament, sign and instrument"[37] of God's continuing mission in the world. Authentic Christian mission will share the characteristics of that divine mission. It will be incarnational and sacrificial. The missionary Church will bear the hallmark of the crucified and risen Christ whose commission she holds.[38] Our relationship with people of other faiths requires the same sort of vulnerable engagement, the same grappling with the ambiguous realities of human history, culture and religious development, as we read in the gospel story. Whether the language of mission is still too laden with colonial associations, as Samartha and others suggest, must be seriously considered, but the concept lies at the heart of Christian faith.

---

36 Bosch, *Transforming Mission*, pp372-3.
37 Bosch, *Transforming Mission*, pp374ff.
38 See Stott, *Christian Mission in the Modern World*.

The too often neglected Johannine version of the "Great Commission" talks of the followers of Christ being sent into the world "as the Father sent me" (John 20:21). To be "sent" by Christ as he was "sent" by the Father means first of all engagement with the particularities and contingencies of human life, for the Fourth Gospel here presupposes all that has gone before in the first nineteen chapters of the Gospel, and which may be summarised in its fundamental affirmation, "The Word became flesh and dwelt among us, full of grace and truth".[39] For Christian theologies of religion there can be no escaping the "scandal of particularity", since the divine love constantly reaches out to humanity within the contingent realities of the human situation. The Godhead is unafraid of the "flesh" regardless of our own inability to come to terms with it!

11.7 Engagement and Particularity

To take such particularity seriously will mean a proper engagement with human history, culture and religion. Christian mission which is true to its divine nature will engage these realities through the processes of incarnation and inculturation. A missiological perspective will therefore require thorough and detailed wrestling with the history and development of religion; this will require academic studies of texts and architecture and artefacts; but more importantly for mission it will be through engagement with people of faith, through immersion in culture and language and climate and geography. This is where true encounter and dialogue take place. This relationship between faith and culture is a fundamental issue for missiology. Of course it is not without difficulty, in fact it contains within itself a tension which is already reflected in the Prologue to the Fourth Gospel, which speaks, almost in the same breath, of the eternal Word's entering into the world of time, history and culture, and the Word's rejection by the world he brought into being, indeed by the very people whom he had called to be his own.[40] This brings us immediately to the "scandal of particularity", with all that it means for the significance of history and culture.

As the debate between Newbigin and Wiles illustrated, Christianity is an historical religion, not simply in the sense in which all religions are historical, that is as the products of the social and cultural life of particular people in a particular place and a particular time. Christianity is an historical religion in the sense that certain historical events are given particular value and weight. For Christian theology in these events, or rather in *the Christ event*, is to be found as Newbigin put it the clue to the meaning of all history. This of course builds on the Jewish tradition that history has purpose and meaning and that history is the sphere of the divine outworking of such purpose, but with the additional point that in *this* event God is involved in a unique way - "the Word became flesh" - thus transforming the human situation, and at the same time touching the very being of God, in a way

---

39 John 1:14.
40 John 1:1-18.

hitherto not experienced. This engagement is understood to have universal implications and is therefore of a different order to that of the old covenant, as the opening verses of the Letter to the Hebrews suggest.[41]

In the Johannine model such engagement is the pattern for all Christian mission. The risen Christ commissions his disciples "as the Father sent me, so I send you"; embracing all that is implied by "the Word becoming flesh", since the risen Lord is identified still by the marks of crucifixion. In missiological terms it is therefore an incarnational model, often referred to as *inculturation* or *contextualization*.[42] This may be defined, in the words of Louis J. Luzbetak, as "the process by which a local Christian community integrates the Gospel message (the 'text') with the real-life context, blending text and context into that single God-intended reality called 'Christian living'".[43] Using an anthropological method Luzbetak identifies three levels of culture, the level of forms, that is the shape of cultural norms in various societies; the level of functions, which refers to the meanings and purposes of such norms; and the level of social psychology in which are uncovered the fundamental assumptions and values of a culture. This third level lies deepest within the subconscious of a community and is rarely questioned by its members, but Luzbetak argues that only when the Gospel is integrated at this level of culture is true contextualization achieved.[44]

As we have seen, culture is not monolithic. There have been, and continue to be, many frameworks by which human beings attempt to give shape to their experience and express the values by which they live and die. Within the major cultures of world history are numerous subcultures and crosscurrents intersecting in many ways. One of the key issues for incarnational models of mission, with their emphasis on the importance of such "local cultures", is how any of these various expressions are to remain true to a cosmic vision of the Christian faith. Michael Nazir-Ali has posed this question in terms of the relationship between the universality and the translatability of the gospel, "In order to be universal, the Gospel must be translatable. This translation, this rendering of the Gospel into the idiom of a particular culture, however, cannot be at the expense of the very universality it was supposed to promote".[45] From both Catholic and Protestant traditions, Luzbetak and Newbigin refer to a three-way conversation between the Gospel, the Church Universal (that is the wider Christian culture) and local culture, as a way of maintaining the integrity and balance of the "faith once given to the saints".

The mission of the Church will be touched by this experience, shaped by historical and cultural movements, just as Jesus himself was shaped by the history,

---

41 Hebrews 1:1-3.

42 Bosch, *Transforming Mission*, views the former as one example of the latter (the other being liberation theology), whereas Luzbetak, *The Church and Cultures* (Orbis, Maryknoll, NY, 1988) uses them synonymously, as does Nazir-Ali in *From Everywhere to Everywhere*, who also adopts the term "identification".

43 Luzbetak, *Church and Cultures*, p133.

44 Luzbetak, *Church and Cultures*, pp74-8.

45 Nazir-Ali, *From Everywhere to Everywhere*, p34.

culture and religion of his day. It is clear that both Kenneth Cragg and Lesslie Newbigin have been deeply shaped by their long experiences in the particularities of their respective situations. Cragg, out of the long history of Christian-Muslim antipathy and aggression, looks for points of contact, places of genuine meeting, possibilities of mutual encounter. Newbigin, from the syncretistic environment of India, draws distinctions in order to clarify the insights of the Christian faith. But in neither case is there an attempt to find some neutral high ground from which the whole field can be surveyed. As we have argued no such vantage point is available. Such an engagement with historical process will also require ongoing reflection on the history of Christian mission and an honest recognition of the imperialisms by which true mission has been betrayed. But repenting of our history is not enough, there must also be an equally open facing-up to the realities of the economic, cultural and military powers with which so-called "Christian civilization" is still all too readily associated in the minds of people from the "two-thirds world", including, as we have argued, the new imperialism of western pluralistic theology.

The Risen Christ of the Johannine Commission, is the Christ identified still by the marks of crucifixion, (the "Jesus of the Scars" in Edward Shillito's moving poem[46]). We have seen in the theology of both Cragg and Newbigin the centrality of the Cross as the essential distinguishing feature of Christian faith and action, and a missiological approach to inter-faith relations will require to be characterized by its truth. To be sent into the world "as the Father sent me" is to be sent to glory as the Fourth Gospel constantly affirms, but only by way of the Cross. Taking history seriously, whether it be the history of religion or the history of mission, is a vital part of such a missiological approach for it is bound up with a Christian philosophy of history which is teleological and therefore eschatological in character, derived from its understanding of the mission of God within the history of the world. The recognition of particularity and contingency, which this method requires, drives the Church to confess its provisional nature, for its mission and the *Missio Dei* are not identical. The mission of the Church points beyond itself, not simply to the Christ-event, but also to the future reign of God of which Christ is the definitive symbol and sign.

The Church, says Bosch, serves the mission of God by "holding up the God-child in a ceaseless celebration of the Epiphany. In its mission, the church witnesses to the fullness of the promise of God's reign and participates in the on-going struggle between that reign and the powers of darkness and evil".[47] We might argue that what is held up to the world is in fact the cross and resurrection through which the destiny of the "God-child" is attained and the purpose of God in creation and redemption

---

46 Published at the end of World War I, and cited by William Temple in his *Readings in St John's Gospel* (Combined Volume, Macmillan, London, 1968) p366. It concludes:
The other gods were strong, but Thou wast weak
They rode, but Thou didst stumble to a throne.
But to our wounds only God's wounds can speak,
And not a god has wounds, but Thou alone.

47 Bosch, *Transforming Mission*, p391.

fulfilled. The scope of the mission of the church is the whole world, for that is the scope of the divine mission, but it is not a world from which God is absent; God is already actively at work through the Spirit and through all the processes of history. The Church does not move into a spiritual void.[48] As we affirmed in the Christological discussion above, the Christ-event does not reveal a God who is otherwise absent, but identifies the God who is ever-present. This highlights the ·character of the Christian confession as *witness*, it speaks of what it knows, yet points beyond itself to the reality of God-in-Christ. But there can be no final divorce between Christianity as a religion and the Christ to whom it claims to witness. The character of the Church must bear some recognizable relation to the Christ whom it confesses. The importance of Newbigin's point about the three-way conversation between Gospel, Church and World is underlined.

The second feature which will be clear in a church "sent as the Father sent me" will be a serious engagement with humanity. Newbigin and Cragg are both concerned that the first step in an adequate theology of religion will be a recognition of our mutual humanity. This will of course reckon honestly with human spirituality in all its multi-faceted manifestations, but will not be beguiled into believing that it is only with the spiritual realm that the Kingdom of God is concerned. If the "enfleshment" of the Logos is anything to go by, and we are arguing that for the Christian it is the crucial thing, then human needs and expressions of our physical, emotional and intellectual life are just as significant as what Western thought tends to isolate, and elevate, as the "spiritual" - as though this could in some way be identified and experienced apart from our physical, emotional and intellectual being. In other words it requires a holistic approach:

> Salvation is as coherent, broad, and deep as the needs and exigencies of human existence. Mission therefore means being involved in the ongoing dialogue between God, who offers his salvation, and the world, which – enmeshed in all kinds of evil – craves that salvation. ... Those who know that God will one day wipe away all tears from their eyes will not accept with resignation the tears of those suffer and are oppressed *now*. Anyone who knows that one day there will be no more disease can and must actively anticipate the conquest of disease in individuals and society *now*. And anyone who believes that the enemy of God and humans will be vanquished will already oppose him *now* in his machinations in family and society. For all of this has to do with *salvation*.[49]

A missiological approach to inter-faith relations will be concerned for a proper contextualization of the issues, not simply in terms of history and culture, but in a humanity accepted and understood in all its material, social, spiritual and intellectual depths. In fact this is central to Christian doctrine. Nothing which truly belongs to humanity is ever finally alien to the missionary God of the Incarnation and the Passion. Even evil, sin and death are met and overcome in the cross and resurrection

---

48 Bosch, *Transforming Mission*, p485.
49 Bosch, *Transforming Mission*, p400

of Christ, for, in the ancient doctrine of the Church "that which is not assumed is not redeemed". The Gospel declaration that the Word became "flesh" is the affirmation that in Christ all human reality has indeed been assumed, transformed and fulfilled.

Here is a crucial pointer for the Church in its engagement with the life of the world: that it is in the whole range of human experience that we should expect to find evidence of the self-giving, self-revealing God. Within the ordinariness of everyday life, in the processes of history, in the rich variety of culture and in the ambiguous complexities of the religions, the Spirit of God may be discerned. For, as another great missionary bishop put it: "The chief actor in the historic mission of the Christian church is the Holy Spirit".[50] The crucial question is by what criterion is this presence of God to be identified and discovered?

Therefore the third feature of a missiological approach to inter-faith relations will be the centrality of Christology. Christians are those who claim that God has chosen to define Godself in Christ as the one in whom is found that absolute and unconditional love which is both the origin and goal of the universe. This love is revealed in its starkest form in the Cross of Christ, but it is characteristic of his whole life and ministry, and normative for his entire understanding of the divine . nature. Yet at the same time there must be acceptance that the God who so *defines* Godself, is not *confined* to the life, ministry, death and resurrection of Jesus.

The significance of the resurrection in this pattern now becomes apparent, since it is the event by which the appropriateness of such Christian affirmations is justified. Newbigin is right in his understanding of the resurrection of Christ as the basis of the Christian position, the *a priori* act of faith behind which it is impossible to go. The resurrection is at once the divine "yes" to all that Christ has said, done and achieved, and the place at which human faith, response and obedience are awakened. To borrow Hick's terminology, the resurrection is the place of eschatological verification, where the ultimate nature of reality is proleptically revealed. There is no inherent reason why this should not happen in the middle of time[51] rather than at the end. The Church, however, must make this confession with due humility, an attitude which Bosch describes as "authentically Christian",[52] for Christianity is a religion of grace and finds its centre in the cross. We might also add that, in the light of history, the Church has much to be humble about! As I have argued elsewhere, such "authentic witness",[53] must be characterized not simply by humility of language, but find expression in matters of life and lifestyle, a "dialogue of life" and not simply of words. This is truly the mission "in the way of Jesus Christ", advocated by the WCC, who was "recognized as Lord and Messiah through his own willingness to suffer and to die, and not by an irresistible imposition of himself on other people".[54]

---

50 John V. Taylor, *The Go-Between God* (SCM, London, 1972) p3

51 As Hans Conzelmann described Luke's presentation of the Gospel: *Die Mitte Der Zeit* (J.C.B Mohr, Tübingen, 1953, ET *The Theology of St Luke*, Faber, London, 1960).

52 Bosch, *Transforming Mission*, p485.

53 The fourth "Principle of Dialogue".

54 Wood (ed), *A Baptist Perspective on Inter-Faith Dialogue*, p14.

11.8 Conclusion

Such an approach is not to abandon the missionary imperative, but to rediscover the true nature of mission. As Newbigin argued, the Church must be missionary but cannot any longer be provincial, in the sense of a solely or predominantly European movement. It must shed its culturally-bound provinciality whilst retaining the particularity that is its essence. Through that very particularity is discovered Cragg's "will to universality", but we must again heed his warning that the message of the cross must be affirmed in the same spirit by which Jesus bore it. This will include the call to conversion, not in any sense of procuring a personal salvation which might otherwise be withheld, but, as Bosch expresses it (referring to both Cragg and Newbigin), "to become a participant in the mighty acts of God".[55] Here we see the double sense of fulfilment: that in the consummation (or fulfilment) of the purposes of God we discover our true human destiny (or fulfilment) both personal and corporate.

Kenneth Cragg is perfectly happy to stand within the fulfilment tradition of Christian missiological reflection, but Lesslie Newbigin was wary of the term, suspecting its too ready acceptance of some sort of evolutionary continuity from human need to divine response. Each, however, recognizes that the Christ-event must determine the Christian approach and this shared emphasis draws them together. Any faith based on an incarnational theology must have a sense of an underlying continuity between the human and the divine. As Cragg has argued, it must be, at the very least, the sort of world, and the sort of divine-human relationship, in which incarnation is possible. Newbigin himself recognized that without such fundamental continuity even basic communication is impossible. Thus, we suggest that Cragg and Newbigin alike, are modifying the stream of biblical and missiological tradition in which each stands, in a convergent direction. Cragg represents the broadly inclusive stream of continuity, but recognises the disjunction of the cross at the heart of the Gospel. Newbigin stands squarely within the stream of radical discontinuity, but concedes that this cannot be total.

The "enfleshment" of the Logos as Jesus of Nazareth led in the end to the cross, and herein lies the root of the discontinuity within the continuum which is present for both our thinkers. The cross of Christ stands over against all comfortable notions of continuity. But it should not be assumed that only the recipients of the Christian proclamation will feel the discomfort and challenge of such a "cruciform missiology"; the first requirement is that it is deeply marked within the Christian self-consciousness. Simon Barrington-Ward, former bishop of the multi-cultural and multi-religious city of Coventry, has expressed it well:

> The Christian task now is to let the Cross of Christ through the action of the Spirit be planted deep within the consciousness of all faiths. But the only way to do this is to plant the Cross again in the heart of the consciousness of Christians themselves. We need a more far-reaching repentance and a self-criticism, a deeper

---

55 Bosch, *Transforming Mission*, p488.

humility, a costlier readiness for long-term loving. We need to learn what it means to take up the Cross and follow, to be 'crucified with Christ' as we are 'plunged into the life' of worlds in crisis. To such a witness (martyria) these worlds are open.[56]

In such a way contemporary Christians may continue to offer faithful witness to the Lordship of Jesus Christ in our world of many faiths.

---

56 S. Barrington-Ward, "Christian Faith in a Pluralist Age", in D. Hardy and P. Sedgwick (eds), *The Weight of Glory* (T&T Clark, Edinburgh, 1991) p263.

Bibliography

Books and Booklets

Anglican Consultative Council *Towards a Theology for Inter-Faith Dialogue* (2nd ed) London: Church House Publishing 1986

Anderson, G. (ed) *The Theology of the Christian Mission* London: SCM Press 1961

Anderson, G. and Stransky, T. (ed) *Christ's Lordship and Religious Pluralism* Maryknoll, NY: Orbis 1981

Anderson, G. and Stransky, T. *Third World Theologies (Mission Trends 3)* Grand Rapids: Eerdmans 1976

Anderson, J.N.D. *Christianity and World Religions* Leicester: IVP 1984

— *Islam in the Modern World* Leicester: IVP 1990

Ariarajah, W. *Not without my Neighbour* Geneva: WCC 2001

— *The Bible and People of Other Faiths* Geneva: WCC 1988

Baillie, D. *God was in Christ* London: Faber & Faber 1956

Banks, R. *Jesus and the Law in the Synoptic Tradition* Cambridge: CUP 1975

Barnes, M. *God East and West* London: SPCK 1991

— *Religions in Conversation* London: SPCK 1989

— *Theology and Dialogue* Cambridge: CUP 1999

Barth, H-M. *Fulfilment* London: SCM Press 1980

Barth, K. *Dogmatics in Outline* London: SCM Press 1949

— *Church Dogmatics* Edinburgh: T & T Clark 1997

Barth, M. *Ephesians* Garden City, NY: Doubleday 1974

Bauckham, R. and Drewery, B. (eds) *Scripture, Tradition and Reason* Edinburgh: T & T Clark 1988

Bauman, Z. *Modernity and Ambivalence* Cambridge: Polity Press 1991

Beaumont, I.M. *Christology in Dialogue with Muslims* Carlisle: Paternoster 2005

Bennett, C. (ed) *Invitation to Dialogue* London: BCC/CCBI 1990

Berger, P. *The Sacred Canopy: Elements of a Sociological Theory of Religion* Garden City NY: Doubleday 1967

— *The Heretical Imperative: Contemporary Possibilities of Religious Affirmation* London: Collins 1980

Bevan Jones, L. *The People of the Mosque* Calcutta: YMCA 1932

Binder, L. (ed) *The Study of the Middle East* New York: Wiley 1974

Bosch, D. *Transforming Mission* Maryknoll, NY: Orbis 1991

Boyd, R.H.S. *India and the Latin Captivity of the Church* London: CUP 1974

Braaten, C. (ed) *History and Hermeneutics* London: Lutterworth Press 1968

Brockington, J.L. *Hinduism and Christianity* Basingstoke: Macmillan 1992

— *The Sacred Thread* Edinburgh: EUP 1981

Brown, D. *All Their Splendour* London: Fount 1982

Brown, J. *Men and Gods in a Changing World* London: SCM Press 1980

Brown, L. *Three Worlds: One World - Account of a Mission* London: Rex Collings 1981

Bruce, F.F. *The Time is Fulfilled* Exeter: Paternoster 1978

Brunner, E. *Revelation and Reason* London: SCM Press 1947

Carey, W. *An Enquiry into the Obligation of Christians to Use Means for the Conversion of the Heathen* Didcot: BMS 1991

Caird, G.B. *Paul's Letters from Prison* Oxford: OUP 1976

Chadwick, H. *The Secularization of the European Mind in the Nineteenth Century* Cambridge: CUP 1975

Chapman, C. *Cross and Crescent: Responding to the Challenge of Islam* Leicester: IVP 1995

Chaudhuri, N.C. *Hinduism: A Religion to Live By* London: Chatto & Windus 1979

Christian, W.A. *Oppositions of Religious Doctrines* London: Macmillan 1972

Clarke, A.D. and Winter, B.W. (eds) *One God, One Lord in a World of Religious Pluralism* Cambridge: Tyndale House 1991

Copleston, F.C. *Religion and the One* London: Search Press 1982

Cotterell, P. *Mission and Meaninglessness* London: SPCK 1990

Council of Churches for Britain and Ireland *In Good Faith - The Four Principles of Inter-Faith Dialogue* London: CCBI 1992

Cracknell, K. *In Good and Generous Faith: Christian Responses to Religious Pluralism* Peterborough: Epworth Press 2005

— *Justice, Courtesy and Love* London: Epworth Press 1995

— *Towards a New Relationship* London: Epworth Press 1986

Cragg, A.K. *The Call of the Minaret* (2nd ed) London: Collins 1986

— *The Christ and the Faiths* London: SPCk1986

— *The Christian and Other Religion* London: Mowbray 1977

— *Christianity in World Perspective* London: Lutterworth Press 1968

— *The Dome and the Rock* London: SPCK1984

— *The Event of the Qur'an* London: Allen & Unwin 1971

— *Islam among the Spires* London: Melisende 2000

— *Faith and Life Negotiate* Norwich: Canterbury Press 1994

— *The House of Islam* Belmont Ca: Dickenson 1969

— *Jesus and the Muslim* London: Allen & Unwin 1985

— *The Lively Credentials of God* London: DLT 1995

— *The Mind of the Qur'an* London: Allen & Unwin 1973

— *Muhammad and the Christian* London: DLT 1984

— *The Qur'an and the West* London: DLT 2006

— *Readings·in the Qur'an* London: Collins 1988

— *The Pen and the Faith* London: Allen & Unwin 1985

— *The Privilege of Man* London: Athlone Press 1968

— *Sandals at the Mosque* London: SCM Press 1959

— *The Secular Experience of God* Leominster: Gracewing 1998

— *To Meet and to Greet* London: Epworth Press 1992

— *Troubled by Truth* Edinburgh: Pentland Press 1992

Cragg, A.K. *What Decided Christianity* Worthing: Churchman 1989
Cragg, A.K. and Speight, R.M. (eds) *Islam From Within* Belmont, Ca: Wadsworth 1980
D'Costa, G. *Christianity and World Religions* Chichester: Wiley-Blackwell 2009
— *John Hick's Theology of Religions* Lanham, Md: UPA 1987
— *Theology and Religious Pluralism* Oxford: Blackwell 1986
D'Costa, G. (ed) *Christian Uniqueness Reconsidered* Maryknoll, NY: Orbis 1990
Dewick, E.C. *The Christian Attitude to Other Religions* Cambridge: CUP 1953
Dodd, C.H. *The Founder of Christianity* London: Fount 1971
Driver, S.R. and Sanday, W. *Christianity and Other Religions* London: Lond & Co 1908
Dunn, J.D.G. *The Partings of the Ways* London: SCM Press 1992
— *Unity and Diversity in the New Testament* London: SCM Press 1977
Edwards, D.L. and Stott, J.R.W. *Essentials - A Liberal-Evangelical Dialogue* London: Hodder and Stoughton 1988
Edwards, J.R. *Is Jesus the only Savior?* Grand Rapids: Eerdmans 2005
Esposito, J.L. *Islam - the Straight Path* Oxford: OUP 1988
— *Unholy War: Terror in the Name of Islam* Oxford: OUP 2002
Farquhar, J.N. *The Crown of Hinduism* London: OUP 1913
Fiddes, P.S. *The Creative Suffering of God* Oxford: Clarendon Press 1988
— *Participating in God* London: DLT 2000
— *Past Event and Present Salvation* London: DLT 1989
— *Tracks and Traces* Carlisle: Paternoster 2004
Fiddes, P.S. (ed) *Faith in the Centre: Christianity and Culture* Macon, Ga: Smyth & Helwys 2001
Forrester, D.B. *Caste and Christianity* London: Curzon Press 1980
Foust, F. Kirk, Hunsberger, J.A. and Ustorf, W.G. *A Scandalous Prophet: The Way of Mission after Newbigin* Grand Rapids: Eerdmans 2002
France, R.T. *Matthew: Evangelist and Teacher* Exeter: Paternoster 1989
Francis, T.D.. and Selvayanangam, I. *Many Voices in Christian Mission: Essays in Honour of J.E. Lesslie Newbigin* Madras: CLS 1994
Gairdner, W.H.T. *"Edinburgh 1910"* London: F.H. Revell 1910
Gibb, H.A.R. *Islam* (Rev.Ed.) Oxford: OUP 1988
Gillis, C. *A Question of Final Belief* Basingstoke: Macmillan 1989
Goddard, H. *Christians and Muslims: From Double Standards to Mutual Understanding* Surrey: Curzon Press 1995
— *A History of Christian-Muslim Relations* Edinburgh: EUP 2000
Gorringe, T. *Divine Spirit* London: SCM Press 1990
— *God's Theatre* London: SCM Press 1989
— *Redeeming Time* London: DLT 1986
Goulder, M.D. *Midrash and Lection in Matthew's Gospel* London: SPCK 1974
Goulder, M.D. (ed) *Incarnation and Myth* London: SCM Press 1979
Green, M. *Do all religions lead to God?* Leicester: IVP 2000
Green, M. (ed) *The Truth of God Incarnate* London: Hodder & Stoughton 1977

Gunn, T. *The Sense of Movement* London: Faber & Faber 1957

Hahn, F. *Mission in the New Testament* London: SCM Press 1965

Hallencreutz, C.F. *Dialogue and Community* Geneva: WCC 1977

— *Kraemer Towards Tambaram* Uppsala: Lund 1966

Hamnett, I (ed) *Religious Pluralism and Unbelief* London: Routledge 1990

Hardy, D.W. and Sedgwick, P.H. (eds) *The Weight of Glory* Edinburgh: T & T Clark 1991

Hargreaves, C. *The Gospel in a World Context* London: BRF 1979.

Harvey, D. *The Condition of Postmodernity* Oxford: Blackwell 1989

Hedges, P. and Race, A. (eds) *Christian Approaches to Other Faiths* London: SCM Press 2008

Hick, J. *Faith and Knowledge* (2nd ed) London: Macmillan 1967

— *God and the Universe of Faiths* London: Macmillan 1977

— *God has Many Names* London: Macmillan 1980

— *An Interpretation of Religion* London: Macmillan 1989

— *Problems of Religious Pluralism* London: Macmillan 1985

Hick, J. (ed) *The Myth of God Incarnate* London: SCM Press 1977

— *Truth and Dialogue* London: Sheldon Press 1974

Hick, J. and Hebblethwaite, B. (eds) *Christianity and Other Religions* London: Fount 1980

Hick, J. and Hebblethwaite, B. (eds) *Christianity and Other Religions* (2nd ed) Oxford: One World 2001

Hick, J. and Knitter, P.F. (eds) *The Myth of Christian Uniqueness* London: SCM Press 1987

Hocking, W.E. *Re-Thinking Missions: A Laymen's Enquiry after One Hundred Years* New York: Harper & Brothers 1932

Hooker, R. and Lamb, C. *Love the Stranger: Christian Ministry in Multi-Faith Areas* London: SPCK 1986

Howard, L. *The Expansion of God* London: SCM Press 1981

Hunsberger, G. R. *Bearing the Witness of the Spirit Lesslie Newbigin's Theology of Cultural Plurality* Grand Rapids: Eerdmans 1998

Hunter, A.G. *Christianity and Other Faiths in Britain* London: SCM Press 1985

Hunter, S. (ed) *Islam: Europe's Second Religion* Westport, Conn: Praeger 2002

Huntington, S.P. *The Clash of Civilizations and the Remaking of World Order* New York: Simon & Schuster 1996

Hussain, M.K. (trans. K. Cragg) *The City of Wrong* Amsterdam: Djambatan 1959

International Missionary Council *The Authority of the Faith (Madras Series Reports — Volume 1)* London: IMC/OUP 1939

Kirk, J.A. *Loosing the Chains: Religion as opium and liberation* London: Hodder & Stoughton 1992

— *What is Mission?* London: DLT 1999

Knitter, P.F. *No Other Name? A Critical Survey of Christian Attitudes Towards the World Religions* London: SCM Press 1985

— *Jesus and the Other Names* Maryknoll, NY: 1989

Knox, J. *The Death of Christ* London: Collins 1959

Kraemer, H. *The Christian Message in a Non-Christian World* (2nd ed) London: IMC Edinburgh House Press 1938

— *The Communication of the Christian Faith* London: Lutterworth Press 1957

— *From Missionfield toIndependent Church* London: SCM Press 1958

— *Religion and the Christian Faith* London: Lutterworth Press 1956

— *World Cultures and World Religions: The Coming Dialogue* London: Lutterworth Press 1960

— *Why Christianity of All Religions?* London: Lutterworth Press 1962

Küng, H. *Christianity and the World Religions* London: SCM Press 1987

— *On Being a Christian* London: SCM Press 1976

Kung, H. and Moltmann, J. (eds) *Christianity among World Religions* Edinburgh: Continuum 1986

Lamb, C. *Belief in a Mixed Society* Tring: Lion 1985

— *The Call to Retrieval: Kenneth Cragg's Christian Vocation to Islam* London: Grey Seal 1997

Lewis, H.D. *Jesus in the Faith of Christians* London: Macmillan 1981

Lewis, P. *Islamic Britain* London: I. B. Tauris 1994 (rev. ed. 2002)

Lindbeck, G. *The Nature of Doctrine* London: SPCK 1984

Ling, T.O. *A History of Religion East and West* London: Macmillan 1968

Luke, P.Y. and Carman, J.B. *Village Christians and Hindu Culture* London: Lutterworth Press 1968

Luzbetak, L.J. *The Church and Cultures* Maryknoll, NY: Orbis 1988

Lyotard, J-F. *The Postmodern Condition* Manchester: MUP 1986

MacIntyre, A. *After Virtue* (2nd ed) London: Duckworth 1985

— *Whose Justice? Which Rationality?* London: Duckworth 1988

Macquarrie, J. *Jesus Christ in Modern Thought* London: SCM Press 1990

— *The Mediators* London: SCM Press 1995

— *Principles of Christian Theology* (2nd ed) London: SCM Press 1972

Maeland, B. *Rewarding Encounters: Islam and the Comparative Theologies of Kenneth Cragg and Wilfred Cantwell Smith* London: Melisende 2003

Marshall, B. *Christologies in Conflict* Oxford: Blackwell 1987

Marty, M.E and Greenspahn, F.E *Pushing the Faith - Proselytism and Civility in a Pluralistic World* New York: Crossroad 1988

Maurice, F.D. *The Religions of the World* London: Macmillan 1886

Meeking, B. and Stott, J. *The Evangelical-Roman Catholic Dialogue on Mission, 1977-1984* Exeter: Paternoster 1986

Meyer, B.F. *The Aims of Jesus* London: SCM Press 1979

Morgan, R. (ed) *The Religion of the Incarnation* Bristol: Classical Press 1989

Moule, C.F.D. *The Origins of Christology* Cambridge: CUP 1977

— *Colossians and Philemon* Cambridge: CUP 1957

Nazir-Ali, M. *From Everywhere to Everywhere: A World-View of Christian Mission* London: Collins/Flame 1991

Nazir-Ali, M. *Frontiers in Muslim-Christian Encounter* Oxford: Regnum 1987

— *Mission and Dialogue* London: SPCK 1989
Neill, S. *Christian Faith and Other Faiths* London: OUP 1961
— *A History of Christian Missions* Harmondsworth: Penguin 1964
— *A History of Christianity in India* (2 vols) Cambridge: CUP 1985
— *Colonialism and Christian Missions* London: Lutterworth Press 1966
Netland, H.A. *Dissonant Voices* Leicester: Apollos 1991
· — *Encountering Religious Pluralism* Leicester: Apollos 2001
Newbigin, L. *Christian Freedom in the Modern World* London: SCM Press 1938
— *A Faith for this One World?* London: SCM Press 1961
— *The Finality of Christ* London: SCM Press 1969
— *Foolishness to the Greeks* London: SPCK 1986
— *The Gospel in a Pluralist Society* London: SPCK 1989
— *Honest Religion for Secular Man* London: SCM Press 1964
— *The Household of God* London: SCM Press 1954
— *The Other Side of 1984* Geneva: WCC 1983
— *The Open Secret* Grand Rapids: Eerdmans 1983
— *The Open Secret* (Rev Ed) London: SPCK 1995
— *Proper Confidence* London: SPCK 1995
— *A South India Diary* London: SCM Press 1951
— *Signs amid the Rubble* (ed. G. Wainwright) Grand Rapids: Eerdmans 2003
— *Sin and Salvation* London: SCM Press 1956
— *Truth to Tell* London: SPCK 1992
— *Unfinished Agenda* Geneva: WCC 1985
— *A Word in Season* (ed. E. Jackson) Edinburgh: St Andrew Press 1994
O'Brien, P.T. *Colossians and Philemon* Waco, Tx: Word 1987
Oden, T. *After Modernity ...What?* Grand Rapids: Eerdmans 1990
Oxtoby, W.G. *The Meaning of Other Faiths* Philadelphia: Westminster 1983
Pannenberg, W. *Basic Questions in Theology* London: SCM Press 1972
— *Jesus - God and Man* London: SCM Press 1968
Pannenberg, W. *et al Revelation as History* London: SCM Press 1965
Pannikar, R *The Unknown Christ of Hinduism* (New Ed) London: DLT 1981
Parrinder, G. *Avatar and Incarnation* New York: OUP 1982
— *Upanishads, Gita and Bible* (2nd ed) New York: Harper & Row 1975
Paul, R.D. *The Cross over India* London: SCM Press 1952
Penner, P.F. (ed) *Christian Witness and Presence among Muslims* Schwarzenfeld: Neufeld Verlag 2005
Polanyi, M. *Personal Knowledge* (Corrected ed) London: Routledge & Kegan Paul 1962
Poole, R. *Morality and Modernity* London: Routledge 1991
Race, A. *Christians and Religious Pluralism* London: SCM Press 1983
— *Interfaith Encounter* London: SCM Press 2001
Radhakrishnan, S. *The Hindu View of Life* London: Allen & Unwin 1927
Rahner, K. *Foundations of Christian Faith* London: DLT 1978
— *Theological Investigations* London: DLT 1964-

Ramachandra, V. *Faiths in Conflict?* Leicester: IVP 1999
— *The Rediscovery of Mission* Carlisle: Paternoster 1996
Robertson, E. *Breakthrough* Belfast: Christian Journals Ltd 1976
Robinson, J.A.T. *Honest to God* London: SCM Press 1963
— *The Human Face of God* London: SCM Press 1973
— *Truth is Two-Eyed* London: SCM Press 1979
Ruthven, M. *Islam: A Very Short Introduction* Oxford: OUP 1997
Samartha, S.J. *Courage for Dialogue* Geneva: WCC 1981
— *One Christ - Many Religions* Maryknoll, NY: Orbis 1992
Samuel, V. and Sugden, C. (eds) *A.D.2000 and Beyond: A Mission Agenda* Oxford: Regnum 1991
Schillebeeckx, E. *Christ* London: SCM Press 1980
— *Jesus - An Experiment in Christology* London: Collins 1979
— *A Schillebeeckx Reader* Edinburgh: T & T Clark 1986
Schnackenburg, R. *Ephesians* Edinburgh: T & T Clark 1991
Schwarz, H. *The Search for God* London: SPCK 1975
Scott, D. *Everyman Revisited - The Common Sense of Michael Polanyi* Lewes: Book Guild 1985
Senior, D and Stuhlmueller, C. *The Biblical Foundations for Mission* London: SCM Press 1983
Sharpe, E.J. *Comparative Religion: A History* (2nd ed) London: Duckworth 1986
— *Faith meets Faith* London: SCM Press 1977
— *Not to Destroy, But to Fulfil* Lund: Gleerup 1965
Slater, T.E. *God Revealed* Madras: Addison & Co 1876
Smart, N. *The Religious Experience [of Mankind]* Glasgow: Collins 1977
— *World Religions: A Dialogue* London: SCM Press 1960
Smith, W.C. *The Meaning and End of Religion* London: SCM Press 1978
Stanley, B. *The Bible and the Flag* Leicester: Apollos 1990
— *The History of the Baptist Missionary Society 1792-1992* Edinburgh: T & T Clark 1992
Stanton, G. *A Gospel for a New People* Edinburgh: T & T Clark 1992
Stewart, W. *India's Religious Frontier* London: SCM Press 1964
Stott, J.R.W. *Christian Mission in the Modern World* Eastbourne: Kingsway 1986
Strecker, G. *The Sermon on the Mount* Edinburgh: T & T Clark 1988
Sykes, S. and Clayton, J. (eds) *Christ, Faith and History* Cambridge: CUP 1972
Taylor, J.V. *For All the World: The Christian Mission in the Modern World* London: Hodder & Stoughton 1966
— *The Christ-like God* London: SCM Press 1992
— *The Go-Between God* London: SCM Press 1972
— *The Primal Vision* London: SCM Press 1963
Thiselton, A.C. *Interpreting God and the Postmodern Self* Edinburgh: T & T Clark 1995
Thomas, D. and Amos, C. (eds) *A Faithful Presence: Essays for Kenneth Cragg* London, 2003

Thomas, M.M. *The Acknowledged Christ of the Indian Renaissance* London: SCM Press 1969
— *Risking Christ for Christ's Sake: Towards an Ecumenical Theology of Pluralism* Geneva: WCC 1987
— *Salvation and Humanisation* Madras: CLS 1971
— *Some Theological Dialogues* Madras: CLS 1977
Toynbee, A. *J Christianity Among the Religions of the World* London: OUP 1958
Tracy, D. *Plurality and Ambiguity* London: SCM Press 1987
Van Engen, C. and Gilliland, D.S. and Peirson, P. (eds) *The Good News of the Kingdom: Mission Theology for the Third Millenium* Maryknoll, NY: Orbis 1993
Wainwright, G. (ed) *Keeping the Faith* London: SPCK 1989
Wainwright, G. *Lesslie Newbigin: a Theological Life* Oxford: OUP 2000
Walker, A. *Enemy Territory - The Christian Struggle for the Modern World* London,: Hodder & Stoughton 1987
Walls, A. *The Missionary Movement in Christian History* Edinburgh: T & T Clark 1996
— *The Cross-Cultural Movement in Christian History* Edinburgh: T & T Clark 2002
Ward, K. *A Vision to Pursue* London: SCM Press 1991
— *Religion and Revelation* Edinburgh: T & T Clark 1992
Warren, M. *I Believe in the Great Commission* London: Hodder & Stoughton 1976
— *The Missionary Movement from Britain in Modern History* London: SCM Press 1965
— *Social History and Christian Mission* London: SCM Press 1967
Watt, W.M. *Muhammad – Prophet and Statesman* London: OUP 1961
Wells, D.F. *The Search for Salvation* Leicester: IVP 1978
Weston, P. (ed) *Lesslie Newbigin: Missionary Theologian* London: SPCK 2006
Westermann, C. (ed) *Essays in Old Testament Interpretation* London: SCM Press 1963
Whaling, F. *Christian Theology and World Religions* London: Marshall Pickering 1986
Wiles, M. *Christian Theology and Inter-Religious Dialogue* London: SCM Press 1992
Williams, S. *Revelation and Reconciliation* Cambridge: CUP 1995
Witvliet, T. *A Place in the Sun* London: SCM Press 1985
Wood, N.J. (ed) *A Baptist Perspective on Inter-Faith Dialogue* Alcester: Joppa Publications 1992
Wood, N.J. *Confessing Christ in a Plural World* Oxford: Whitley 2002
WCC *The Church's Witness to God's Design* London: SCM Press 1948
— *Guidelines on Dialogue* Geneva: WCC 1979
— *Your Kingdom Come: Mission Perspectives* Geneva: WCC 1980
Zacharius, R. *Jesus Among Other Gods* Nashville TN: Word Publications 2000

Zaehner, R.C. (ed) *The Concise Encyclopaedia of Living Faiths* London: Hutchinson 1971
— *Hindu Scriptures* London: J.M. Dent & Sons 1968
— *Hinduism* Oxford: OUP 1969

Articles and Essays

Anderson, G.H. 'Theology of Religions and Missiology' in C. Van Engen, D. Gilliland and P. Pierson (eds) *The Good News of the Kingdom* Maryknoll NY: Orbis 1993

Banks, R. 'Matthew's Understanding of the Law: Authenticity and Interpretation in Matthew 5:17-20' *Journal of Biblical Literature* 93, 1974

Barrington-Ward, S. 'Christian Faith in a Pluralist Age' in D. Hardy and P. Sedgwick (eds) *The Weight of Glory* Edinburgh: T & T Clark 1991

Bradshaw, T. 'Grace and Mercy: Protestant Approaches to Religious Pluralism' in A. Clarke and B. Winter (eds) *One God, One Lord* Cambridge: Tyndale House 1991

Bruce, F.F. 'The Epistle to the Colossians' *Bulletin of John Rylands Library* 48, 1966

Byrne, P. 'John Hick's Philosophy of World Religions' *Scottish Journal of Theology* 35, 1982

Bultmann, R. 'Prophecy and Fulfilment' in C. Westermann (ed) *Essays in Old Testament Interpretation* London: SCM Press 1963

Cragg, K. 'The Central College of the Anglican Communion' *Anglican & Episcopal History* (Vol LIX.2), 1990
— 'Islam and Incarnation' in J. Hick (ed) *Truth and Dialogue* London: Sheldon Press 1974

D'Costa, G. 'Christ, the Trinity and Religious Plurality' in G. D'Costa (ed) *Christian Uniqueness Reconsidered* Maryknoll NY: Orbis 1990

Forrester, D. 'Professor Hick and the Universe of Faiths' *Scottish Journal of Theology* 29, 1976

Gorringe, T.J. 'Sacraments' in R. Morgan (ed) *The Religion of the Incarnation* Bristol: Classical Press 1989

Griffiths, P.J. 'The Uniqueness of Christian Doctrine Defended' in G. D'Costa (ed) *Christian Uniqueness Reconsidered* Maryknoll NY: Orbis 1990

Hebblethwaite, B. 'The Moral and Religious Value of the Incarnation' in M.D. Goulder (ed) *Incarnation and Myth* London: SCM Press 1979

Hick, J 'Eschatological Verification Reconsidered' *Religious Studies* XIII, 1977

Moule, C.F.D. 'Fulfilment-Words in the New Testament: Use and Abuse' *New Testament Studies* 14, 1967
— 'Pleroma' *Scottish Journal of Theology* 4, 1951
— 'The manhood of Jesus in the New Testament' in S. Sykes and J. Clayton (eds) *Christ, Faith and History* Cambridge: CUP 1972

Newbigin, L. 'The Basis, Purpose and Manner of Inter-faith Dialogue' *Scottish Journal of Theology* 30, 1977
— 'Christ and the Cultures' *Scottish Journal of Theology* 31, 1978
Newbigin, L. 'The Centrality of Jesus for History' in M.D. Goulder (ed) *Incarnation and Myth* London: SCM Press 1979
— 'The Christian Faith and the World Religions' in G. Wainwright (ed) *Keeping the Faith* London: SPCK 1989
— 'The Church in its World Mission' in L.G. Champion (ed) *Outlook for Christianity* London: Lutterworth Press 1967
— 'Religion of the Marketplace' in G. D'Costa (ed) *Christian Uniqueness Reconsidered* Maryknoll NY: Orbis 1990
Pannenberg, W 'The Revelation of God in Jesus of Nazareth' in J.M. Robinson and J. Cobb (ed) *Theology as History* London: Harper & Row 1967
Rossano, P 'A Roman Catholic Perspective' in G. Anderson and T. Stransky (eds) *Christ's Lordship and Religious Pluralism* Maryknoll NY: Orbis 1981
Scott, W '"No Other Name" – An Evangelical Conviction' in G. Anderson and T. Stransky (eds) *Christ's Lordship and Religious Pluralism* Maryknoll NY: Orbis 1981
Smart, N 'Truth and Religions' in J. Hick (ed) *Truth and Dialogue* London: Sheldon Press 1974
Sugden, C. 'Evangelicals and Religious Pluralism' in I. Hamnett (ed) *Religious Pluralism and Unbelief* London: Routledge 1990
Sykes, S.W. 'The theology of the humanity of Christ' in S. Sykes and J. Clayton (eds) *Christ, Faith and History* Cambridge: CUP 1972
Surin, K 'Towards a "materialist" critique of "religious pluralism"' in I. Hamnett (ed) *Religious Pluralism and Unbelief* London: Routledge 1990
Wiles, M. 'In what sense is Christianity a"Historical" Religion?' *Theology* Vol. LXXXI No.679 1978
— 'Does Christology rest on a mistake?' in S. Sykes S and J. Clayton (eds) *Christ, Faith and History* Cambridge: CUP 1972
Williams, R. 'Trinity and Pluralism' in G. D'Costa (ed) *Christian Uniqueness Reconsidered* Maryknoll NY: Orbis 1990
Wood, N.J. 'Inculturating Christianity in Postmodern Britain' in *Faith in the Centre: Christianity and Culture* P.S. Fiddes, (ed) Macon, Ga: Smyth & Helwys 2001
Wright, D. 'The Watershed of Vatican II' in A. Clarke and B. Winter (ed) *One God, One Lord* Cambridge: Tyndale House 1991
Zimmerli, W. 'Promise and Fulfilment' in C. Westermann (ed) *Essays in Old Testament Interpretation* London: SCM Press 1963

Abbreviations and General Index

Abbreviations

218   *Abbreviations and General Index*

Paternoster Biblical Monographs
(All titles uniform with this volume)
Dates in bold are of projected publication

Joseph Abraham
Eve: Accused or Acquitted?
A Reconsideration of Feminist Readings of the Creation Narrative Texts in Genesis 1–3
Two contrary views dominate contemporary feminist biblical scholarship. One finds in the Bible an unequivocal equality between the sexes from the very creation of humanity, whilst the other sees the biblical text as irredeemably patriarchal and androcentric. Dr Abraham enters into dialogue with both camps as well as introducing his own method of approach. An invaluable tool for any one who is interested in this contemporary debate.
2002 / 0-85364-971-5 / xxiv + 272pp

Octavian D. Baban
Mimesis and Luke's on the Road Encounters in Luke-Acts
Luke's Theology of the Way and its Literary Representation
The book argues on theological and literary (mimetic) grounds that Luke's on-the-road encounters, especially those belonging to the post-Easter period, are part of his complex theology of the Way. Jesus' teaching and that of the apostles is presented by Luke as a challenging answer to the Hellenistic reader's thirst for adventure, good literature, and existential paradigms.
2005 */ 1-84227-253-5 / approx. 374pp*

Paul Barker
The Triumph of Grace in Deuteronomy
This book is a textual and theological analysis of the interaction between the sin and faithlessness of Israel and the grace of Yahweh in response, looking especially at Deuteronomy chapters 1–3, 8–10 and 29–30. The author argues that the grace of Yahweh is determinative for the ongoing relationship between Yahweh and Israel and that Deuteronomy anticipates and fully expects Israel to be faithless.
2004 / 1-84227-226-8 / xxii + 270pp

Jonathan F. Bayes
The Weakness of the Law
God's Law and the Christian in New Testament Perspective
A study of the four New Testament books which refer to the law as weak (Acts, Romans, Galatians, Hebrews) leads to a defence of the third use in the Reformed debate about the law in the life of the believer.
2000 / 0-85364-957-X / xii + 244pp

Mark Bonnington
The Antioch Episode of Galatians 2:11-14 in Historical and Cultural Context
The Galatians 2 'incident' in Antioch over table-fellowship suggests significant disagreement between the leading apostles. This book analyses the background to the disagreement by locating the incident within the dynamics of social interaction between Jews and Gentiles. It proposes a new way of understanding the relationship between the individuals and issues involved.
2005 / 1-84227-050-8 / approx. 350pp

David Bostock
A Portrayal of Trust
The Theme of Faith in the Hezekiah Narratives .
This study provides detailed and sensitive readings of the Hezekiah narratives (2 Kings 18–20 and Isaiah 36–39) from a theological perspective. It concentrates on the theme of faith, using narrative criticism as its methodology. Attention is paid especially to setting, plot, point of view and characterization within the narratives. A largely positive portrayal of Hezekiah emerges that underlines the importance and relevance of scripture.
2005 / 1-84227-314-0 / approx. 300pp

Mark Bredin
Jesus, Revolutionary of Peace
A Non-violent Christology in the Book of Revelation
This book aims to demonstrate that the figure of Jesus in the Book of Revelation can best be understood as an active non-violent revolutionary.
2003 / 1-84227-153-9 / xviii + 262pp

Robinson Butarbutar
Paul and Conflict Resolution
An Exegetical Study of Paul's Apostolic Paradigm in 1 Corinthians 9
The author sees the apostolic paradigm in 1 Corinthians 9 as part of Paul's unified arguments in 1 Corinthians 8–10 in which he seeks to mediate in the dispute over the issue of food offered to idols. The book also sees its relevance for dispute-resolution today, taking the conflict within the author's church as an example.
2006 / 1-84227-315-9 / approx. 280pp

Daniel J-S Chae
Paul as Apostle to the Gentiles
His Apostolic Self-awareness and its Influence on the Soteriological Argument in Romans
Opposing 'the post-Holocaust interpretation of Romans', Daniel Chae competently demonstrates that Paul argues for the equality of Jew and Gentile in Romans. Chae's fresh exegetical interpretation is academically outstanding and spiritually encouraging.
1997 / 0-85364-829-8 / xiv + 378pp

Luke L. Cheung
The Genre, Composition and Hermeneutics of the Epistle of James
The present work examines the employment of the wisdom genre with a certain compositional structure and the interpretation of the law through the Jesus tradition of the double love command by the author of the Epistle of James to serve his purpose in promoting perfection and warning against doubleness among the eschatologically renewed people of God in the Diaspora.
2003 / 1-84227-062-1 / xvi + 372pp

Youngmo Cho
Spirit and Kingdom in the Writings of Luke and Paul
The relationship between Spirit and Kingdom is a relatively unexplored area in Lukan and Pauline studies. This book offers a fresh perspective of two biblical writers on the subject. It explores the difference between Luke's and Paul's understanding of the Spirit by examining the specific question of the relationship of the concept of the Spirit to the concept of the Kingdom of God in each writer.
2005 / 1-84227-316-7 / approx. 270pp

Andrew C. Clark
Parallel Lives
The Relation of Paul to the Apostles in the Lucan Perspective
This study of the Peter-Paul parallels in Acts argues that their purpose was to emphasize the themes of continuity in salvation history and the unity of the Jewish and Gentile missions. New light is shed on Luke's literary techniques, partly through a comparison with Plutarch.
2001 / 1-84227-035-4 / xviii + 386pp

Andrew D. Clarke
Secular and Christian Leadership in Corinth
A Socio-Historical and Exegetical Study of 1 Corinthians 1–6
This volume is an investigation into the leadership structures and dynamics of first-century Roman Corinth. These are compared with the practice of leadership in the Corinthian Christian community which are reflected in 1 Corinthians 1–6, and contrasted with Paul's own principles of Christian leadership.
2005 / 1-84227-229-2 / 200pp

Stephen Finamore
God, Order and Chaos
René Girard and the Apocalypse
Readers are often disturbed by the images of destruction in the book of Revelation and unsure why they are unleashed after the exaltation of Jesus. This book examines past approaches to these texts and uses René Girard's theories to revive some old ideas and propose some new ones.
2005 / 1-84227-197-0 / approx. 344pp

David G. Firth
Surrendering Retribution in the Psalms
Responses to Violence in the Individual Complaints
In *Surrendering Retribution in the Psalms*, David Firth examines the ways in which the book of Psalms inculcates a model response to violence through the repetition of standard patterns of prayer. Rather than seeking justification for retributive violence, Psalms encourages not only a surrender of the right of retribution to Yahweh, but also sets limits on the retribution that can be sought in imprecations. Arising initially from the author's experience in South Africa, the possibilities of this model to a particular context of violence is then briefly explored.
2005 / 1-84227-337-X / xviii + 154pp

Scott J. Hafemann
Suffering and Ministry in the Spirit
Paul's Defence of His Ministry in II Corinthians 2:14–3:3
Shedding new light on the way Paul defended his apostleship, the author offers a careful, detailed study of 2 Corinthians 2:14–3:3 linked with other key passages throughout 1 and 2 Corinthians. Demonstrating the unity and coherence of Paul's argument in this passage, the author shows that Paul's suffering served as the vehicle for revealing God's power and glory through the Spirit.
2000 / 0-85364-967-7 / xiv + 262pp

Scott J. Hafemann
Paul, Moses and the History of Israel
The Letter/Spirit Contrast and the Argument from Scripture in 2 Corinthians 3
An exegetical study of the call of Moses, the second giving of the Law (Exodus 32–34), the new covenant, and the prophetic understanding of the history of Israel in 2 Corinthians 3. Hafemann's work demonstrates Paul's contextual use of the Old Testament and the essential unity between the Law and the Gospel within the context of the distinctive ministries of Moses and Paul.
2005 / 1-84227-317-5 / xii + 498pp

Douglas S. McComiskey
Lukan Theology in the Light of the Gospel's Literary Structure
Luke's Gospel was purposefully written with theology embedded in its patterned literary structure. A critical analysis of this cyclical structure provides new windows into Luke's interpretation of the individual pericopes comprising the Gospel and illuminates several of his theological interests.
2004 / 1-84227-148-2 / xviii + 388pp

Stephen Motyer
Your Father the Devil?
A New Approach to John and 'The Jews'
Who are 'the Jews' in John's Gospel? Defending John against the charge of antisemitism, Motyer argues that, far from demonising the Jews, the Gospel seeks to present Jesus as 'Good News for Jews' in a late first century setting.
1997 / 0-85364-832-8 / xiv + 260pp

Esther Ng
Reconstructing Christian Origins?
The Feminist Theology of Elizabeth Schüssler Fiorenza: An Evaluation
In a detailed evaluation, the author challenges Elizabeth Schüssler Fiorenza's reconstruction of early Christian origins and her underlying presuppositions. The author also presents her own views on women's roles both then and now.
2002 / 1-84227-055-9 / xxiv + 468pp

Robin Parry
Old Testament Story and Christian Ethics
The Rape of Dinah as a Case Study

What is the role of story in ethics and, more particularly, what is the role of Old Testament story in Christian ethics? This book, drawing on the work of contemporary philosophers, argues that narrative is crucial in the ethical shaping of people and, drawing on the work of contemporary Old Testament scholars, that story plays a key role in Old Testament ethics. Parry then argues that when situated in canonical context Old Testament stories can be reappropriated by Christian readers in their own ethical formation. The shocking story of the rape of Dinah and the massacre of the Shechemites provides a fascinating case study for exploring the parameters within which Christian ethical appropriations of Old Testament stories can live.

2004 / 1-84227-210-1 / xx + 350pp

Ian Paul
Power to See the World Anew
The Value of Paul Ricoeur's Hermeneutic of Metaphor in Interpreting the Symbolism of Revelation 12 and 13

This book is a study of the hermeneutics of metaphor of Paul Ricoeur, one of the most important writers on hermeneutics and metaphor of the last century. It sets out the key points of his theory, important criticisms of his work, and how his approach, modified in the light of these criticisms, offers a methodological framework for reading apocalyptic texts.

2006 / 1-84227-056-7 / approx. 350pp

Robert L. Plummer
Paul's Understanding of the Church's Mission
Did the Apostle Paul Expect the Early Christian Communities to Evangelize?

This book engages in a careful study of Paul's letters to determine if the apostle expected the communities to which he wrote to engage in missionary activity. It helpfully summarizes the discussion on this debated issue, judiciously handling contested texts, and provides a way forward in addressing this critical question. While admitting that Paul rarely explicitly commands the communities he founded to evangelize, Plummer amasses significant incidental data to provide a convincing case that Paul did indeed expect his churches to engage in mission activity. Throughout the study, Plummer progressively builds a theological basis for the church's mission that is both distinctively Pauline and compelling.

2006 / 1-84227-333-7 / approx. 324pp

David Powys
'Hell': A Hard Look at a Hard Question
The Fate of the Unrighteous in New Testament Thought
This comprehensive treatment seeks to unlock the original meaning of terms and phrases long thought to support the traditional doctrine of hell. It concludes that there is an alternative—one which is more biblical, and which can positively revive the rationale for Christian mission.
1997 / 0-85364-831-X / xxii + 478pp

Sorin Sabou
Between Horror and Hope
Paul's Metaphorical Language of Death in Romans 6.1-11
This book argues that Paul's metaphorical language of death in Romans 6.1-11 conveys two aspects: horror and hope. The 'horror' aspect is conveyed by the 'crucifixion' language, and the 'hope' aspect by 'burial' language. The life of the Christian believer is understood, as relationship with sin is concerned ('death to sin'), between these two realities: horror and hope.
2005 / 1-84227-322-1 / approx. 224pp

Rosalind Selby
The Comical Doctrine
The Epistemology of New Testament Hermeneutics
This book argues that the gospel breaks through postmodernity's critique of truth and the referential possibilities of textuality with its gift of grace. With a rigorous, philosophical challenge to modernist and postmodernist assumptions, Selby offers an alternative epistemology to all who would still read with faith *and* with academic credibility.
2005 / 1-84227-212-8 / approx. 350pp

Kiwoong Son
Zion Symbolism in Hebrews
Hebrews 12.18-24 as a Hermeneutical Key to the Epistle
This book challenges the general tendency of understanding the Epistle to the Hebrews against a Hellenistic background and suggests that the Epistle should be understood in the light of the Jewish apocalyptic tradition. The author especially argues for the importance of the theological symbolism of Sinai and Zion (Heb. 12:18-24) as it provides the Epistle's theological background as well as the rhetorical basis of the superiority motif of Jesus throughout the Epistle.
2005 / 1-84227-368-X / approx. 280pp

Kevin Walton
Thou Traveller Unknown
The Presence and Absence of God in the Jacob Narrative
The author offers a fresh reading of the story of Jacob in the book of Genesis through the paradox of divine presence and absence. The work also seeks to make a contribution to Pentateuchal studies by bringing together a close reading of the final text with historical critical insights, doing justice to the text's historical depth, final form and canonical status.
2003 / 1-84227-059-1 / xvi + 238pp

George M. Wieland
The Significance of Salvation
A Study of Salvation Language in the Pastoral Epistles
The language and ideas of salvation pervade the three Pastoral Epistles. This study offers a close examination of their soteriological statements. In all three letters the idea of salvation is found to play a vital paraenetic role, but each also exhibits distinctive soteriological emphases. The results challenge common assumptions about the Pastoral Epistles as a corpus.
2005 / 1-84227-257-8 / approx. 324pp

Alistair Wilson
When Will These Things Happen?
A Study of Jesus as Judge in Matthew 21–25
This study seeks to allow Matthew's carefully constructed presentation of Jesus to be given full weight in the modern evaluation of Jesus' eschatology. Careful analysis of the text of Matthew 21–25 reveals Jesus to be standing firmly in the Jewish prophetic and wisdom traditions as he proclaims and enacts imminent judgement on the Jewish authorities then boldly claims the central role in the final and universal judgement.
2004 / 1-84227-146-6 / xxii + 272pp

Lindsay Wilson
Joseph Wise and Otherwise
The Intersection of Covenant and Wisdom in Genesis 37–50
This book offers a careful literary reading of Genesis 37–50 that argues that the Joseph story contains both strong covenant themes and many wisdom-like elements. The connections between the two helps to explore how covenant and wisdom might intersect in an integrated biblical theology.
2004 / 1-84227-140-7 / xvi + 340pp

Stephen I. Wright
The Voice of Jesus
Studies in the Interpretation of Six Gospel Parables
This literary study considers how the 'voice' of Jesus has been heard in different periods of parable interpretation, and how the categories of figure and trope may help us towards a sensitive reading of the parables today.
2000 / 0-85364-975-8 / xiv + 280pp

Paternoster
9 Holdom Avenue,
Bletchley,
Milton Keynes MK1 1QR,
United Kingdom
Web: www.authenticmedia.co.uk/paternoster

Paternoster Theological Monographs
(All titles uniform with this volume)
Dates in bold are of projected publication

Emil Bartos
Deification in Eastern Orthodox Theology
An Evaluation and Critique of the Theology of Dumitru Staniloae
Bartos studies a fundamental yet neglected aspect of Orthodox theology: deification. By examining the doctrines of anthropology, christology, soteriology and ecclesiology as they relate to deification, he provides an important contribution to contemporary dialogue between Eastern and Western theologians.

1999 / 0-85364-956-1 / xii + 370pp

Graham Buxton
The Trinity, Creation and Pastoral Ministry
Imaging the Perichoretic God
In this book the author proposes a three-way conversation between theology, science and pastoral ministry. His approach draws on a Trinitarian understanding of God as a relational being of love, whose life 'spills over' into all created reality, human and non-human. By locating human meaning and purpose within God's 'creation-community' this book offers the possibility of a transforming engagement between those in pastoral ministry and the scientific community.

2005 / 1-84227-369-8 / approx. 380 pp

Iain D. Campbell
Fixing the Indemnity
The Life and Work of George Adam Smith
When Old Testament scholar George Adam Smith (1856–1942) delivered the Lyman Beecher lectures at Yale University in 1899, he confidently declared that 'modern criticism has won its war against traditional theories. It only remains to fix the amount of the indemnity.' In this biography, Iain D. Campbell assesses Smith's critical approach to the Old Testament and evaluates its consequences, showing that Smith's life and work still raises questions about the relationship between biblical scholarship and evangelical faith.

2004 / 1-84227-228-4 / xx + 256pp

Tim Chester
Mission and the Coming of God
Eschatology, the Trinity and Mission in the Theology of Jürgen Moltmann
This book explores the theology and missiology of the influential contemporary theologian, Jürgen Moltmann. It highlights the important contribution Moltmann has made while offering a critique of his thought from an evangelical perspective. In so doing, it touches on pertinent issues for evangelical missiology. The conclusion takes Calvin as a starting point, proposing 'an eschatology of the cross' which offers a critique of the over-realised eschatologies in liberation theology and certain forms of evangelicalism.
2006 / 1-84227-320-5 / approx. 224pp

Sylvia Wilkey Collinson
Making Disciples
The Significance of Jesus' Educational Strategy for Today's Church
This study examines the biblical practice of discipling, formulates a definition, and makes comparisons with modern models of education. A recommendation is made for greater attention to its practice today.
2004 / 1-84227-116-4 / xiv + 278pp

Darrell Cosden
A Theology of Work
Work and the New Creation
Through dialogue with Moltmann, Pope John Paul II and others, this book develops a genitive 'theology of work', presenting a theological definition of work and a model for a theological ethics of work that shows work's nature, value and meaning now and eschatologically. Work is shown to be a transformative activity consisting of three dynamically inter-related dimensions: the instrumental, relational and ontological.
2005 / 1-84227-332-9 / xvi + 208pp

Stephen M. Dunning
The Crisis and the Quest
A Kierkegaardian Reading of Charles Williams
Employing Kierkegaardian categories and analysis, this study investigates both the central crisis in Charles Williams's authorship between hermetism and Christianity (Kierkegaard's Religions A and B), and the quest to resolve this crisis, a quest that ultimately presses the bounds of orthodoxy.
2000 / 0-85364-985-5 / xxiv + 254pp

Keith Ferdinando
The Triumph of Christ in African Perspective
A Study of Demonology and Redemption in the African Context
The book explores the implications of the gospel for traditional African fears of occult aggression. It analyses such traditional approaches to suffering and biblical responses to fears of demonic evil, concluding with an evaluation of African beliefs from the perspective of the gospel.
1999 / 0-85364-830-1 / xviii + 450pp

Andrew Goddard
Living the Word, Resisting the World
The Life and Thought of Jacques Ellul
This work offers a definitive study of both the life and thought of the French Reformed thinker Jacques Ellul (1912-1994). It will prove an indispensable resource for those interested in this influential theologian and sociologist and for Christian ethics and political thought generally.
2002 / 1-84227-053-2 / xxiv + 378pp

David Hilborn
The Words of our Lips
Language-Use in Free Church Worship
Studies of liturgical language have tended to focus on the written canons of Roman Catholic and Anglican communities. By contrast, David Hilborn analyses the more extemporary approach of English Nonconformity. Drawing on recent developments in linguistic pragmatics, he explores similarities and differences between 'fixed' and 'free' worship, and argues for the interdependence of each.
2006 / 0-85364-977-4 / approx. 350pp

Roger Hitching
The Church and Deaf People
A Study of Identity, Communication and Relationships with Special Reference to the Ecclesiology of Jürgen Moltmann
In *The Church and Deaf People* Roger Hitching sensitively examines the history and present experience of deaf people and finds similarities between aspects of sign language and Moltmann's theological method that 'open up' new ways of understanding theological concepts.
2003 / 1-84227-222-5 / xxii + 236pp

John G. Kelly
One God, One People
The Differentiated Unity of the People of God in the Theology of
Jürgen Moltmann
The author expounds and critiques Moltmann's doctrine of God and highlights the systematic connections between it and Moltmann's influential discussion of Israel. He then proposes a fresh approach to Jewish–Christian relations building on Moltmann's work using insights from Habermas and Rawls.
2005 / 0-85346-969-3 / approx. 350pp

Mark F.W. Lovatt
Confronting the Will-to-Power
A Reconsideration of the Theology of Reinhold Niebuhr
Confronting the Will-to-Power is an analysis of the theology of Reinhold Niebuhr, arguing that his work is an attempt to identify, and provide a practical theological answer to, the existence and nature of human evil.
2001 / 1-84227-054-0 / xviii + 216pp

Neil B. MacDonald
Karl Barth and the Strange New World within the Bible
Barth, Wittgenstein, and the Metadilemmas of the Enlightenment
Barth's discovery of the strange new world within the Bible is examined in the context of Kant, Hume, Overbeck, and, most importantly, Wittgenstein. MacDonald covers some fundamental issues in theology today: epistemology, the final form of the text and biblical truth-claims.
2000 / 0-85364-970-7 / xxvi + 374pp

Keith A. Mascord
Alvin Plantinga and Christian Apologetics
This book draws together the contributions of the philosopher Alvin Plantinga to the major contemporary challenges to Christian belief, highlighting in particular his ground-breaking work in epistemology and the problem of evil. Plantinga's theory that both theistic and Christian belief is warrantedly basic is explored and critiqued, and an assessment offered as to the significance of his work for apologetic theory and practice.
2005 / 1-84227-256-X / approx. 304pp

Gillian McCulloch
The Deconstruction of Dualism in Theology
With Reference to Ecofeminist Theology and New Age Spirituality
This book challenges eco-theological anti-dualism in Christian theology, arguing that dualism has a twofold function in Christian religious discourse. Firstly, it enables us to express the discontinuities and divisions that are part of the process of reality. Secondly, dualistic language allows us to express the mysteries of divine transcendence/immanence and the survival of the soul without collapsing into monism and materialism, both of which are problematic for Christian epistemology.

2002 / 1-84227-044-3 / xii + 282pp

Leslie McCurdy
Attributes and Atonement
The Holy Love of God in the Theology of P.T. Forsyth
Attributes and Atonement is an intriguing full-length study of P.T. Forsyth's doctrine of the cross as it relates particularly to God's holy love. It includes an unparalleled bibliography of both primary and secondary material relating to Forsyth.

1999 / 0-85364-833-6 / xiv + 328pp

Nozomu Miyahira
Towards a Theology of the Concord of God
A Japanese Perspective on the Trinity
This book introduces a new Japanese theology and a unique Trinitarian formula based on the Japanese intellectual climate: three betweennesses and one concord. It also presents a new interpretation of the Trinity, a co-subordinationism, which is in line with orthodox Trinitarianism; each single person of the Trinity is eternally and equally subordinate (or serviceable) to the other persons, so that they retain the mutual dynamic equality.

2000 / 0-85364-863-8 / xiv + 256pp

Eddy José Muskus
The Origins and Early Development of Liberation Theology in Latin America
With Particular Reference to Gustavo Gutiérrez
This work challenges the fundamental premise of Liberation Theology, 'opting for the poor', and its claim that Christ is found in them. It also argues that Liberation Theology emerged as a direct result of the failure of the Roman Catholic Church in Latin America.

2002 / 0-85364-974-X / xiv + 296pp

Jim Purves
The Triune God and the Charismatic Movement
A Critical Appraisal from a Scottish Perspective
All emotion and no theology? Or a fundamental challenge to reappraise and
realign our trinitarian theology in the light of Christian experience? This study
of charismatic renewal as it found expression within Scotland at the end of the
twentieth century evaluates the use of Patristic, Reformed and contemporary
·models of the Trinity in explaining the workings of the Holy Spirit.
2004 / 1-84227-321-3 / xxiv + 246pp

Anna Robbins
Methods in the Madness
Diversity in Twentieth-Century Christian Social Ethics
The author compares the ethical methods of Walter Rauschenbusch, Reinhold
Niebuhr and others. She argues that unless Christians are clear about the ways
that theology and philosophy are expressed practically they may lose the ability
to discuss social ethics across contexts, let alone reach effective agreements.
2004 / 1-84227-211-X / xx + 294pp

Ed Rybarczyk
Beyond Salvation
Eastern Orthodoxy and Classical Pentecostalism on Becoming Like Christ
At first glance eastern Orthodoxy and classical Pentecostalism seem quite
distinct. This ground-breaking study shows they share much in common,
especially as it concerns the experiential elements of following Christ. Both
traditions assert that authentic Christianity transcends the wooden categories of
modernism.
2004 / 1-84227-144-X / xii + 356pp

Signe Sandsmark
Is World View Neutral Education Possible and Desirable?
A Christian Response to Liberal Arguments
(Published jointly with The Stapleford Centre)
This book discusses reasons for belief in world view neutrality, and argues that
'neutral' education will have a hidden, but strong world view influence. It
discusses the place for Christian education in the common school.
2000 / 0-85364-973-1 / xiv + 182pp

Hazel Sherman
Reading Zechariah
The Allegorical Tradition of Biblical Interpretation through the Commentary of
Didymus the Blind and Theodore of Mopsuestia
A close reading of the commentary on Zechariah by Didymus the Blind
alongside that of Theodore of Mopsuestia suggests that popular categorising of
Antiochene and Alexandrian biblical exegesis as 'historical' or 'allegorical' is
inadequate and misleading.
2005 / 1-84227-213-6 / approx. 280pp

Andrew Sloane
On Being a Christian in the Academy
Nicholas Wolterstorff and the Practice of Christian Scholarship
An exposition and critical appraisal of Nicholas Wolterstorff's epistemology in
the light of the philosophy of science, and an application of his thought to the
practice of Christian scholarship.
2003 / 1-84227-058-3 / xvi + 274pp

Damon W.K. So
Jesus' Revelation of His Father
A Narrative-Conceptual Study of the Trinity with Special Reference to
Karl Barth
This book explores the trinitarian dynamics in the context of Jesus' revelation of
his Father in his earthly ministry with references to key passages in Matthew's
Gospel. It develops from the exegeses of these passages a non-linear concept of
revelation which links Jesus' communion with his Father to his revelatory words
and actions through a nuanced understanding of the Holy Spirit, with references
to K. Barth, G.W.H. Lampe, J.D.G. Dunn and E. Irving.
2005 / 1-84227-323-X / approx. 380pp

Daniel Strange
The Possibility of Salvation Among the Unevangelised
An Analysis of Inclusivism in Recent Evangelical Theology
For evangelical theologians the 'fate of the unevangelised' impinges upon
fundamental tenets of evangelical identity. The position known as 'inclusivism',
defined by the belief that the unevangelised can be ontologically saved by Christ
whilst being epistemologically unaware of him, has been defended most
vigorously by the Canadian evangelical Clark H. Pinnock. Through a detailed
analysis and critique of Pinnock's work, this book examines a cluster of issues
surrounding the unevangelised and its implications for christology, soteriology
and the doctrine of revelation.
2002 / 1-84227-047-8 / xviii + 362pp

Scott Swain
God According to the Gospel
Biblical Narrative and the Identity of God in the Theology of Robert W. Jenson
Robert W. Jenson is one of the leading voices in contemporary Trinitarian theology. His boldest contribution in this area concerns his use of biblical narrative both to ground and explicate the Christian doctrine of God. *God According to the Gospel* critically examines Jenson's proposal and suggests an alternative way of reading the biblical portrayal of the triune God.
2006 / 1-84227-258-6 / approx. 180pp

Justyn Terry
The Justifying Judgement of God
A Reassessment of the Place of Judgement in the Saving Work of Christ
The argument of this book is that judgement, understood as the whole process of bringing justice, is the primary metaphor of atonement, with others, such as victory, redemption and sacrifice, subordinate to it. Judgement also provides the proper context for understanding penal substitution and the call to repentance, baptism, eucharist and holiness.
2005 / 1-84227-370-1 / approx. 274 pp

Graham Tomlin
The Power of the Cross
Theology and the Death of Christ in Paul, Luther and Pascal
This book explores the theology of the cross in St Paul, Luther and Pascal. It offers new perspectives on the theology of each, and some implications for the nature of power, apologetics, theology and church life in a postmodern context.
1999 / 0-85364-984-7 / xiv + 344pp

Adonis Vidu
Postliberal Theological Method
A Critical Study
The postliberal theology of Hans Frei, George Lindbeck, Ronald Thiemann, John Milbank and others is one of the more influential contemporary options. This book focuses on several aspects pertaining to its theological method, specifically its understanding of background, hermeneutics, epistemic justification, ontology, the nature of doctrine and, finally, Christological method.
2005 / 1-84227-395-7 / approx. 324pp

Graham J. Watts
Revelation and the Spirit
A Comparative Study of the Relationship between the Doctrine of Revelation and Pneumatology in the Theology of Eberhard Jüngel and of Wolfhart Pannenberg
The relationship between revelation and pneumatology is relatively unexplored. This approach offers a fresh angle on two important twentieth century theologians and raises pneumatological questions which are theologically crucial and relevant to mission in a postmodern culture.
2005 / 1-84227-104-0 / xxii + 232pp

Nigel G. Wright
Disavowing Constantine
Mission, Church and the Social Order in the Theologies of John Howard Yoder and Jürgen Moltmann
This book is a timely restatement of a radical theology of church and state in the Anabaptist and Baptist tradition. Dr Wright constructs his argument in dialogue and debate with Yoder and Moltmann, major contributors to a free church perspective.
2000 / 0-85364-978-2 / xvi + 252pp

Paternoster
9 Holdom Avenue,
Bletchley,
Milton Keynes MK1 1QR,
United Kingdom
Web: www.authenticmedia.co.uk/paternoster

July 2005